Projects and Their Consequences

Reiser + Umemoto

———

Projects and
Their Consequences

———

PRINCETON ARCHITECTURAL PRESS · NEW YORK

This book is dedicated to the life and work of
our son, Zeke, who left us far too early:
your brilliant spirit pervades us
and everything we do.

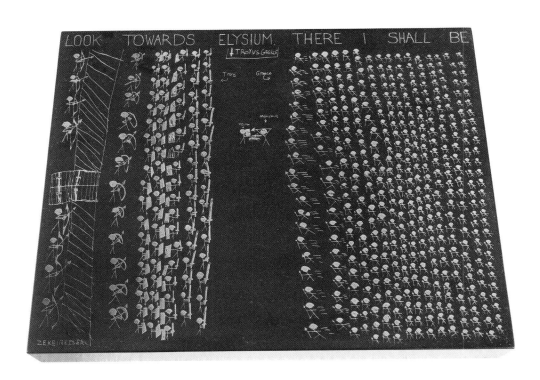

Published by
Princeton Architectural Press
A McEvoy Group company
202 Warren Street
Hudson, New York 12534
Visit our website at www.papress.com

Princeton Architectural Press is a leading publisher in
architecture, design, photography, landscape, and
visual culture. We create fine books and stationery of
unsurpassed quality and production values. With more
than one thousand titles published, we find design
everywhere and in the most unlikely places.

This publication is made possible in part from
the Barr Ferree Foundation Fund for Publications,
Department of Art and Archaeology, Princeton University.

Editor: Sara Stemen
Design concept: Liyan Zhao
Design and typesetting: Reiser + Umemoto

Special thanks to: Paula Baver, Janet Behning, Abby Bussel,
Benjamin English, Jan Cigliano Hartman, Susan Hershberg,
Kristen Hewitt, Lia Hunt, Valerie Kamen, Jennifer Lippert,
Sara McKay, Parker Menzimer, Eliana Miller, Nina Pick,
Wes Seeley, Rob Shaeffer, Marisa Tesoro, and Joseph Weston
of Princeton Architectural Press
—Kevin C. Lippert, publisher

Library of Congress Cataloging-in-Publication Data
Names: Reiser, Jesse. | Umemoto, Nanako. | Benjamin,
Andrew E. | Berman, Ila (Ila Leslie), 1960– | Lynn, Greg. |
Somol, Robert. | Steele, Brett.
Title: Projects and their consequences.
Description: First edition. | New York : Princeton Architectural
Press, 2018.
Identifiers: LCCN 2018007250 | ISBN 9781616897192
(hardcover : alk. paper)
Subjects: LCSH: Reiser + Umemoto.
Classification: LCC NA737.R4455 P76 2018 | DDC 721—dc23
LC record available at https://lccn.loc.gov/2018007250

Contents

Preface

Projects and Their Consequences, a title suggested by our good friend and interlocutor Jeffrey Kipnis, has been an ongoing project in our studio since 2006. It was originally meant to be a record of twenty years of work. The book, which will be the first of three volumes, has passed through many brilliant and capable hands since its inception and has gone through at least three major incarnations of organizing and naming the heterogeneous work our studio has engaged in under the overall rubric of architecture.

The structure we settled upon, while not ideal, appears to us the most adequate way of presenting the Gordian knot of multiple accounts, histories, scales, media, formats, and programmatic types that describe our now thirty-plus years of practice. But (as the title of the introduction suggests) it could always have been otherwise. For the sake of clarity, we chose to present each group of projects through the dominant lens of a particular theme or interest. In truth, those themes and interests could apply in varying degrees to virtually any of our projects. We must leave it to the reader to make the connections.

The book is organized around four thematic sections, with projects organized roughly chronologically. Interspersed between and among them are works of punctuation: short projects, films, cartoons, theoretical arguments, et cetera, which we hope will illuminate the thematic sections by way of contrast. The succeeding volumes will refrain those themes in variation with other projects as the architectural ideas evolve over time. The anachronistic structure of Orson Welles's *Citizen Kane* was the model. As with our *Atlas of Novel Tectonics*, we do not expect the reader to begin at the beginning. We invite all who are interested to enter and exit as they please. We hope the projects, like buildings being experienced, stand on their own without theory or commentary. However, for those interested in a wider and deeper range of written speculations, these are included as well.

Besides presenting a record of our work, we feel it is very important to give the reader our sense of the context in which it was produced. As a part of the "consequences," we have included selections from contemporaneous articles by colleagues to provide other perspectives on the projects in their time. This book is about telling our story but also is a plea for the continuation of an architectural culture that is presently under threat from corporate domination from above and the quotidian profession from below. We find ourselves thrust into the unenviable position of being conservatives—that is, calling attention to the importance of the extended family of disciplines in and around architecture itself and the vital importance of the continuity of those relationships, recognizing that it might take a lapse of only one generation for the five-hundred-year-old experiment to come to an end.

After 1991 our work was done while teaching at various universities. Aside from the huge benefit of providing a stable income, the work and discourse among us and colleagues across many schools was absolutely invaluable to our formation. It was and remains the only viable way to sustain a speculative practice and culture in architecture in the United States. We think ourselves fortunate to have worked under the direct and indirect influence of exceptional colleagues, masters, friends, and family, both living and dead. Our work, such as it is, would have been unthinkable without them. For that reason also, we are compelled to give voice to the importance of that continuity.

Jesse Reiser & Nanako Umemoto   Harlem, NY, March 2017

Regular dinners at Brio: Jesse Reiser, Sanford Kwinter, Zeke Reiser, Jeffrey Kipnis, and Nanako Umemoto

Acknowledgments

Research for this book was supported by grants from the Graham Foundation for Advanced Studies in the Fine Arts, the Princeton University Committee on Research in Humanities and the Social Sciences, and the Princeton University Barre Fennue Fund. We also thank Eliss Jafee and Jeffrey Brown for their continuing support over the long gestation period of this book. The thirty-plus years of our collaboration was initiated during Jesse's fellowship at the American Academy in Rome in 1985. We are thankful to the Academy for providing a place for work and thought, and to Aldo Rossi for inviting us to show the product of that year at the 1985 Venice Biennale. My experience working for Rossi, first as an intern in 1979 and later as an employee in 1985, was absolutely formative in instilling the notion of what a speculative practice in architecture should be. We bear an enormous debt of gratitude to John Hejduk, who by verbal and nonverbal means transmitted a sense of cultural depth in architecture, and to my teacher Daniel Libeskind—the upholder of a tradition of radicality—whose work and ideas inspire us by continuously challenging architecture's most enduring certainties.

Special thanks for Kikue Hirota and Debora Reiser, the first architects of our worlds, who independently in Kyoto and New York instilled in each of us an ethics and an aesthetics of architecture and life that are surprisingly similar. We are the lucky beneficiaries of their unstinting generosity and good counsel to this day.

Architecture as a cultural practice extends beyond the architectural studio. Our work is indebted to the theorists and historians with whom we have had the pleasure of being colleagues, some of whom have written about our work. Our deep thanks to those who have contributed contemporaneous essays to this book: Robert Somol, Greg Lynn (as theorist), Brett Steele, Ila Berman, and Andrew Benjamin. Our appreciation to Jeffrey Kipnis, who suggested, among other things, a title for the book; Sanford Kwinter and Ed Eigen, for their theoretical and practical insights; Cynthia Davidson for her cogent advice on all things monographic; Beatriz Colomina, for her historical acumen, especially on the discipline of architecture; and Architects Steven Holl and Bernard Tschumi for enthusiastically advocating grant funding for this book.

Our gratitude to a triumvirate of Princeton deans: Stan Allen, Alejandro Zaera-Polo, and Mónica Ponce de León, whose continuous support made this book possible.

Special thanks to Kevin and Jennifer Lippert of Princeton Architectural Press, who went all out supporting our ambitions for this volume. We share our enthusiasm for beautiful books with them. Our abiding thanks to our editor at Princeton Architectural Press, Sara Stemen, who shepherded this volume through many a rough patch and whose careful yet gentle edits improved the final version enormously.

Special note should be made of Liam Lee's contribution, not only to this volume but to the series as a whole. He assisted us tremendously in shaping the form, structure, and content of all three volumes—a daunting endeavor. His collaboration with the primary graphic designer, Liyan Zhao, interpreted the content and the visual materials brilliantly. Many have contributed their graphic and editorial talents over the course of this book's long development, including Reto Geiser, Emily Cass, Sonia Flamberg, Shota Vashakmadze, Yotam Ben Hur, Fanyi Pan, Becky Quintal, and Jieun Doe.

We extend our thanks to Niall Hobhouse, Tina Di Carlo, and the staff of Drawing Matter.

Special thanks to our old friend Hal Schwartz, who made exquisite final refinements on the images and graphic design.

Our gratitude to Steven Kyle Cook, who assisted in shaping the introductory text and diagrams. He served as an intelligent and critical sounding board, placing our often disparate observations into a coherent order.

Our debt to present and past collaborators at RUR over the course of over thirty years; the group has grown into an extended family, many of whom have their own practices and positions in academy. There are too many to create a complete list here, but notables include David Ruy, Yama Karim, Jose Sanchez, Rhett Russo, Wolfgang Gollwitzer, Hisa Matsunaga, Taiji Miyasaka, John Kalleher, Marcelyn Gow, Noma Yehia, Jason Payne, Neil Cook, Kutan Ayata, Michael Young, Ciro Najle, Steven Lauritano, Michael Loverich, Akari Takebayashi, Jason Scroggin, Efra Xanthouli, Max Orzi, Joy Wang, Cooper Mack, Ryosuke Imaeda, Marcelo Spina, Michael Overby, Jasmine Lee, Jonathan Solomon, Juan DeMarco, Hilary Simon, Eva Perez De Vega, Kris Hedges, and many others who gave countless hours to the design work in our office and in doing so substantially shaped our work and thought.

Finally, our deepest thanks to our dear son, Ezekiel, who was so much a part of our lives and the life of our office.

INTRODUCTION

It Could Always Be Otherwise

One thing is certain: architecture will become ever more itself while at the same time becoming everything other than what architecture is today. The discipline of architecture is ramifying. There are, and will be, many architectures—alas, not of equal value. Some will be short-lived; some will persist longer. We are witnessing the demise of the belief in singular, dominating ideologies, as well as a loss of confidence in the teleology of technological improvement.

The profession of architecture has ineluctably moved away from holding any significant position within the discipline to being defined purely in a legal sense, centered exclusively on building; we are witnessing the almost complete subsumption of the profession into laws, codes, performance criteria, and regimes of compliance. That which resists rationalization and quantification, which is to say architecture as a cultural form, must of necessity be rigorously excluded. Insofar as it intersects with the legal system (a perverse form of interdisciplinarity), it must be represented in the abstract as intellectual property, without regard to the specific cultural content it protects.

Architecture has arguably not been coextensive with technology in the pure sense since the days of the great fortifications. Being solely the instrument of its military function, fortress architecture was the precise embodiment of the war machine, including the nascent social media of command and control. And just as the cathedrals gave up their semantic role to the printed book and later to film, radio, television, and the manifold platforms on the web, the fortification has long since given up the ghost to technologies too mobile and subtle to be contained in material structures.

And yet humans can still be confined behind physical walls as effectively as they can still be ravaged by edged weapons. The myth of technological improvement and belief in technological succession gives way to the sobering reality of simultaneity. People somewhere on this planet are living a Stone Age existence. Troglodytes share this world with humans on the verge of technologies that will obviate the need for a body at all. And it's more than a fair bet that the future human, if privileged enough, will pay through the nose for the opportunity to inhabit a body (or many bodies), while the average soul will have to make do with consignment to the heaven or hell of pure consciousness. Meaning in architecture will run the gamut from standard (i.e., the intolerable symbolism of the Freedom Tower) to works of unsettling subtlety and nuance. The future will arrive soon—it already has.

Architecture being first and foremost a serious cultural phenomenon is as ridiculous as, say, opera or sports would seem if seen by an alien. Like opera, architecture is an unstable compound of arts and practices drawn from many areas of life and knowledge, improbably condensed into a singular discipline, having its own universe with its own peculiar way of hosting and manifesting everything else. Serious architecture simultaneously addresses real-world demands (clients, codes, economies, et cetera), as must all building, while at the same time going beyond it—proffering, in manifold ways, a fictive universe whose peculiar version of physics, mathematics, space, time, the social, the political, philosophy, history, et cetera, characterizes its particular architecture and is quite distinct from orthodox disciplinary definitions.

Great architecture will recast the physical world and its laws into what it ought to be, not what it is, but it must do so through what is. Rather than representing other disciplines metaphorically or allegorically, the best architecture today reoriginates them. Metaphysical in the literal sense, architecture embodies the burning desire to transcend with its own panoply of devices and effects, which seek in various ways to go beyond literal physical and spatial limits—a sure signal of crossing over from building to architecture. This transcendence does not give the pragmatic issues priority or make them foundational to the metawork—the architecture in that schema being a surplus over building. No, quite the opposite: the architectural is foundational, and the functions the surplus! In other words, architecture is something an eagle, a bat, or a dog would never be enchanted or perplexed by. The prefix *meta* should, indeed, precede all of the disciplines mentioned above, even life.

This gives rise to many misunderstandings. Interdisciplinarity today is invoked ad nauseam as a self-evident good, especially in academic contexts. Institutionally, interdisciplinary endeavors are applauded as ensuring a diversity of opinions and debate, and as a counter to parochialism (which is true enough in theory). But most of the time, the conversants talk past one another and at worst share only in cynical opportunism.

We contend, conversely, that the periodic rush by architects to outside disciplines is a sign of the onset of a period of weakness. We have enough trouble with other architects, let alone other disciplines! Indeed, intradisciplinary differences are often so profound that one wonders sometimes if other architects are even in the same field.

The problem is that architectural design, as opposed to architectural discourse or rhetoric, deals with a dumb and recalcitrant medium. Architecture's hallmark is that it must convert whatever outside discipline it engages into its own terms. The muteness of the architectural object—as opposed to the clear messages of discourse—parallels the distinction Gershom Scholem makes between mysticism and prophecy in *Major Trends in Jewish Mysticism*. Hence the perennial complaints by historians, philosophers, social scientists, and others that architects never get their concepts right—though perhaps there is an ur-architect out there who might! However, if the discipline's focus is on a particular area—for example, Derridean philosophy, which had a good decade to be digested by the best minds in the field—then it would be fair to say that the result is in essence what architecture could do with Derridean philosophy, at least within the perspective of that period (the salient outcome in that particular period being physical allegories of deconstruction). That, in itself, would establish clear philosophical limits and points to what the limits are with other outside disciplines as well.

O-14
Concrete-exoskeleton tower

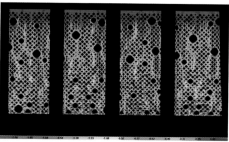

O-14
Trickle-down engineering

Unlike an opera (that is, if it is to stay the same opera), architecture can, distressingly to some, be separated from its authors' discourse and rhetoric and even its functions—time will do all three. As one of our most insightful colleagues, Stan Allen, has said, the best interdisciplinary collaborations for architects happen when all parties stay within their own discipline. Engagements like our long collaborations with engineers are indeed crucial, both as precise indicators of disciplinary limits and also as goads—heuristic prods to invention, defining clearly when the invention is truly an architectural one, not simply the physics of building.

Our experience designing the shell of the O-14 tower is a pure example. A fairly simple set of elements were in play: a concrete shell and a normative diagrid, both of which come directly from structural engineering. The effects we sought to wrest from the system were, however, the result of our architectural desires. The design process was basically a dance

Debora K. Reiser, 1966. Photograph by Hans Namuth (posthumous reproduction from an original negative; detail cropping.) This image was originally published in a *New York Times* article entitled "And a Corner for Mother." Photograph shows architect Debora Reiser at work with Jesse Reiser, age eight, in background. The photo was later adapted as a poster by Design Research and displayed in the window of their Manhattan store.

Poster in Design Research's storefront. Debora Reiser, 1966

between engineer and architect. Our project, at some level a critical one, was to perturb the normative system of diagrid concrete shell to its limit. Why? A host of architectural reasons: to vary the scale of the fenestration from large multifloor openings to fields of small openings for diffuse lighting and to vary the ambient conditions in what are typically homogeneously lit office floors, and on the exterior, to animate what in a typical diagrid building are unchanging patterns of solid and void from top to bottom and to bring a shifting sense of scale to the tower, imparting a visceral sense of a pullulating cascade. All these effects fall, at some level, into the category of expression.

The architectural expression of forces in relation to structure has typically vectored towards expressionism, that is, the foregrounding of structural muscularity. We sought quite the opposite, there being a wide spectrum of nuanced and even contradictory effects now possible in the medium that more closely resemble symptoms in the medical sense. We knew, too, that diagrids are inherently redundant, which allowed us to expand holes or create nonstructural zones in ways that normally trabeated structures would not permit. The forces would almost inevitably find another way to run, and the structure would still stand. This gave us flexibility up to a point, but we wanted to push past that. For the first time in our practice, we were able to plumb and push past those limits through productive struggle with the engineer.

The field of contest was the structural analysis program. We would deliver an insult to the system, and the system controlled by the engineer would respond. For example, our choosing to expand openings in a specific zone could induce a cascade of effects, even to areas remote from the change, a rejigging of the pattern—sometimes a good thing but more often bad! So there was a continual exchange between what we wanted and what physics wanted the structure to do. Our criteria were formal, organizational, and

Eight-year-old Jesse's first airplane model, a gift from *New York Times* editor Elizabeth Sverbeyeff to distract him during photo shoot

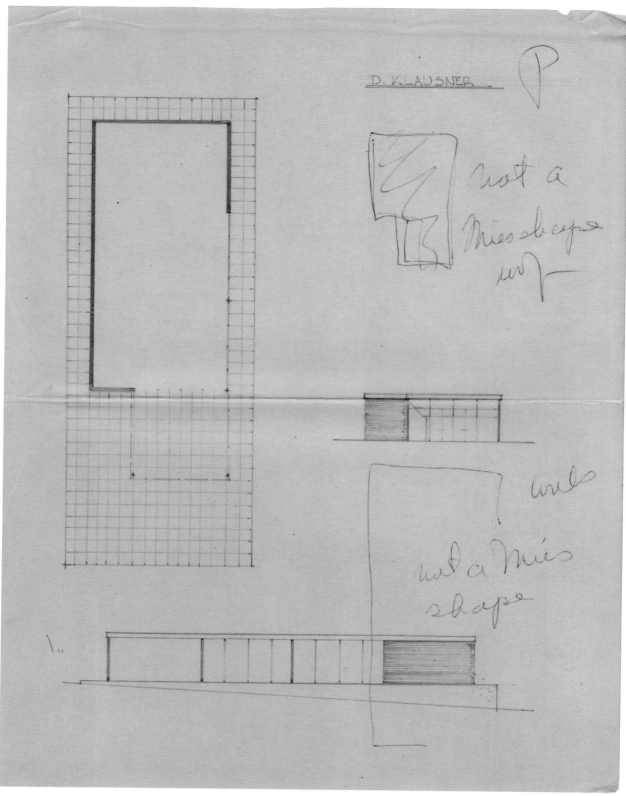

Debora Reiser's homework, assigned by Philip Johnson at Pratt Institute

One Turn Too Many

I came upon this exercise that was done by my mother at Pratt in the spring of 1948. Philip Johnson was the instructor for a course entitled "Mies, Wright, and Le Corbusier." He assigned exercises to draw pavilions in the manner of those masters. Johnson's criticism of my mother's Miesian pavilion had to do with the fact that she put one too many turns into the wall. His comment: "Two turns would have been fine, but three is totally un-Miesian." Johnson was enormously influential to her. He was the first instructor she had who approached architecture from an aesthetic perspective. Her professors were mainly young graduates from Harvard, Walter Gropius disciples who were orthodox functionalists, and she found that dismal and uninspired. Johnson appeared like a sprite, talking about architecture and its connection to beauty. She was smitten and to this day feels he saved her.

compositional—that is, architectural. The response was material. If the engineer dialed up concrete strength, then the holes could expand and the material between holes could be reduced, likewise the thickness of the shell. Increasing material strength also allowed greater freedom for the holes to drift off the grid lines, which we wanted, as we were trying to defeat the inherent tendency of engineering diagrids to emphasize literal and visual paths of least resistance, that is, the engineering imperative of getting forces out of the building as quickly and efficiently as possible. We wanted to slow everything down, both physically and perceptually. Our engineer, being a devoted Reaganite, called our design "trickle-down engineering." At no time did we pretend to be amateur engineers, and at no time did our engineer, Ysrael Seinuk, pretend to be an architect. Our engineer was the avid mind behind the matter.

An entirely different interdisciplinary dynamic would apply to, for example, today's ethical imperative to design net zero buildings—in essence, a problem of engineering. The good derived in this case is a statistical one, thankfully independent of the architecture in question, which could be good, bad, or indifferent and still contribute to a net zero world. From architecture's perspective such imperatives are rather minimal expectations, typically written into building codes related to health and safety (for example, standards to prevent designing firetraps).

As one example, both Thom Mayne's Cooper Union building and Robert A. M. Stern's George W. Bush Library meet LEED Platinum criteria, but the two buildings occupy entirely different architectural universes. In practice, then, architecture is an entirely independent variable. Whether to advertise sustainability with windmills, green roofs, or photovoltaics becomes a question of expression or even good taste. Our primary anxiety rests with a political climate where the ignorance of even the best-intentioned decision makers leads to demands for an architecture that signals sustainability. Sadly, this must be seen as an unnecessary infringement on freedom of architectural expression, with potentially homogenizing consequences for the public realm.

While the disciplines of architecture and engineering are often closely intertwined, their ethical and social imperatives are quite distinct. In short, engineers strive for a livable world, while architects strive for a world worth living in. A crucial distinction, indeed, especially if we agree with the predictions that we are living in the environmental end time! How, then, would one want to go out? Who and how would one mediate life support? Restricting one's responsibilities to the built world to the role of a blind carbon accountant (which is to say, regarding architecture purely as a problem of engineering) would be to abrogate our ethical responsibilities as architects. So while we follow the precepts of sustainability (in case the doomsday can be averted), our aim accords with Epicurus's, toward the poignantly human art of living and dying well.

I have been personally inspired by the three-hundred-year-old house in Kyoto in which Nanako grew up. We've stayed in this house for extended periods over the years, during winters and summers. Kyoto is famously hot in summer and quite cold in the winter— cold enough to see your breath inside. For an American, this period of cold in the house is akin to winter camping four months per year. It is typical to be colder inside the house than out of doors. The house is environmentally and aesthetically spare and uncompromising, and it has formed its inhabitants that way. It is also about as far away from American interior comfort zone engineering as one can imagine. Yet it works brilliantly. Heat and light are delivered to the body only where needed and no further. The *kotatsu*, a shrouded table sunk into the floor, traditionally heated by a hibachi, warms the body but leaves the head cool ("Better to think!"). Heaven help you if you don't take the nightly bath, for it is not a cultural affectation but a functional necessity: the body must be superheated to last through the night. Likewise, cooking in a hot pot and the conviviality it brings does the double duty of cooking food and heating the diners, a physical and social effect impossible to import to an overheated Manhattan apartment! The logic of that traditional house was carbon neutral *avant le mot* and achieved it without reducing architecture and its effects to mere numbers.

Beyond quotidian building, architects must wrestle, through paradox, the demands of liaising the possible with the impossible, fact with fiction, in the same space. Indeed, architecture may be classed as a factual fiction—a problem that was broached but received less than adequate treatment in twentieth-century avant-garde theater. Serious architecture breaks the fourth wall. Its legacy as "mother of the arts" has historically

The homework opposite was found in Johnson's assigned course book, Alberto Sartoris, *Encyclopédie de l'architecture nouvelle: ordre et climat méditerranéens* (Milan: Ulrico Hoepli, 1948).

Two architectural universes, same LEED Platinum rating: Thom Mayne's Cooper Union (top) and Robert A. M. Stern's George W. Bush Library (bottom)

Kyoto house: Nanako Umemoto and her brothers

burdened it with the weight of classical representation, a legacy still pathetically in operation today in projects like the Freedom Tower. That is why the greater the architecture, the greater the divide between knowing and seeing, as in magic. And like life itself, the discipline moves through times of strength and health, when its hold on the world is sufficient unto itself, to periods of weakness and dissolution, when the two-headed beast of history and a surfeit of representational thinking cause it to be consumed both from within and without.

Projects are this life. By *project* we mean a sustained engagement bordering on obsession with a spatio-formal erotic. Such models must inevitably address the vicissitudes of sites, functions, programs, client demands, sustainability, and the like, but they are never the consequence of them. Strictly speaking, they only incidentally and fortuitously intersect with building at all. The vast majority of architectural projects are unbuilt, but like unperformed symphonies, certain ones (or more often, chains of them) become significant markers—if not for the general public, then, alas, to the interested.

And like symphonies, architecture may be enjoyed, despised, or passed through with indifference, without the audience knowing or having to care what is significant about them. In other words, architecture can remain a black box, as most cultural and scientific disciplines are to the public, with no ill effects whatsoever. We know of clients in full physical possession of a project, who live in them, who comprehend less of them than colleagues who know the project only through drawings. Architecture hides in plain sight, and its form of intelligibility confers a measure of autonomy and possessability to anyone with an interest; it is a currency beyond what can be held materially.

This shared inheritance distinguishes architecture (and perhaps musical composition) from most of the art world, in which the divide-and-conquer effect of the market is so profound that it has effectively severed or stopped artistic lineages. Not so, paradoxically, with architecture. Despite its fundamental proximity to wealth and power (or because of it), the culture persists—perhaps because the stakes are so low. Architecture in built form is not typically portable; as opposed to other art, it is rarely even preserved. Architectural works, which are essentially information in the form of drawings and models—the instructions, so to speak—have little value either as artifacts or in the mass market. Most architectural projects are basically expensive one-offs, prototypes that very rarely get even close to mass production.

The market, however, does massively intervene when architects promote themselves, which is why they are often so reluctant to acknowledge other architects, especially contemporaries, as influences. But make no mistake—the best ones are watching each other like hawks. Their public rhetoric typically foregrounds unique invention, especially as it pertains to answering client needs or pragmatic concerns. (All true enough. We do it ourselves.) However, the rhetoric rarely gets to the deeper cultural substratum, which is a pity. Imagine a culture alive and well (maybe)—a legacy of projects connecting many architects that the public, the press (especially the press), most curators, and the profession are completely ignorant of or indifferent to. The public consequences are unfortunate as well. Building becomes the only bona fide to the press and profession alike. What is not recognized is that a built design is rarely identical with the project that made it possible. The legacy of the unbuilt project(s) that preceded it are never discussed.

There's a certain democracy of objects; the object could be dog shit! On this, certain cultures are more articulate than others. I remember talking to the French architectural theorist Antoine Picon about form and realizing that his sense of form related more closely to ideal or platonic forms. Those were form to him. He might see clods of earth or stones or natural material as belonging to the unformed world. China or Japan, by contrast, have cultures that are extremely articulate about those materials; they belong to a world of form and can be discussed as such.

John Hejduk knew this well. He would intuit the form of an object as having a kind of energy: slightly open, slightly closed, everything in the object generating a certain energy as a form of expression. I learned this from my mother, too—that an object would possess a kind of degree-zero energy that relates to classicism. Not too open, not too closed—hitting a sweet spot at the level of form making, where no part or inflection would draw attention from the whole.

I would see it constantly as a child: my father would choose a wineglass at the store, and my mother would look over at me, and I could see she meant, "It's going too much like *this*!" But those conditions are actually impersonal conditions. For instance, the Baccarat Perfection pattern, which was designed for the French wine industry, was designed within the constraints of neoclassical aesthetics, and yet it feels intuitively perfect. This may be devolvable into simple geometry, but people regard this as a special series of glasses. It isn't whim or fancy, and it has nothing to do with money, since there are hundreds of other series from that glassmaker, probably more expensive ones, and they're horrible. And they're all well crafted, too. You can train people to be more sensitive to these things, and first they will understand, then they will feel it. It's most challenging to actually create it. Philip Johnson was a connoisseur in this regard. He could see it, but many times he wasn't able to do it. He had a very good eye for things other people were doing.

This intuition or ability comes from being extremely sensitive to the object world. It's basically visual training or mainly about vision. You see this in other cultures. I remember being struck by it in Milan: you'd see groups of men standing in front of storefronts, looking at a pair of shoes and discussing the proportions of shoes. You'd never see that in New York. I remember buying a pair of shoes in Milan, and all the men in Aldo Rossi's office, where I was working at the time, knew where I'd gotten them.

I also experienced Hejduk doing this. I was working on an elevation drawing for his Devil's Bridge project. There were elements of the approach stairs that were taken more or less directly from Mies van der Rohe; they were the stairs leading up to the Farnsworth House. I then put in a more or less Miesian rail—a tubular rail you might find at the Seagram Building. What Hejduk did to the rail was shocking to me. He took my more orthodox description from the Farnsworth House and eliminated one of the uprights, then put the support at the center of the rail. He shifted it to one T-shaped upright with an inclined plane, then bent the two ends, and so it immediately took on a strange animistic quality that the Miesian rail didn't have. It had a weirdness to it, but it also strangely mimicked the treads holding the stone slabs in the Miesian design. It would have vibrated like crazy, like a tuning fork, which I'm sure would have amused him a lot. It was no longer a frame, but this was evident in retrospect—I don't think he ever conceived of it in those terms. Hejduk was fond of those kinds of extractions and transformations, but he had a knack for making them strange.

Hejduk would give us sketches to draw up. He gave us a rough pen-and-ink sketch of a birdcage-like object with a tail on top. It was a very crude sketch. It was another example of my being a dutiful student (though I had graduated), but it was a turning point in terms of my education. I got the sketch, took it back, and drafted it up in the most literal way. I knew that what I drew was not good, but it was a dutiful representation of what he literally drew. And he looked at me—looked through me. He said something like, "You know that I know that you know what's going on here: get the fuckin' proportions right." So I said, "OK." I did the drawing, and it was fine. It was a very interesting moment—I did know that there was something wrong with the first drawing.

At the time, he wanted very specific elements drawn from both architecture and painting. For his *Victims* project, Hejduk wanted to reference a particular streetcar from a Paul Delvaux painting. So I went to the *Traction Handbook for Model Railroads*, and I drew some streetcars up, and I connected them to the European type and got the representation close to what he was thinking about. It was a lot of fun.

———

Unlike in the sciences, greater knowledge of, say, scripting languages in computation will not produce a better architecture any more than the relatively rudimentary state of knowledge of the human brain in Shakespeare's time hampered his invention of subjectivity. Amending the black box analogy from computer science, inputs (for us a chain of influences) are important insofar as they establish working assumptions about where a project stands. What has already been done? Can we see how it might be advanced—or not, or not yet?

Despite a multitude of technologies available today, the cultural dimension of architecture is essentially indifferent to technology's two-hundred-year-old embrace of the teleology

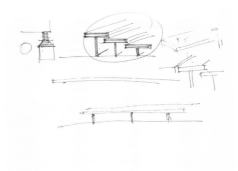

Studies of stair treads for the Devil's Bridge, John Hejduk, 1982

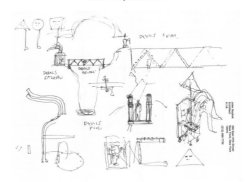

Studies for the Devil's Bridge: Devil's Seat and Devil's Gazebo, John Hejduk, 1982

Study for the Devil's Bridge with Gazebo, John Hejduk, 1982

of improvement. Technology is far older than science and was advanced for millennia as technique prior to scientific explanation. Material processes like cooking or ceramics have enabled artisans to skillfully and precisely direct chemistry or physics without formal knowledge of them.

I am not advocating a willful ignorance of science, which is always salutary. Rather, I wish to make clear that an entirely different knowledge set must be mobilized. In many situations the architect must reasonably draw a line between design at the level of materials science and at the scale of architecture. Doubtless there are occasions when design at the microscale affects design at the macro, as was the case with our design team's use of superplasticizers in the concrete mix used in the O-14 tower. However, a distinction should be drawn between the engineers of micromaterial performance and the architects guiding those materials at the scale of building. Asking the architect to engineer materials is like expecting André Courrèges to synthesize PVC for his miniskirts! We enjoy pushing material limits in our designs, but properly, it is the chemist's job to invent them and our engineers' job to suggest them, and only when necessary.

Despite attempts to connect architecture to recent art-world theorization, architecture has never been medium specific. Rather, architecture is inherently a polymedia practice involving information and matter. Architectural design connects to the concept of format that David Joselit developed in response to new forms of mediation in art, but at some level architecture has been implicated in format since at least the Renaissance. Today, of course, architecture's embedment in new media amplifies its reach, saturation, and, inversely, duration. Thus pre- or postfixes relative to media or mediums are in architecture not so relevant since they are always in operation. Falling heavily on the informational side of the equation, architectural design, especially now, traffics in codifications that even prior to any actual material engagement are open, mainly through the currency of matter-inflected geometry, to rapid changes in material systems or even type.

Today architectural design continuously rehearses its possible entanglements with matter through emulations long before any material is literally moved and sends out multiple iterations modifying the model that it ultimately instrumentalizes. What is unique to architecture's complex of entanglements with the world is that its medium is information; it bundles and influences multiple information streams at once. The nexus of this complex of information does the work in the world of building and as such has a primacy that secondary representations don't possess. Architecture regularly throws off multiple visible representations of itself in much the same way that a physical process such as an explosion can be endlessly imaged; today the image has become exponentially more ubiquitous through the agency of social media. Social media's saturation has also enormously amplified and increased the complexity of what was once quaintly termed "site and context" in the same measure that it has shrunk the half life of images to almost nothing. The image will never produce the physical explosion of architecture. It may, however, serve as a source for creating or modifying a design, but it must do so through the agency of entrained nonrepresentations, which architectural design uniquely mediates.

One redeeming quality of architectural design is the significant slowing of the image through knowledge and practice. One of the most notable instances of this phenomenon is Daniel Libeskind's *Chamber Works*, a series of rigorously abstract drawings depicting the systematic emergence and collapse of multiple geometric worlds out of and back into a line. At the time he drew the *Chamber Works*, Libeskind conceived architectural drawing as autonomous production sufficient unto itself. These drawings make no reference to illusionistic space. The subsequent thirty-year history of Libeskind's use of the *Chamber Works* is even more remarkable: they have served as an almost inexhaustible catalogue of geometric source material for actual building projects, a practice unique in the history of architecture. I am reminded of the quip attributed to James Joyce: it took him a lifetime to write *Finnegan's Wake*, and so it should take the reader a lifetime to read it.

How different Libeskind's masterful development of the line was to the excess of lines typically applied to drawings of conventional architecture of the same period, a practice we then termed "compensatory graphics." A similar yet slightly more rigorous version of such drawing was the ostentatious display of geometric construction lines—communicating, no doubt, that the architect was guided always by reason!

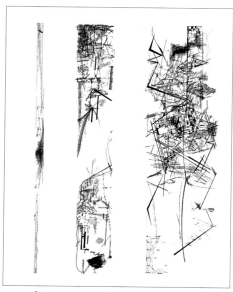

Selections from *Chamber Works* suite,
Daniel Libeskind, 1983

As active producers rather than passive consumers we are thankfully armed with a relative immunity to the seductions of the endless bombardment of advertising. Indeed, we are unenchanted by practically everything we see and thus have the urge to redesign everything to our own liking. However, when we finally see something that we like, we become attached to it to an almost pathological degree. For me, the Italian bicycle-parts maker Campagnolo's mid-1980s Corsa Record Gruppo (particularly the first-generation crankset and the prototype Delta brakes) was so achingly beautiful that time literally stopped. To my mind, no components' aesthetics before or after have surpassed their precarious balance between complexity and simplicity—like that of a good English suit or the form of an Mk. 1 Spitfire.

Thoroughbred lines: the Spitfire Mk. 1

The Corsa Record group was created at a critical moment, when Campagnolo's forty-year dominance as a producer for the racing fraternity was under real threat from Japanese component manufacturers whose designs by massive, computationally driven R & D departments outstripped Campagnolo both in terms of price and sheer performance. Campagnolo's design response was to counter the performance threat with beauty. Their artisans or designers in Vicenza, assisted by traditional tool-and-die makers, were asked to make parts that looked like a computer had generated them! Would that a computer could ever design such marvels! In a situation analogous to the famous crafted intersections of Mies's Barcelona Chair, aesthetic performance outstripped functional performance. (Extreme functional performance at a world-class level in cycling is a nonissue in any case to anyone but top athletes, whose success relies on a tenth of a second faster shift times and a few grams less weight.) Later, I learned there exists a Campagnolo subculture (large enough for the *Wall Street Journal* to label it a "cult") in complete accord with my aesthetic reaction; websites endlessly parse minutiae, and there is a precise consensus around the very parts I am talking about. Even today I do not tire of staring at those parts for hours, a practice I have learned the great Italian cyclist Paolo Bettini would do in his hotel room before a race. But I digress.

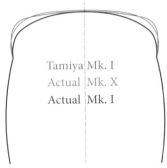

Tamiya Mk. I
Actual Mk. X
Actual Mk. I

Small differences mean everything: comparative geometric descriptions of Spitfire models' Cowling cross sections redrawn from Yoyuso Airplane Model

A sensibility trained to appreciate small differences, to discriminate, is but a step toward mobilizing it for design. By itself it is a receptive art that is good enough for the connoisseur or a good client. Before 1968 it was an assumed piece of equipment among people of a certain social and economic class or those working in the design arts, but in my experience it is a capacity fairly well distributed across the class and economic spectrum. In public school, I perceived that the working-class kids who naturally had a talent for it tended to be closer to production or because of economic circumstances had to develop a sensibility themselves; the majority of the upper-middle-class kids benefited or suffered from a particular form of taste training through the privilege of being detached consumers. For lack of a better term, one could call it "taste culture."

Designers of the Spitfire

The airframe: Reginald Mitchell, creator of a lineage of Schneider Trophy race planes that evolved into the Spitfire

All of this went by the wayside, ideologically at least, in the wake of the upheavals of 1968. Nanako and I independently and quite beyond our wills were steeped in it essentially from birth such that—like so many skills learned in youth—it became reflexive. You see, you understand, you accept, reject, or (most challenging of all) change. The temptation facing a designer who is so immersed is the inclination to follow one's *natural affinities*, which at some level inoculate one from making major mistakes—to adhere to the quotidian *good taste* one finds in well-detailed minimalist projects, white-box museums, and the like, which are so seductive in their claims to timelessness. The problem for an architect seeking to create something beyond the accepted canon is where taste becomes proscriptive, an aesthetic straitjacket.

The engine: Beatrice Shilling, inventor of "Miss Shilling's Orifice," a crucial modification of the Rolls Royce Merlin

We have no problem exercising taste judgments, but they are useful only as a design ethos, as opposed to as a set of fixed standards. Instead of closing down avenues of exploration through inflexible standards of correctness, we have sought at every opportunity to find a more generous and expansive path through the world. This often means deliberately working against intuitive inclinations and wrestling with the counterintuitive and the ugly. Edgar Degas remarked, "When everything is perfect, nothing is perfect." Again, an ethos becomes more a dynamic corrective, always running very close to failure; it will often mean embracing an extreme situation and then finding in it a precarious balance. Having started with a trained sensibility, we found this way of internalizing the outside a difficult way forward, for it meant embracing elemental forces and strange proclivities and

Cult image of the C-Record crankset

The triumph of aesthetic performance over functional performance: Campagnolo Corsa Record group, 1985

John Hejduk

First collaboration: Jesse Reiser and Nanako Umemoto

seeing in the most unpromising things a life or how, as a designer, to extract a life from disenchanted material.

I vividly recall seeing John Hejduk at night in the empty studio at Cooper Union picking up a Coke can by the top like a tiny toy. He was a giant of a man, almost seven feet tall, with huge hands, so he was in some way estranged from the scale of everyday things. He touched it so gingerly, brought it up to his eyes bemused and laid it down again, pulling his hand away rapidly as if it were burning. Amazing that he could extract something out of even a Coke can—and so un-pop a response! I realized he was a sensitive, someone who was attuned to the strange element in things.

His was a way I understood without theorization. It was more basic than that. Far from being a state of psychic arrest, as postulated by psychoanalysts, this primitive felicity could potentially enchant the world anew, in an ever-broadening chain of fetishes, polymorphic affections. It was a stunning lesson all the more poignant because it had always been with me, assumed and unacknowledged. It continues to inform our work, despite the changes in formal and organizational motives over the years. In a sense it is the ultimate enduring criterion, irrespective of program, site, or even the dynamics of materiogeometrics. It is also our rejoinder to the oft-cited stopping problem. For us it has never been a dilemma at all. Our work is not based upon arrested movement or processes that involve it. As most of our work is static, the common motive beyond aesthetics is to impart a sense of potential, a potential energy most closely allied to the dynamics of animism, which acquires its greatest power in arrest. Indeed, dynamic architecture becomes visible only when mediated in films or video or better yet as still images or flattened into silhouette; literal movement in architecture is routinely uninteresting and almost imperceptible, lost in the movement that continuously surrounds us anyway. Redeemed by architecture's congenital belatedness, its inherent slowness thankfully never quite allows it to be brought up to the speed of other media except in reproduction.

Above all, what is important is the output: the architectural object. The architectural object tells what the design is doing and suggests where the project might be going as a result. What comes in between is opaque, chaotic, and full of contradiction. Therefore, accounts of the process of generation, such as its sequence, reasoning, or history, are beside the evaluative point. This is not to say that a project terminates in unreason and chaos, full of contradiction—only if one wants. We rather evaluate a project solely on its effects. Recalling Jorge Luis Borges's reading of Novalis, "the greatest wizard would be the one who bewitched himself to the point of accepting his own phantasmagoria as autonomous apparitions." The currency and power of great architecture are such that the phantasmagoria is communal.

Often in my long collaboration with Nanako Umemoto and our group, I cannot say who is precisely author of what. It is active consensus that advances an architectural project, like a jam unfolds in jazz. Architectural will, fortitude, or effort to sell a project is another issue entirely. Projects shape humans as much as they are shaped by them. This can be literal—as the legs of people who grew up in traditional Japanese architecture can attest—or it can be indicated by the habits, the sensibilities, and the very cognitions of all of us. Certain architects thus become their own avant-garde: when designing, and through what they design, they are the first to witness consequences. In the same way, Manhattan Project scientists foresaw a terrible new source of heat and light before any of the hardware was made.

The opacity of the human applies equally to architects. Architects are not in a privileged position vis-à-vis their own work. In our experience, the state of design is essentially egoless, with the architect witness, enabler, and manager of what is (ideally) an unfolding process and state of play. Some projects live and die without ever being built, or even more typically are realized so belatedly that they are past forgetting by the cognoscenti even as press and public celebrates their newness. Chains of projects play out in time and in imaginary space especially. Projects may pass through the minds and hands of many architects. In this respect the discipline is akin to a river whose streams feed mainstreams feeding tributaries: a ramifying obsession sometimes shared by multiple architects, sometimes sustained within a single practice.

Capsule house designed by Yoshio Higashikata
Nanako Umemoto's first work experience: sales guide for capsule houses

MIGRATION OF A DIAGRAM

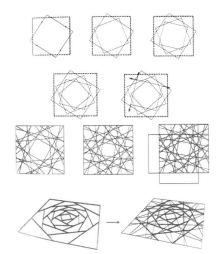

Cecil Balmond's structural geometry
for Toyo Ito's Serpentine Pavilion, 2002

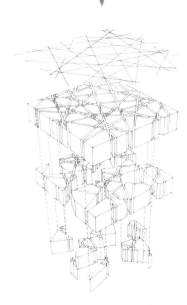

Toyo Ito colors in Balmond's diagram
and turns the structure into infill, 2002.

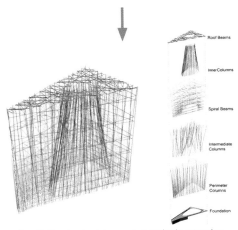

Sou Fujimoto stretches and massively upscales
Balmond's diagram for the Taichung Tower, 2011.

A contemporary work may retroactively connect a new constellation of past architectural works by authors separated in time and space, otherwise unrelated and unknown to one another. This Borgesian model of history making applies as much to architectural authors as it does to writers and involves a dynamic process of constant reconfiguration. As opposed to static hierarchies or genealogies, this lineage looks backward to create a history or forward to project a future.

However, a project is not indefinite. Some architects are notable for initiating projects and others for ending them. Call them beginners and enders, but whether one begins, ends, or jumps in midway is relatively unimportant. Most sustained projects are polyauthored anyway because their trajectory, even for new projects, comes from a legacy of those previous—even if in reaction against that legacy, always from others. Indeed, projects, like the circumstances around them such as site, program, budget, changing client preferences, et cetera, could always be otherwise. Arbitrariness at some level is the sea in which architects swim. Things always could and do go otherwise, but this by itself in no way dooms a project. So projects like writing have no ideal starting point, as Roland Barthes keenly observed in *Writing Degree Zero*. It is not a question of where one starts. One could start anywhere, it being more important how one moves in a project and ultimately to flesh everything out. The inevitable unchanging situation, like life, is of being thrown into a historical situation not of our choosing, and we enter a project, or not, wherever it happens to be. Tragic, indeed, are those who waste their efforts doing over projects that have already been done, by vain recourse to a linear logic based on *first principles*.

The paradox of authorship is stranger still: generally, the most universal and grandly impersonal works come from single authors or at most small groups—certainly not from focus groups. What is important is the intuition and receptiveness to move a project somewhere new—to open up new territory within the project itself, seeing a way forward.

Only a limited number of projects are actively in play at any one time. Not every project undertaken by an architect is part of this active list; the vast majority of architecture is merely perpetuated. Most architects will simply repeat models without contributing anything fundamentally new. This is more the rule than the exception—the profession is built on that practice. Repeatability in scientific experimentation is the sine qua non—in culture it is just treading water. At best, cultural repetition acts as a form of preservation, especially when projects are done well. Schools traditionally perform this essentially conservative function of sustaining cultural inertia, transmitting information through unchanging repetition, until eventually, a fortuitous confluence of disruptive influences meets an architect who would craftily knot them together and an audience who would be receptive to the madness.

As with all cultural pursuits, however, moving to novelty once excellence is achieved is easier said than done. Not all projects show promise, and it takes something close to informed intuition to know where to leap. I am reminded of a story related to me by the accomplished biochemist Olga Blumenfeld, who would be approached regularly by her postdoc students about lines of experimentation that she knew in advance would go nowhere. Sometimes a decade of experimentation, papers, and grants would go by before they, too, reached the same conclusion!

To be sure, those who theorize a project may not be the best designers of them, and that is nothing new. To be heretical, while Leon Battista Alberti may have delivered the most coherent theory of architecture in the Renaissance, he does not stand at the same level as an architect as Donato Bramante or Filippo Brunelleschi. In recent history it is ironic, indeed, that some of those who theorized and advocated for complex form were among the least capable of doing it well. Ironic, too, is that as we are now separated by at least four generations from an art and architectural tradition that imparted the sensibility and skills to handle complex form making, we are at last in possession of tools that could easily effectuate it, but most are incapable of doing anything well with it; hence the plethora of taffy projects. On reflection it is not that surprising. There are craft traditions with unbroken technical histories, such as ceramics or glassblowing, and yet there will always be far more terrible designs perfectly crafted than great designs imperfectly crafted.

In a shocking example of forgetfulness, one of the principal achievements of modernism was to eclipse over four hundred years of perspectival representation. Modern subjectivity, it was recognized, found the social and political confluence of human subject and object intolerable and had torn free of that correlation. Photography and film in particular devised strategies like montage to break free of the determinism of the optical/perspectival projection inherent in the medium and mechanisms of film. To be clear, we regularly create perspectives for presentational purposes. For better or (mainly) worse, perspectives and animations have become mandatory in practically every competition and presentation we do; clients and juries expect increasingly photorealistic renditions. We regard perspective essentially as propaganda. In our studio we are careful never to use them generatively.

Details from *Walls of the Second Theater,* bronze reliefs, Jesse Reiser, 1984

With the digital turn, the very real achievements of modernist abstraction, among them the revival of discrete metrical space, were suddenly replaced again by the sham spatiality of perspective and, for the architect, the design *space* of the perspective window. It is not clear whether this wholesale return to perspective was the accidental consequence of using Hollywood animation software as a design platform, or, more likely, the mistaken belief that in software one could design in *real space*. This perception is so ubiquitous, especially now that a vast plurality of the world lives in solipsistic gamespace, that it appears as common sense. Forgotten by architects is the difficult mental achievement of understanding and correlating the metrically based conventions of plan, section, and elevation. The general public may not be expected to read them, but only a generation ago it was a minimal expectation for architects. I am not advocating a simple return to those conventions, or worse, middlebrow sectional perspectives, but the baby should not be thrown out with the bathwater. Rather, I would advocate putting the convention on steroids.

The basis for this skill has been imparted by the five-hundred-year-old art of drawing. A complex body such as the human body had to be primarily known and secondarily seen to be drawn. Bones, musculature, viscera, and skin had to be understood as a complex dynamic system in interchange. This knowledge continuously informed observation. In truth, direct observation would act only as a check on knowledge, as the outward presentation of a nude model conveyed very little information at all. In a nonweightlifter, only vague shadows hint at the underlying anatomy. The body would thus first be understood by the draftsman systematically and as a myriad of anatomical landmarks: bones, muscles, tendons, and their insertions in imaginary space. Many times, as in the drawings of Michelangelo, superficial muscle groups, the ones visible on a living model, would be ignored completely in favor of deeper invisible structure that created a more vivid effect of a body in action, the science of expression taking an entirely different course than medical anatomy. It was this knowledge that was in play: a complex of gross anatomy, stylistic convention, vision, and the corporeal memory and action of the draftsman. The body was thus conceived in a complex and purely metrical space, permitting it to be drawn from memory, from any angle and attitude.

Two salient factors emerged that have a bearing on the current situation in architectural design. The first is the nonrepresentational aspect of this mode of drawing; bodies here are primarily presented rather than represented. In essence, they are designed. Second, they are primarily understood as dynamic systems in metrical space and only later and only sometimes represented in perspective *space*. However, given the inherent complexity of the body and the geometric undecidability of garments and drapery, even in the Renaissance, they carve out a local counterspatiality to the architecture of regular bodies that comprised the normative perspectival field. Taken to its limit by Michelangelo in the Sistine ceiling and even more so in the *Last Judgment*, a single regulating perspectival space is essentially eliminated in favor of a strange carnal spatiality, defined by a *lost and found* geometric framework in which multiple episodic perspectives and nonperspectives weave into and out of organic space.

The line itself has historically been utilized as the sensitive index of multiple cultural, material, and technical influences. To give a famous example, the lines defining the wet drapery clothing the frieze figures of the Parthenon incorporate what is in essence a multidimensional force field, registering with continuously changing degrees of relative intensity the impress of dynamic idealized bodies, the surface tension effects of the wet fabric, gravity forces, and conventionalized formal traits of drapery then in vogue—all graven through obdurate stone. This capacity for complex encoding with any number of technical, material, and cultural dimensions is now part of the architect's toolbox. The informed line functions beyond the gravity-based conventions of plan, section, and elevation, which were adequate to describe the regular bodies of modernism but are inadequate in the new context of architectural form making. Our method, derived directly from classical drawing and from there to spatial carving, consists of dynamically coordinating literally hundreds of essentially two-dimensional measured profiles, carefully corrected from every aspect, to create space and form, thus avoiding the distortions and formal abortions of the perspective window.

Ultimately, the complex feats of coordination and control among seeing, knowing, and acting that drawing mobilizes—like crossing the blood/brain barrier—are mappable into other architectural relations as well. The relations logically become totally separable from the terms—the historical analogy between bodies and buildings, structure/skin relations, et cetera, being only the most obvious. The digital turn also made possible for the first time a radical revision of one of modernism's most effective and productive critiques of modernity. As Jeffrey Kipnis points out (admiring Manfredo Tafuri), mass production and standardization, the sine qua non of modernity, were mobilized ideologically against the "malaise and existential despair of modernity itself…to wrest architecture from its historic servitude to wealth and power and redirect it into the service of the masses."

With computation, however, came the heretofore unthinkable (at least among serious modernist architects and theorists) instrumentality, which, among other things, would embrace bourgeois tailoring through the new technology of mass customization. It also went a long way in obviating the argument over what a modernist would not do for ideological reasons and what I suspect they could not do as a practical matter. Strange, indeed, that the immediate effect of a mass-customized thing was nearly indistinguishable from that of an old-style custom product, the virtue residing, beyond the practical achievement, in the abstract belief that if more variations existed cheaply somewhere else in the world, then having the unique thing would be politically acceptable. Almost as strange in retrospect are the canonical handmade prototypes of modernism, for example, Mies van der Rohe's Barcelona chair, which was handwrought to look like a machine had produced it, presumably by the thousands!

In terms of architectural production, it is well not to think in too ideological terms about the technology or technique. Architecture as we practice it is done in a very similar way to a cottage industry. Our small team can do the work that once required an army of draftsmen. Anachronistic craft ethos, while today vanishing from the jobsite, is essential

Michelangelo's study of the *Last Judgment*, 1534–36

Wet draperies, Birth of Athena, East Pediment, Parthenon, 447–32 BCE

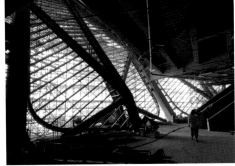

Taipei Pop Main Hall Glazing based on MK VIII RAF goggles, RUR Architecture, 2018

to the design process. Craft has not therefore been superseded, as was thought a virtue in modernism; rather, it has migrated to the design studio, where medieval craftsmanship links to computation and mass customization, thus weaponizing and systematizing craft practices in ways that no traditional craftsman could have imagined. With computation, human limits are exceeded at both ends of the spectrum, from extremely fast feats of coordination and integration to processes so slow that no human would be capable of (or interested in) sustaining them.

Which returns us to the most poignant use of mass customization in architecture. Unlike the mass customization of products like dress shirts, which can be offered to individual customers in custom-tailored variations, the most effective mass customization in architecture occurs when a population of varying components are used in concert in a single building.

It is only recently that architecture could express a world increasingly shaped by invisible forces and statistical determinations, so that a statistical condition in action could be made visible. Strange, too, that the so-called decadent art nouveau already had a version of mass customization in the ancient technology of founding and stamping, which in turn emerged out of repetitive practices such as weaving and embroidery—activities so mind-numbing, so redolent of malaise and despair (and also, interestingly, the tasks historically assigned to women) that Michelangelo places them at the very bottom of his hierarchy of the arts. Indeed, it is this very indifference of technology to style that reveals so much about the cultural employments of technology. The machine aesthetics of modernism put forward the image of the machine as a truer and better representation of modernization than the art nouveau or neobaroque or neo-Adirondack, although all of them and more were, in greater or lesser degrees of fidelity to their models, mechanized for the market.

There are special cases where a project begins and ends with a single work—the project being too comprehensive and intractable to advance further. Architectural projects have their own form of identity in this sense: some concatenation of objective factors that incidentally bear a unique stamp only retrospectively known as authorship. The best are as marvelously impersonal as nature, and for that reason, their very inhumanity (in the most poignant cases) results in the most humane architecture. Projects come to an end through an exhaustion of possibilities. They die or become foreclosed for a time until something, some counterintuitive factor, sets them into motion again—or perhaps not.

One of my mentors, Aldo Rossi, argued the foreclosure of the whole modernist project as the principal existential situation facing his generation. In his case it also yielded one of the most perfect and unrepeatable overall projects in a period dominated by postmodernist eclecticism. I postulate that had Rossi's project been delivered to the world, say, seventy-five years earlier, it would have supplanted full-blown modernism, or at the least would have posed a serious challenge to its hegemony. In actuality, his project was itself circumscribed by the limits of his time (the 1970s and '80s), the place (northern Italy), and a specific building culture that today is largely gone. In the early part of the twentieth century, the same project would have been more or less universally applicable, but by the end of Rossi's time it was constrained by a locus and by the perfection of death. By the mid-1980s, when his work became internationally recognized, it went from being a clarion call to an elegy in short order. The classical dictum that nothing could be added or subtracted applied so well to Rossi's model that although some talented younger practitioners, Steven Holl and Thom Mayne, tried for a time to extend and transform his project into their own, after an initial period of infatuation, they each abandoned the endeavor; it was too perfect to advance. Too perfect even for Rossi himself, who could only copy himself at the end. The project did not travel well.

———————

Nanako and I were fortunate to come onto the scene, as it were, during a period of disciplinary confusion not unlike today. As a result, in some sense, we want every student of architecture to have the experiences we did with orthodoxy. Orthodoxy protects a designer from theory for a while: students could become indoctrinated or opinionated and simply enjoy designing, after which they would gain the strength to be exposed to a critical approach. "Imitation to emulation to jealousy" is a better model for young designers than are critical frameworks. The approach is old-fashioned, but it stems

Aldo Rossi

from love—to be ravished by someone's work, which is not critical; to be completely overcome by someone's work and then want to do it yourself. The appreciation turns into frustration. You'll take it in, believing it, then begin to disbelieve it. After all that, you have something to be critical about.

With a critical mindset, it's difficult to decide to design anything at all. At Princeton, where I teach, it's typical for students to be so well-read and so smart that they steer themselves toward criticism and away from practice. The education of a designer is not the development of discursive intelligence but of a certain attitude. They're suddenly confronted with a range of problems that are not architectural per se. They're confronted with massive world problems, and there's an ethical question in many cases as to whether architecture is even the right tool to address those urgent problems. To paraphrase my friend Jeff Kipnis, it's like asking an aspiring chef to begin by solving world hunger.

I first dealt with these problems through drawing and painting, which I loved. I even transferred out of the architecture school after my first year into the painting department, so my first experience of copying and also of drawing and thinking through other sensibilities came by way of that rather than architecture. Attempting to master drawing and attempting to master *master* drawings was a big deal, and it was an obsessive pursuit. The whole five years I was at Cooper Union, I kept taking more than the required drawing classes because once I started confronting that kind of description, I couldn't stop. It was also extremely difficult, as I was not a natural draftsman.

Theoretical discourse, while rigorous in its own terms, offers only a tenuous, language-based framework when it comes down to actual problems confronting design. When one is suddenly subjected to all the ramifications of the actual work at hand, a thousand decisions separate the construct from the practice and the final result. It takes a thousand decisions, many of which elude reason, and often they must be made quickly. Intuition is important, but not as a vague condition—rather, a precisely guided intuition is required, operating within very small constraints. One could talk about what separates a mediocre Sebastiano Serlio painting from a Raphael. Serlio technically followed each precept of neoclassicism coming out of the Renaissance and would produce an average work. His rules could be followed by architects, and they wouldn't go too wrong, but they wouldn't go too right, either. The precepts don't necessarily produce great work.

————

In Japan, before Jesse, I studied at Osaka University of the Arts under Harvey Shapiro, a disciple of Ian McHarg. I wasn't focusing when they taught that stuff (although my best friend used McHarg's charting methods for business and money, and he said they work really well). Shapiro did not want to talk to me, because I designed things, and he said he did not believe in people who design things. I had to take many of his classes, and I got C's on everything. Planning, urban planning, environmental planning: everything was a C.

When it came to design studio, everything was an A. Design studios involved small-scale projects, since it was an environmental design school. I liked the design instructor; he had just come from the United States, and he was a disciple of Lawrence Halprin. Kinsaku Nakane was a so-called garden designer. Nothing is fixed in landscape, because the trees are growing, water is running, soil is changing, and moss is growing. Everything is growing and dying. He did lots of restorations of famous temples in Kyoto, but there is no way to restore their original designs because they might have been designed five hundred years ago and have kept growing. That was his specialty. He assigned design problems.

After I went to college for environmental planning, I realized that what I really wanted to do was architecture. But I didn't have a degree, so I couldn't get a job; at that time, especially for a woman, it was very hard to get in. But I was hired to design furniture in product design. So I did lots of full-scale drawing. That's how I learned connections and how to draw curves at one-to-one scale. We were making rattan furniture, which has almost no joints; the joints are always bound together. If there's a flat piece, you have to curve it to wrap it. So almost everything had a curve. My boss would do the sketches, and I would blow them up to full scale to make a template for prototypes. He would never draw it because he would be out watching baseball or at the sushi bar he designed, eating sushi. So I was always working.

Ian McHarg at Osaka University of the Arts, 1971

Harvey Shapiro leads seminar on regional development, June 1972. Nanako Umemoto, bottom left

Nanako Umemoto, far right, with classmates at Osaka University of the Arts

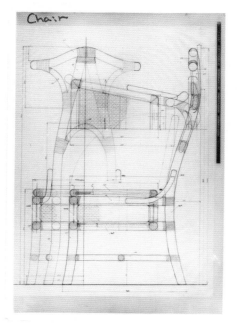

Rattan Chair, full-scale working drawing, Nanako Umemoto, 1979

Kinsaku Nakane, Nanako's professor of garden design, was named a Certified Preserver of Important Intangible Cultural Properties by Japan's ministry of culture.

But I was frustrated not doing architecture, so I would go to help at my professor's office in Tokyo. They worked every day, so I would go on weekends. He was a disciple of Antonin Raymond, who was a disciple of Frank Lloyd Wright. You had to take a test in order to work for Raymond, then once you passed, they would teach you how to eat. It was like Wright: very formal dinners served in the office. Raymond's test was to draw a running horse—that was the drawing exam. He couldn't afford his own office, so it was an office shared with three other architects. So I befriended those guys, too. I would be helping everyone at the same time, and I was helping the landscape design firm next door, too. I was trying to hang on to architecture that way. In Japan there was no going back to architecture once you had a degree in planning or something else.

I came to the United States, and someone told me to go to Cooper Union. And I said, "Oh, that's good—it's a union school." I didn't know it had nothing to do with unions. I just applied as a transfer student. I had no idea how hard it was to get in to that school—I thought it was like a hobby school, so I would get in for sure. I would pass by the building every day, but I didn't know what it was. But somehow they took a transfer student that year. I already had parts of the degree, but I was placed to study with people who were eighteen years old…so I'd have to do eighteen-year-old things, like going to parties wearing lots of makeup. That was how I learned American culture.

In Japan only the thesis had a jury system; otherwise, you just turned in your work. When I came here, I had to present things, so that was horrible for me. At Cooper Union you had to talk about your project, do lots of drawings and model making. I couldn't speak English well. (I was the first student they took directly from Japan. Normally the school was for local kids.) So I made sure that every time I had an assignment, I produced a lot so I wouldn't need to talk. I would make everything correct, and all the requirements would be satisfied. It worked. But my classmates would say it didn't make any sense—they didn't know what I was talking about. Shigeru Ban was a student at the same time; he worked the same way, but he'd had two years of Sci-Arc education, so he had skill already in model making and things like that. When I went to Cooper I had no skill, or very limited skill. In Japan they used sticks, so everything was essentially a wood structural model. I had no idea how to make a model of a site, which was required, so I asked Shigeru to teach me to use his foam cutter, and in the end he just cut everything for me. Then I put on too much paint, so everything became rounded, oozing paint, and he said I was destroying the model.

When I got to know Jesse, I would look at how he made models. I didn't ask anything—I would just look. He would make very precise models, and after a couple months of watching, I started to learn how to do it. Everything was so precise. Shigeru would use a box cutter, but Jesse would use X-ACTO blades, and he would say, "You have to use #11 blades. Throw all the other blades out." So I did, and after that I became quite a good model maker.

———

The cultural dimension of architecture is bound up with impossibilities. Addressing things that could never be resolved is precisely where architecture becomes architecture, as opposed to building or engineering. Architecture has its own definition of mathematics and physics, which is entirely irrational from the point of view of engineering or those disciplines because it's a cultural reading of the state of physics—what physics ought to be rather than what it is. There would be an architectural way of dealing with the infinite. It wouldn't be endless, but would produce the effect of endlessness in a finite thing. Not weightless, but would produce the effect of weightlessness in something extremely heavy. These kinds of issues would be architectural issues, which would relate more to magic than to science.

We became preoccupied with the problem of the continuous surface, which was almost a kind of virus moving through the architectural world, where everyone was absolutely fascinated with the notion of boundlessness. The topological problem—the "surface problem"—in architecture seemed to connect to that fascination. The S-shaped section became a peculiar motif repeated again and again in projects—some well, some not so well. Working through the problem, you would almost want to break through the problem rather than staying within its constraints.

The constraint of an orthodoxy is useful only insofar as it's something to transcend or transgress. This is very different from, for instance, colonial architecture, where there's a form of assimilation—acquiring motifs and assembling them in a neoclassical way. In contrast, if you look at Michelangelo's transformations of classicism, he breaks through—goes beyond the orthodoxy. It's no longer an assimilative project. He produces a different kind, rather than degree, of architecture. It's unsettling, even now, to see those spaces.

In the process of designing, you make a certain set of assumptions that could be attached to more or less any architect making those choices. A crude type might suggest, for instance, two horizontal planes as a provisional organizational strategy for a two-story building—two floating planes with program in between. Such an entity wouldn't be a classical typology but a flexible structure. In the process of design it could either remain as the predominant diagrammatic organization or it might undergo such pressure as to assimilate into another crude type. It might be as malleable as wax.

For our Angewandte project for the University of Applied Arts Vienna, we were going to do some form of a bar fusing with the existing building. With the Sagaponack House, early versions were like a Miesian pavilion floating over the ground; then our desire to make the pavilion distinct from the ground changed. The first moves were geometric; then there were physical consequences, which were factored back in. Architecture is continually saved by the recalcitrance of matter. The organizations we are interested in apply across scales and equally across sites and programs. So they resist categorization, nor could they be understood in a chronological way.

Periodically, an inchoate desire—for boundlessness, for instance—runs through the discipline. There is a political dimension to the notion of boundlessness, which overlaps notions of transparency, openness, and freedom. The desire for boundlessness attempts to bring freedom to the inertia of architecture, which is conventionally finite, bounded, and lacking in dynamism. The bundle of desires is the thing that interacts—they're like political sentiments bound up in space. These motivate the desire for the project and can then connect to concrete examples: for instance, the model of the parking garage embodying the impossibility of a road folded up into a building. This becomes the generative model for a building that would incorporate movement in a new way.

The other aspect of what we are calling the surface project is attached to atmospheres and the desire that the S-shaped section would present no hard corners or hard distinction between floor, wall, and ceiling. One's eyes do the walking, and one achieves some sense of boundlessness. This lineage is understood to come from OMA, and even before that, the oblique architecture of Claude Parent. FOA and MVRDV took it up in a topological aspect. Then the problem came to Columbia, and that's where our office intersected with it, with our Kansai Library (a year after FOA's Port Terminal was submitted in competition but before it was actually built). The library threw us off of the surface project.

A project becomes hardened into an orthodoxy after there are no possibilities left. If it becomes an orthodoxy, it loses its sense of freedom and has diminishing effects. Orthodoxy also becomes ideological because it establishes a set of rules that extends beyond any particular case. This is because orthodoxy is word-based. The particular instantiations of a design are never congruent with orthodoxy's theorization or rules.

There was, for instance, a new lease on life given to realism by the pop movement after the triumph of abstract painting had presumably ended five hundred years of realism. There was a sense in the 1990s that the period of architectural projects commenting on themselves via eclecticism and historicism could be ended. So there were fifteen years or so where there was a period of new health. We're back now in a period of commentary.

These cycles are similar to what happened during the Cultural Revolution in China, where history took a back seat to immediate developments—so there was less of a burden of historicism or representational thinking. I use a kind of right-wing technique to turn those things around. I always chafed at the idea that one gender or certain social groups could take claim to a particular space, because to me it always smacked of the talk that the Nazis made about "Jewish physics." In the 1930s the findings of Einstein and others were dismissed because so-called German physics dealt with mechanics and problems of the real world. That, of course, ended with the atomic bomb, when "Jewish physics" became a problem of the real world. I always found it offensive when groups would make disturbing ideological claims in that vein. I don't know what a group is—I don't even know what a human is! I really don't know how to construct those boundaries.

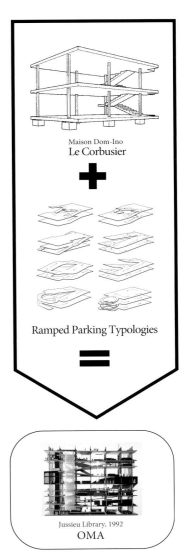

Maison Dom-Ino
Le Corbusier

+

Ramped Parking Typologies

=

Jussieu Library, 1992
OMA

Dom-Ino + parking lot = Jussieu
The lineage of continuous-surface projects might be seen to start with two projects of Rem Koolhaas. Alternately, these projects are themselves the sum of Le Corbusier's Maison Dom-Ino and *Architectural Graphic Standards*'s ramped parking typologies.

University of Applied Arts Vienna,
RUR Architecture, 2012

If one interrogates many of the contemporary socially driven projects, they're typically quite conservative as architecture. They assume a certain normative technological character and are generally not connected to any kind of formal invention or exuberance. This might relate to an ossification of the norm. It's also dialectical in a way—that whatever transgressions happen to the system, they must happen dialectically to what is so-called normal, which is a representational way of thinking. The program is transgressive, and the form—that of "The Man"—would be normative. And so it rarely plays out as anything other than a prohibition on invention. One could make a counterargument that their formalism yielded more radical, revolutionary, and disturbing consequences than radical programs in normative spaces. Because program is essentially invisible, it doesn't rock the boat at all. It doesn't take any form, and so it's less threatening.

––––––––––

The paradox in our attitude toward authorship is that, in a way, the most unauthored work doesn't come from data-mining, collection, or authorship. Realizing how existentially contingent one really is already dismantles the notion of any coherent author or source. It would come from a sense that what you are made up of is influences. In any particular project one is tapping into a fairly impersonal set of conditions that come from the discipline. They're not really you. We're tapping into an existing set of cultural projects and then looking carefully for ways of extending the project or turning it upside down or inside out. It isn't our project but something inherited. It's not as though we originated the problems, but we're taking on problems that already exist, or maybe new issues develop out of them to create a new lineage, but they don't come from nothing. Not a work of solitary genius.

Architecture isn't ever the sole production of one person. Codes, systems, materials, and clients push back. We estimate that at any one time at least six architects are working on a particular problem. At the level of the work itself, it's mediated; one is designing through systems of construction and of representation, neither of which is subjective. And so we're working through a set of conditions or language that is more objective than subjective, which pushes back on whatever we—or any architect—does. When it comes to a specific work, we know what the consequences of groupthink are. Most work coming out of focus-group conditions—American cars, for example—are mediocre. This is where I would locate the paradox: the most objective work comes from the most subjective engagement.

The issue of authorship is probably explained best not by politics but by theology or philosophy. There's nothing coherent about the subject, anyway. Within modernism there are techniques of deauthorizing work, even that of a single author, which range from drugs to automatic writing to the manipulation of already-given material through forms such as collage or montage, among other operational techniques that inherently work in a productive way against authorial will. So there's already a long history within single-authorial production—and architecture's even more distant than most art production.

––––––––––

Matter's refractory behavior, its limits and logics, is the milieu in which architecture gets developed. It would not be wrong to say that architects think through matter and in certain cases are thought by it. Matter sometimes thinks for itself—it then acts as a computer. Indeed, matter is so implicated in architecture that it underlies even the projects predicated on dematerialization, Peter Eisenman and Michael Graves being two outstanding yet diametrically opposed practitioners of that art. Unlike philosophy, which can be based solely on abstract concepts, architecture is wedded to specific situational, material, and even geometric problematics. Design can never be entirely preconceived. As Peter Cook once astutely observed, "If architecture could be preconceived, then what's the point of doing it in the first place?" And Gertrude Stein's observation on writing holds as well: "Naturally one does not know how it happened until it is well over beginning happening." In truth, concepts deliver, at best, only the vaguest outline of a problem.

In the event, a design is never completely what you thought it was, anyway. Carles Vallhonrat, a gracious and talented former colleague, notably the principal designer of Louis Kahn's Salk Institute, recalled his first desk crit with Kahn as a student at Penn. Carles, anxious to talk, presented some preliminary site sketches and quickly put them aside, thinking that he would impress Kahn with his ideas. After some time, Kahn gestured that he had heard enough. "Next time you have an idea, work without it." Clearly,

Louis Kahn was not an architect bereft of concepts or anti-intellectual; rather, his order to Carles spoke to the omnipresent gap between abstract concepts and material practices that require work to understand what the concept actually is and where the project might go. Like in war, overall strategies quickly move into tactical situations, where initial assumptions are tested and either persist or are changed, incrementally or suddenly. This strange moment of duration breaks out of the continuum, often when insight flowing out of material expression breaks with historic or cultural continua. One has a moment of clarity, seeing something for the first time untethered.

A minor version of this happened to me at Cranbrook while working in the metal shop run by Richard Thomas—one of the last of a generation of classical metalsmiths. His studio was run very much like a medieval workshop, where the exacting art of raising metal to create hollowware from flat sheets was taught. The hand tools—anvils, irons, stakes, and hammers—indeed, had not substantially changed since the medieval period. They had strange names: the beakhorn, the cow's tongue, the snarling iron, the extinguisher, the tunnel, the blowhorn, the planisher. The first thing his students were required to do was to make their own set of tools, which would be their initiation into the art as well as their lifelong equipment. They were each given a box of rough iron sand castings, which they had to shape and smooth with files, stones, and strops, until their work surfaces acquired a mirror-smooth finish. Hammerheads were also hardened and tempered in oil, then fixed to ash handles. All extremely labor-intensive work: every piece had to exactly match the classical pattern, and if it didn't, it would be discarded and begun again.

I was a fortunate stranger architect in the metals shop—my entrée was through a former student of Thomas's, Wayne Felgar, who had graduated from Cranbrook in the 1950s. I had worked under Felgar as teenager in the early 1970s as a junior counselor at the socialist-oriented Buck's Rock Work Camp. I knew my way around most of the tools in Thomas's shop, having taught basic metalsmithing and assisted Felgar during off-hours, customizing firearms for members of the New Milford Police Department. I judged myself competent, though not nearly at the level of expertise Thomas expected of his students—he doubtless came to the conclusion that I would not ruin anything or be a danger to myself or anyone else. I was allowed to work there and complete my bronze thesis models, as long as I didn't get in the way. I remember one particular occasion when I simply could not find the right-shaped stake to form a cleft in the body of the piece I was working on. I realized the edge of the wooden work bench offered precisely the correct angle. I looked around to see if anyone was watching. All clear, I whacked the piece down hard on the bench edge: perfect result. Thomas came by some hours later, saying "I saw what you did." I braced myself for a dressing down. The metals students around me were snidely amused that the interloper from architecture would get a talking to from the master. With a wry smile he said, "Jesse, if the bench works like a stake, then use it."

This was a signal moment for me. A real expert, one of the last of the old-school metalsmiths, a man who felt the weight of the history and the orthodoxy, told me it was OK to abuse: to make a table a tool. I have been abusing tools ever since. Like using the Mona Lisa as an ironing board, as Duchamp advised (a transgressive moment) or the ashtray as the murder weapon (an opportunistic moment), architecture at critical moments reoriginates its tools and itself. It delivers the ahistorical opening—momentarily short-circuiting custom, culture, and history—for something to be visible for what it is, or what it wants to be or do, as if for the first time: for something new to emerge. Reason and purpose behind the tools are not important. The software I and my whole generation abused in the 1990s was in reality an opportunistic use of tools designed by, for example, the entertainment industry. We cobbled together whatever software would work to achieve our architectural goals, the primary driver being what we wanted to achieve—we couldn't have cared less what the software was designed to do or that what we were doing was in any way transgressive. That's why it could be said that we reoriginated the use. It was about where the project would go—not a comment on what it was or the originally intended use of the tools that got us there.

Today, practitioners such as Michael Meredith legitimate their abuse of software on cultural grounds—in essence, the Duchampian transgressive mode is crucial to his project. This represents a return to a meaning-based paradigm that celebrates the transgressive dialectic between proper and improper use. While Duchamp postulated the radical effects of the Mona Lisa transgression in his notes, he cleverly never acted

Richard Thomas, photographed by Harvey Croze
© Cranbrook Archives, Neg.# AA2895-45

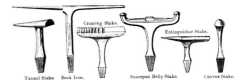

Metalsmithing stakes

Study of gutter for Ero/Machia/Hypniahouse,
bronze, 1988

Study of Long Pig,
masonite, die-formed bronze, 1988

The competitors, from left: Ben van Berkel,
Peter Eisenman, Cedric Price, Thom Mayne,
Nanako Umemoto, Jesse Reiser

The jury (Philip Johnson, Rafael Moneo,
Phyllis Lambert, Frank Gehry, Arata Isozaki,
Liz Diller) and the design team (Jesse Reiser,
Nanako Umemoto, Ysrael Seinuk)

West Side Convergence, RUR Architecture, 1999

on them. Today, this shopworn form of dialectic has been institutionalized, first in art criticism, then practice, and latterly in architectural criticism and practice. Analogous is the institutionalizing of adolescent rebellion: we see rebel acts everywhere in popular, commercial, and fine art contexts alike. These instances of acting out against symbols of the man while at the same time always being beholden, tied to, and limited by the object of the rebellion ensure that nothing new comes out of it. It becomes yet another institutional and artistic stock in trade repeated over and over again, perhaps as cynical as the art representing the ruling taste it protests.

Architecture, being first and foremost an affirmative practice, suffers under this regime even more than the predominantly representational arts because it relinquishes its powerful capacity to engender positive change by projecting forward into the future, as opposed to taking the retrospective stance of the critical project that relies on maintaining the continued existence of the problem to perpetuate itself and its practitioners.

Interesting that the seemingly eternal oscillation between meaning-based procedures and effective ones mirrors the state of the discipline. The breathless sense of becoming, of immediacy in everything, that we experienced with our generation was in effect a benign Cultural Revolution; history, meaning, and interpretation for a while took a back seat. How could anyone ever really historicize soap bubbles? Our corner of the discipline, then in rude health, was expansive—evolving largely in autonomy. At that time the objective standard was the international competition. We and a group of like-minded colleagues teaching at Columbia University—Stan Allen, Greg Lynn, Ben van Berkel, Caroline Bos, Alejandro Zaera-Polo, and Farshid Moussavi—would enter the same competitions, knowing in advance that we stood very little chance of winning. The primary reason was that we could compete with each other, advancing specific architectural ideas under the constraints of a site, a program, and a deadline not of our choosing. The postmortem presentations among ourselves, along with withering criticism by critics and theorists such as Jeffrey Kipnis and Sanford Kwinter, were the most interesting part. It also represented a way of advancing a coherent direction in architecture, which we could present to the world as a group and as individuals through publications and exhibitions. And finally, since these high-profile competitions typically attracted the best in the discipline, our work had to stand in comparison to theirs.

The work then, even the best of the projects, was inherently problematic, as all overall projects are at their inception; separating the dazzle of the new technologies from the more enduring lessons was almost as difficult as not getting lost in purely technical problems or thinking that technical solutions would answer cultural questions, and in so doing forgetting about architecture altogether. The international scope of the surface project in architecture (the Japanese ultimately solved it, in some sense, twenty years later), which in many ways sums up the materio-spatial desires of the period, resonates with so many other boundless forces unleashed at that time: the end of history, globalization, the internet, the European Union, et cetera.

In opposition to an object-centered architecture, architects focused on territories, realms, and scapes, domains that would exceed boundary and in their real world instantiations curiously elude permanent definition or ownership. For such domains as the sea, the air, the desert, the steppe—at best, impermanently held and by force alone—transmutation into architecture bespeaks a desire to transcend boundaries and the creation of objective symbols. Transmuted into architecture, such domains exemplified the desire to exceed even ideological determination, at the end of history; any group could plant a flag and claim the territory as a pure expression of power and magnitude without symbols—a determination quite similar to the Stalinist decision to appropriate a grandiose Palace Style for the Moscow subways. Their physiognomy, likewise, would be impermanent, manifesting fugitive features in structures like weather, waves, light, and the fluctuations of growth and decay. While such boundless models were mapped back into landscape and infrastructure, their most enduring successes were at the scale of architecture, a scale most resistant to the model and hence the most interesting to experimenters in the discipline. For, by definition, buildings are objects par excellence: bounded and finite. The twenty-year (and counting) life and ramifications of the surface project forms a section of this book. Suffice it to say here that the longevity of the overall project is proof of the model's tantalizing impossibilities.

Today we are in an involutionary period. As in the late 1980s, the discipline feeds on itself through endless quotation and revival. Representation rules, as opposed to presentation, while at the same time architecture grasps outward in an attempt to gain leverage from other disciplines.

In between, a generation emerged in reaction to the perceived abuses and excesses that resulted from the combination of dishonesty and irrationality of the 1990s black boxers who thought to begin architectural computation anew through a systematic scientific/technocratic approach. Part of that generation (the talented and the lucky ones) spent almost twenty years in the computational desert, trying to find their own way, thinking that their greater mastery and rigor in computation over their teachers would lead to a new architecture. It didn't. Fortunately, some realized that architecture as a cultural discipline was distinct from purely technical or computational regimes, and their work is beginning to emerge. Not surprisingly, it involves a return to objects. As with the surface project, there are ample real-world correlates: resurgent nationalism, the closing down of borders, a philosophical movement that makes objects of everything.

Compounding the difficulty with philosophy and its longstanding relationship with architecture is the question of philosophy's general ambition to describe all the world and one's conduct in it, which is a general claim to all things and practices, good, bad, and indifferent; viewed as such it has little value to architecture. If it is merely a specific set of claims, prescriptions, and proscriptions, then it would stop being philosophy and become—theory? I am thinking specifically of the latest philosophical trend to interest a generation of architects, object-oriented ontology: Do its claims apply to all objects in the world or to some specific set of objects that display some enhanced aspect of objecthood? "OOO" would appear to be a more adequate description of the ineffable quality of the architectural object that Le Corbusier observed. One test for OOO would be whether it could be used to say something that has not already been said about, for example, Le Corbusier's Villa Stein—it being more difficult to make verifiable claims for old work than new!

But beyond the representational or allegorical recourse to philosophy, there is the work itself, which in the best cases, such as the work of Tom Wiscombe, Jason Payne, Mark Foster Gage, David Ruy, Marcelo Spina, and Georgina Huljich, requires no explanatory context to legitimize its power. Interestingly, in some examples, boundless features (tectonics) are reinscribed onto finite objects, like the endless worlds traditionally painted on ceramic vessels. Our own office has been around long enough to have gone through a 1980s version of objects as well as the 1990s nonobjects. Our Kaohsiung Port Terminal employs both models. Retrospectively, object architecture is just what the surface project needed all along!

Kaohsiung Port Terminal aerial view, RUR Architecture, 2018

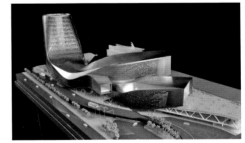

Kaohsiung Port Terminal model, RUR Architecture, 2010

Kaohsiung Port Terminal under construction, RUR Architecture, 2018

For others in the second generation, technocratic ideology prevails, surprisingly similar to what my mother encountered at Pratt in the late 1940s from the disciples of Gropius. For the technocrat, architecture emerged from problem solving: the problems to be solved would be stated clearly beforehand, the processes clearly monitored, and the results based upon verifiable performance criteria. In this regime, process prevails over product—the assumption being that contributions to an overall database would be slow and incremental.

The most extreme proponents of this sensibility advocated dissolving architecture altogether into a rubric of universal design or polymedia practices—architecture being too culturally laden and too disciplinary and design being objective, scientific, and applicable to all human problems. These are the orthodox types who insist on writing their own bespoke scripts.

But there is a deeper problem inherent in a will to pure performance. As Kazimir Malevich and later Theodor Adorno pointed out, performance ultimately seeks to make whatever performs invisible behind what is accomplished. For the most part, this is an unattainable desire—architectural artifacts are overwhelmingly bound up with material of some sort. However, the practical consequences of this ideology are very much with us and from an aesthetic perspective well-nigh disastrous. Things don't become invisible; they just enter the vast, now-dominant realm of the subvisual—becoming still more contributions to the sea of shit around us. The quest for ultimate performance elevates the invisible reason over the visible artifact, a common trait of ideal thinking that regards the invisible as somehow higher and more truthful than the visible. Supported by a train of reasons and process justifications, this pervasive ideology blinds architects to what they have actually created. There are, of course, scales (both very small and very large) and regimes that exceed embodied experience, whose very existence throws our lived experiences into doubt. However, that doubt can quickly change to corrosive nihilism toward any architecture, for those not bathed in cynicism or presumably shielded from doubt by practically religious recourse to invisible entities like the economy.

I recall a thesis review with Sylvia Lavin where she quite rightly corrected a student discussing the aesthetics of strip malls. She pointed out that the aesthetics, such as they were, essentially were automatic byproducts of economic forces indifferent to aesthetics. They were by no one for no one. Of course, for more than seventy years a wing of critical theory and of artwork and belatedly architecture has existed that has celebrated the now-superannuated conversion of this automatism: it is called pop. Again it arises in the wake of high modernism as a resurgence of representational thought over and against modernist abstraction. On the art historical/political level it celebrates the material generically as symptomatic of the state socioeconomic superstructure, any particular work, like money, being essentially interchangeable with another.

Guild House, Robert Venturi, 1963

High-Rise City, from *Großstadt Architektur*, Ludwig Hilberseimer, 1927

From an architectural perspective, pop is even more disconcerting, for it is a symptom of a loss of faith in the affirmative dimension of architecture—the ability to create a positive world. Understandable, perhaps, in the representational arts but particularly disturbing, since architecture as Alberti theorized it is the only one of the arts that is not obligated to represent any nature (including man's), but only itself.

The situation in architecture became even more peculiar as pop entered the discipline as a representation of a representation, as signage on an architecture already in the popular field. In other words, it re-represents what is relentlessly pumped into the world anyway, with or without architects. Of course, there are particularly powerful examples. I would count Robert Venturi's Guild House as the quintessence of architectural nihilism, far more affective in this regard than, say, Ludwig Hilberseimer's *Großstadt Architektur*.

There is also some sense of cultural slumming in all of this, a sense that pop serves the high bourgeois as an inoculation of low culture—a frisson redolent of lax sentimentality for those who always have had the luxury of escaping it. Perhaps I am conflating too much the subject of pop with the object, but in effect, the two are the same for those who must live day in and day out in the grinding, soul-destroying milieu of spaces of mass consumption. This is as much about the attitude toward the artifact as the artifact itself.

Ah yes, but they're functional, justifiable, user-friendly, convenient! Like McDonald's, where one is consuming an idea rather than a meal. Doubtless a public so formed by the technologies of popular culture will be receptive and buy into the *both and* of easy architecture that is the latest incarnation of pop. *Both and* for the architects being projects far more marketable than modernism and intellectually defensible, in a cynical sort of way.

Unlike in a military operation, an architect must select and invent the field of action as well as the weapon systems and the maneuvers within it. The contours and terrain of the problem—internal and external—set the limits and constraints. Projects evolve (I say this advisedly) through unrelenting, counterintuitive challenges to their stability and inertia—a form of random selection consisting of an accumulation of mainly small differences, which in the rarest of cases move from differences in degree to differences in kind. Most challenges, however, are discarded, not incorporated—sometimes for naught, recalling Edward Hopper's favorite quote of Ralph Waldo Emerson: "In every work of genius we recognize our own rejected thoughts: they come back to us with a certain alienated majesty."

This situation may lead to an objective concatenation of design ideas or motives that by their seeming inevitability define a particular author. I don't know how many times we unintentionally channeled Le Corbusier, aghast, as if confronting a black hole; his work seems to engulf every line of escape! Specific projects, especially mature ones, tolerate a limited number of ideas at once.

On a more mundane note, some projects' external constraints overcome the best-intentioned concepts laid down by the architect. I am thinking specifically of the side wings of Bernard Tschumi's Lerner Hall at Columbia University. Here the planning and contextual constraints determined by the McKim, Mead & White campus code (regulating, for example, cornice lines, building scale, and materials) led to a form of auto-postmodernism. Combine old geometry with a newer tectonic, and that is what you get. (Thankfully, the main building is not so afflicted!) To be clear, Tschumi's work heroically went against the tide of the historicist postmodernism that represented the mainstream of that period, but however sophisticated his argument was in this case, the objective factors—what was actually in play, over and against authorial intentions—prevailed over his concepts.

———

Everyone gets everything he wants. I wanted a mission, and for my sins they gave me one.
—Apocalypse Now

Historically, inertia has acted on both poles of disciplinary production. As in physics, projects in motion tend to stay in motion, and projects at rest tend to stay at rest unless acted on by an outside force. The medium, whether physical or virtual, is where this desire plays out. If concepts are of limited value, desires are even more treacherous. Anachronism is necessary to explain this. The range of human desires throughout history has been strictly limited, the personal as constructed in, say, perfume ads or pornography being the most generic of all. Those applying to architecture are even more so. Architectural desire, as mentioned earlier, was heretofore held in check largely by the recalcitrance of matter. Matter has historically provided a necessary resistance to dream images of unmediated fulfillment. Even so, we are shocked to see old masterworks cleaned of their patinas. Their vividness delivers an intimation of what was to come and perhaps what they were after all along. We are witnessing the advent of an unprecedented period in architecture, when the technology has become so sophisticated and so frictionless, and representation so hyperreal, that the dream image so long held in abeyance by the pushback of physical stuff can emerge unfettered in extrareal space.

There have been precursors—warnings, as it were—of this situation. The climactic scene of *Raiders of the Lost Ark*, where Jewish angels devour the Nazi defilers, is nothing if not the fulfillment of a Baroque mis-en-scène. Angels morphing into demons, melting and exploding transgressors, would have been exactly what Saint Ignatius Loyola dreamed of. *Raiders of the Lost Ark* was released almost forty years ago, and at that point, the effects its director, Steven Spielberg, had at his disposal were predominantly analog: the angels were double-exposed puppets; the melting exploding Nazi heads, waxwork models sequentially sped up and slowed down; all were captured on chemistry-based film stock. Today, CGI and nascent virtual reality have obviated the need for the physical analogues. The dream

Architecture for popular music need not be pop: Taipei Pop Music Center under construction, RUR Architecture, 2018

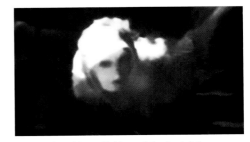

Angel from *Raiders of the Lost Ark*...

...becoming demon, 1981

Melting Nazi head from *Raiders of the Lost Ark*, 1981
Courtest of Lucasfilm Ltd. LLC

is becoming real. The gap between the paradoxical terms that ensured a redeeming impossibility is closing. The symptoms become clearer in the remarkable phenomenon of thirst for the actual—as opposed to CGI—in film: the real armies of *Dunkirk* over the digital armies of *Troy* or the vitality of live broadcast (or even scheduled programming!) as opposed to the atemporal programmability of Hulu and its ilk. There will come a time in the not too distant future when we will look back with nostalgic yearning for the almost real. The uncanny valley effect is a foretaste of what we will get, both in future perfect and in visceral revulsion to beings not quite right.

Today we are left with the all too human: the drive to tattoo the body in order to gain some moment of reality in pain and to memorialize it ("not someone else's life and dreams, but mine") and to display it ("See before you: I was there, I suffered, I'm real."). But that is just a holding action. The next theater is the human itself, in its limits, its potential affiliations, modifications, and extensions far beyond violations and inscriptions to the natural body. My former classmate Karl Chu has prognosticated that all the gross material movement that architecture has traditionally entailed will be obviated by a pill that would induce architectural phantasmagoria quickly and economically—to say nothing of the potential new polis who could enjoy communion through this shared vision and argue a politics in the new net-distributed, drug-induced agora.

I have secretly shared Aldo Rossi's ethos (all architects have their limits) of leaving well enough alone. He spoke eloquently about this in reference to his housing project at Gallaratese, where he asserted that at a certain point, people's choices (regarding interior design) should be none of his business. Similarly, the decision about when and where design leaves off was a crucial issue for him.

The creation of community, now both a local and global urgency, is perhaps the highest calling of an architect, as it requires the architecture to be neither under- nor overdetermined. For instance, the overdesigned street furniture, lampposts, and trash cans that populate the streetscape of post-Olympics Barcelona display this kind of cloying overdesign. The overpowering sense is of generic artifacts that have been updated to an absurd degree—even as the old generic production does what it needs to do so well—but have not produced a new kind of life: hence, the resulting pathos. Perhaps I am betraying my deep affection for modernism, but at any scale our desire is to create a new generic, however elaborated and different the new generic must be. Under this constraint it is difficult yet necessary to seek out how and where and what kind of newness matters. It brings to mind Robert De Niro's character's *sachlich* moment in *The Deer Hunter*, when he holds up a cartridge and says, "This is this." There have been a few happy moments when we could say of our work, "This is this"—when it is new and expresses not only difference in degree but difference that makes a difference.

However, there are certain thresholds to the new that should be crossed with extreme caution. To go one step further (because the world has done so, while architecture has doubtless played a major role in modifying our brains and subjectivities), I draw a line between creating what happens before our eyes and messing around with the gray matter behind them. For we are facing a future where there will be no qualms about crossing over.

Today, we have the intimation of what comes next in inertia without matter: image as concept generating a velocity so extreme that, like trying to draw articulately in a spin art environment, the irresistible pull renders everything the same. We are on the cusp of creating buildings that literally float, fly, mutate, are invisible, and more…The age-old dreams thus realized become visible for what they, as dreams, always were: kitsch. Stéphane Mallarmé was right in insisting on a necessary indirectness as he intuited the direct path, coming at the tail end of four hundred years of fraught perspectivalism. We are not, however, advocating a reactionary return to the old modernism or a naive craft ethos. Eliding the two, how many more well-crafted museums with spaces indistinguishable from Zara can we tolerate? And for that matter, how much art created expressly for the Zara spaces can we continue to entertain? The most interesting architecture today must negotiate a path dangerously close to multiple black holes without falling in or, even worse, being sucked into a representational eddy from which there is no escape.

Sachlich moment: Robert De Niro
in *The Deer Hunter*, 1978

Out of this frictionless phantasmagorium we witness the strange, short-lived reemergence of 1980s architectural techniques as last hurrahs before they sink back into oblivion for the last time: postmodern collage, now divested of its will to signify complexity, contradiction, or anything; cartoons without humor, cuteness; objects of hysterical levity—wood-grain contact paper rendered in puce covering the walls, floors, furnishings, inhabitants of a suburban rumpus room of no one's choosing, seemingly resurrected out of Susan Sontag's lists of camp.

If we regard these not as concepts or as things no longer effectively enunciating the life of a disenfranchised group but now a general symptom of being adrift in a Candy Land universe of sugar and surfaces without a past or a certain future (except a future without descendants), a symptom of irresistible forces far more insidious than surveillance, continuously infantilizing us with free-floating delusions of immortality, the signs become clear. (Japan is socially, culturally, and demographically in the unfortunate position of being in the avant-garde in all of this.) And so, the architectural stage is set for the reduction of the human to emojis, vast tableaux of catalogue furniture groupings without architecture, typically seen from above, showing cartoon versions of sociality: people and potted plants straight out of Williamsburg coffee shops enacting a user-friendly, innovative politics.

———————

Rejected ideas are consigned to the to-do list, perhaps to be drawn upon later; they stake out vectors of future development. Thus, an overarching project may start as one thing and become another. Concepts in isolation are fairly easy to formulate, and almost any intelligent person can create them. Form and composition, on the other hand, are monstrously hard; that is why they are reviled by so many.

In fact, good ideas most often yield mediocre, sometimes bad, and very rarely good architecture. What separates ideas from architecture are a thousand small problems and a thousand small decisions. The difference between being on point or off—totally off—is infinitesimally small. Hence, the stories of Jean-Auguste-Dominique Ingres tearing his hair out over the angle of a hand or, more directly pertinent to architecture, the image of Mies staring at the lines on a plan for hours and then adjusting them a few millimeters. How is this not the image of the pastime of a madman? It is what separates the Seagram building from its mediocre lookalikes a few blocks away. This is also the difference that separates architectural ideology from implementation: the divide between a particular building type, promulgated for mass production, and the specific prototype that spawned it.

Here it is important to distinguish the two architectural politics: the first, which underpins the ideological project as a general program of building, and the second, which informs the specific case of architecture as ideological object. Paradox, at least from the architectural perspective, rules here as well. In the first, you have the pathos of an ideal, yet generalized program, for and by the masses and therefore open to a world of vicissitude—not the least being the talent level of the architects into whose hands the project lands, a certain formula for mediocrity, or worse. And in the second, the ideological object, you have a fiery compound combining a dystopia of the present and utopia of the future—a potent object of the here and now that also points forward to a possible world only if and when the project and political program extend beyond the prototype to full social implementation.

The twentieth century saw both things happen. The former were paradigms of the architect's political commitment, with ofttimes unforeseen, often negative consequences, and the second, paradigms of how architecture itself renders politics—often in objects of unsurpassed provocation and unsurpassed excellence. A further distinction between the former and the latter can be drawn. The former tends to a politics predicated on programs, for example, ones demonstrating social responsibility, such as social housing. Social programs being nominally a good thing in and of themselves, they are well-nigh uncriticizable, however good or bad their architecture. The second, more difficult case is essentially a politics inherent in the architecture itself, quite independent of the use program. This moves into the territory of the politics of form, as opposed to formal politics. Formal abstraction, to be precise, is an arena of surprisingly durable volatility

Self Portrait, Jean-Auguste-Dominique Ingres, 1850

Mies van der Rohe at Riehl House, 1912

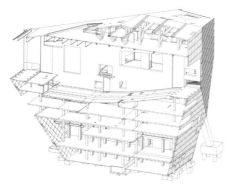

The same form, radically different programs: two projects by OMA. Y2K House, 1998 (top), and Casa da Música, Porto, 2005 (bottom)

encompassing the left, the right, and the in-between. Witness the fate of the Russian constructivists who, after a short postrevolutionary flowering, were officially denounced, deprived of a vocation, sent to factories, or, in the case of Vsevolod Meyerhold, summarily executed. An equally tragic fate befell many in the maw of the Third Reich, forced into professional silence, exile, or worse. *Formalism* as a pejorative indeed has a long history, the latest manifestation, even in highly regarded schools of architecture (and even by some good formalists), being the obligatory renunciation of form in the lecture preamble as proof of social responsibility and serious intent. Contrarily, it may be asserted that the almost universal ire aroused by the best formal projects is proof of their political efficacy. To open up, if even only for an instant, a clearing in a lifeworld so regimented by quotidian routine that the radical effects of play are denied expression is reason enough.

To be clear, most formal projects—that is, those dealing in complex form—are bad, simply because form is so difficult to do well. It receives scant attention in the schools, mainly because most of the teachers are ill-informed or inept themselves. All architecture must have a form, so it is not as if there exists an alternative, form-free architecture. So the problem beyond naive functionalist arguments related to form and function, which are unnecessary to rehearse yet again here, is the historical question of form itself. The theorist Sanford Kwinter hits the nail on the head in his aptly titled essay "Who's Afraid of Formalism?" He points out that the obligatory attacks on form reduce form to an object. *Poor formalisms* are really just unextended formalisms: parodic analytical methods derived from the great and genuine aesthetic and epistemological innovations of the modern avant-gardist tradition, but which have simply forgotten what they are. For the poverty of what is collectively referred to by the misnomer of *formalism* is more than anything else the result of a sloppy conflation of the notions of form with those of object. This violent reduction of form to a mere thing voids what is crucial to a politics of form. "Indeed there is not, and has never been, any such thing as meaning or ideology, not, in any case, one separate from the physics of history and power: a physics, not incidentally, which is always a physics of forms, be it the form of an idea, the form of an epoch, or the form of a tool."

On the level of practice, where even those with avant-gardist pretensions typically premiate program, the ideological reduction and demotion of form leads to an unfortunate outcome. Wittingly or unwittingly, practitioners fall prey to the purely aesthetic reduction of form exemplified by mid-twentieth-century corporate modernism. In a popular architectural book today, Bjarke Ingels's *Yes Is More*, architectural design and practice become more or less indistinguishable from the exhortations of Dale Carnegie. Practice becomes just another form of bureaucratic management, and architects function as "creative conceptuals" or art directors.

Form thus never emerges in the context of an overall project, but since a project must have a form, it is taken or cherry-picked from practices that do. A number of prominent architects today operate quite successfully on this model, much to our chagrin. Interestingly, the rhetoric mobilized behind what is at base eclecticism is that they create a new idea and a new form for every project! This unfortunate model has become increasingly the norm in schools of architecture as well—the facile opposition of program (good) and form (bad) being the operant trope. However, those in the discipline know (or ought to!) that beyond the first- or second-adopter activities of these practices, there are those who truly advance the discipline.

Perhaps the most ethically dubious excess associated with programmatic projects is when a political problem is addressed through architectural symbolism. It thus becomes a question whether architecture is the best tool for addressing the problem at all. In certain architecture schools, the border problem is a favorite: Palestine/Israel, United States/Mexico, North/South Korea, and, once upon a time, the Berlin Wall. The paradox here is thinking that designing more architecture, or more stuff, addresses a problem truly solvable only with policy. Beyond being a case of mobilizing the wrong tools for the problem, it strangely monumentalizes the problem both as a physical and institutional artifact. At best, such projects describe the architect's political commitments, and at worst they devolve into a stock in trade, what David Ruy precisely termed "architectural ambulance chasing."

It is virtually impossible for an architectural educator to criticize such projects, any criticism of the architecture per se being interpreted as support of the political status quo! Thus, there have emerged evolutionary schools, whose overall project consists of collective experimentation led by professors on extended formal projects. An analogy in art is the work of Paul Cézanne, whose program was conventional—still lifes, landscapes, portraits, et cetera—but whose innovations lay in the evolution of form and space. In counterpoint to the evolutionary school is the conceptual school, as exemplified by the work of Marcel Duchamp. But that would do a disservice to Duchamp's actual project! Such schools could be described as discursive, embodying all of the contradictions that separate words and concepts from vision. Unlike in the evolutionary schools, where visual talent is a prerequisite, such gifts in a conceptual school are looked upon with suspicion or even derision.

Such a situation would be unheard-of in a conservatory or in most any of the other arts or sports, where talent is assumed as a matter of course. And skill or range of formal repertoire would be a point of admiration—not derision. Architectural practices that stake their entire claim on advancing their social or political commitments without any other evident ability are rightly disregarded in the same way any segment of the public rightly would not tolerate a lack of skill in sports or inept musicianship. In any case, it is a situation, especially within the United States, brought about by misplaced assumptions about democracy and equality extending to the realm of talent, as well as an evident discomfort reconciling the existence and the perceived unfairness of unearned gifts.

Fortunately, the distribution of talent (clearly independent of race, class, or gender) is at odds with the technocratic thrust of mass education and mass society, which apply normalizing regimes to the production of the professional architect and where architectural—that is to say, cultural—values, because they resist quantification, are systematically excluded in favor of the *real issues* of health, safety, and welfare. In fact, only about 3 percent of building in the United States is done by architects, and of that group far less than 1 percent bring what I would loosely call a critical approach to the discipline. So we're talking about a very small group, even worldwide, who bring about significant change.

It is also a matter of the speed of change. An observation sticks in my mind, made by Philip Johnson at the 1992 Columbia University exhibit celebrating the sixtieth anniversary of *Modern Architecture: International Exhibition* at the Museum of Modern Art. He related his surprise at the durability of the modern movement. Had he projected back sixty years from 1932, the architecture of 1872 would have looked really antique. Not so with the work in the show from 1932, which still looked modern and quite similar architecturally, if not technologically, to what was being produced in 1992.

Quotidian modern architecture today, twenty-five years later, is even more similar to 1992 than different. From this we put forward a counterintuitive thesis: that the rate of innovative architectural production is actually slowing down—slowing down and becoming more localized and attenuated, though given the admittedly exponential speeding up and diffusion of information, the notion of what is local has been radically transfigured. As opposed to the old norms of broadcast, the practice and production of the genuinely new in architecture is now both widely distributed yet narrowly focused. We can count, maybe on two hands, colleagues across the world who are actually contributing work of vital importance to us; they are our local. Genuinely new architecture is far less pervasive quantitatively than in 1932. Likewise, the rate of change, while not diminished, is more on the order of steady state—or maybe slower.

As a comparison, the High Renaissance in architecture in Italy lasted at most twenty years and was practiced by roughly fifty significant individuals—a short enough span for many of the major proponents to move on to mannerism. The major work associated with the "digital turn" in the 1990s, produced by roughly the same number of individuals worldwide, was created within about seventeen years. Despite the fantastic speed and spread afforded by computation and new media, the time for the discipline to actually work through the problems was essentially the same. Why? My only conjecture is that the limiting factors are the speed and bandwidth of the human brain and the cultural depth, which, irrespective of relative technological power and change of content, is astonishingly similar.

That is not to say that all decisions are made at a snail's pace. Many times (as with the combat pilot or the samurai swordsman), if you have to think, you're dead. Architects can play fast and loose or slow and precise with many things, including history. One of the great privileges of the discipline—and not merely at the level of style—is the freedom to be dangerously ahistorical, though I prefer to think of it in the terms of Gertrude Stein, with all history being a function of the continuous present. Certainly at a techno/material level, all eras are happening somewhere on earth at this very moment. Successful or not, right or wrong, everything inevitably becomes history. Ask Palladio.

Nanako Umemoto and Jesse Reiser
drawn by a Tsinghua University student, July 2017

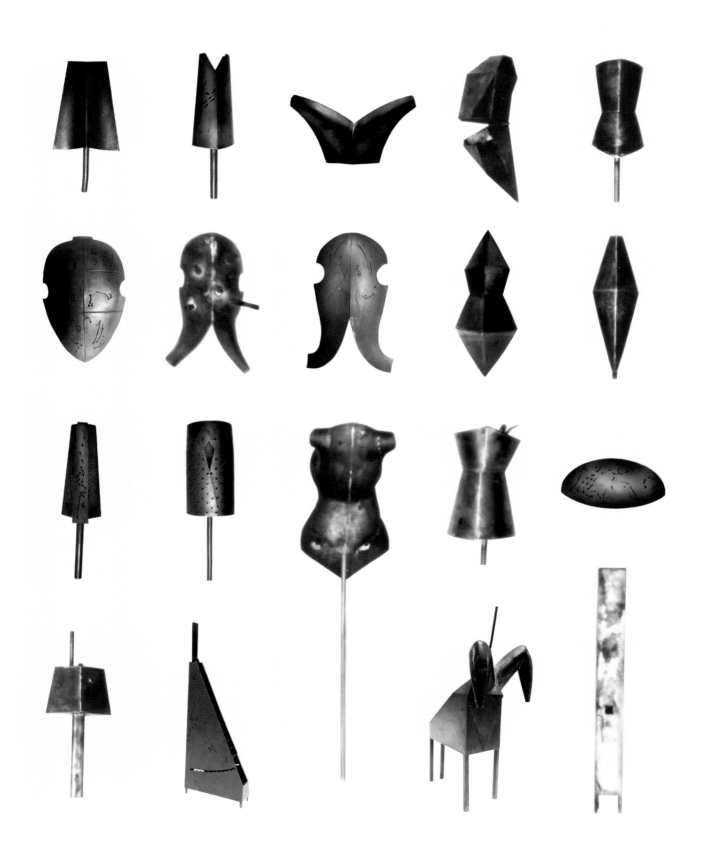

Mnemonic Objects

PLATES

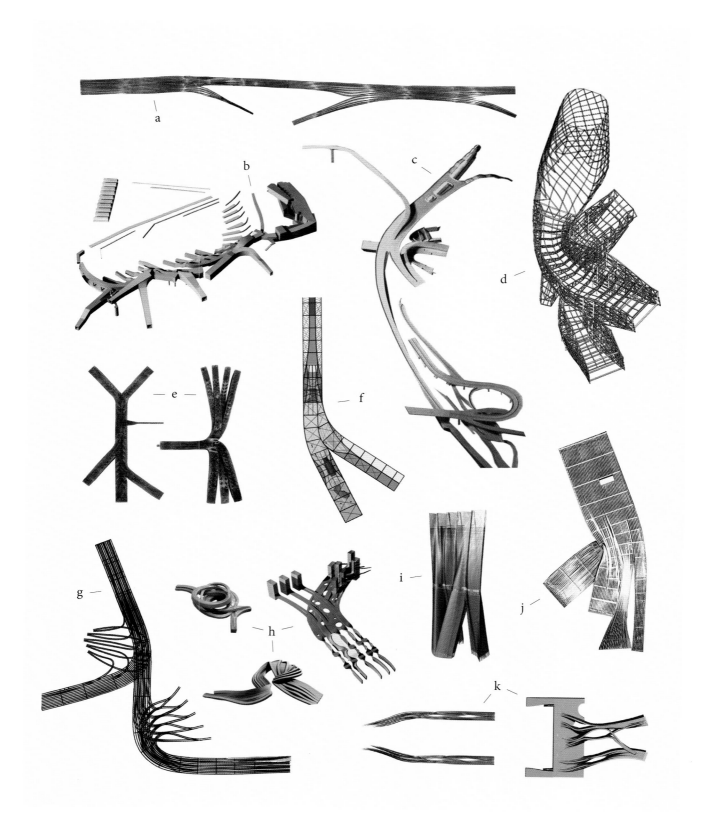

Branches

Branches

a United Nations Cultural Center, East River Corridor
b Venice Gateway
c Indoor/Outdoor Performance Space, East River Corridor
d Kaohsiung Port Terminal
e Airport for the Year 2080
f Alishan Tourist Routes
g Alishan Tourist Routes
h Foshan Sanshui Urban Plan
i Aeon
j Sagaponack House
k West Side Convergence

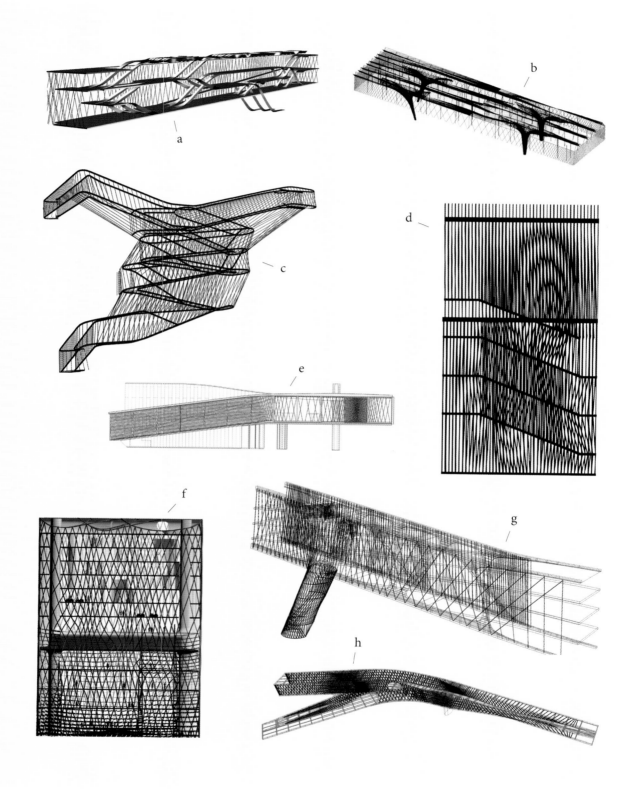

a

b

c

d

e

f

g

h

Rod-Net System

<u>Rod-Net System</u>

a Children's Museum of Pittsburgh
b Kansai Kan National Diet Library
c Staircase, Taipei Pop Music Center
d New Museum
e Sagaponack House
f Eyebeam Museum
g University of Applied Arts Vienna
h Alishan Tourist Routes

Bricolage

<u>Bricolage</u>

a Ero/Machia/Hypniahouse
b Venice Gateway
c Ero/Machia/Hypniahouse
d Yokohama Port Terminal
e BMW Leipzig
f Cardiff Bay Opera House

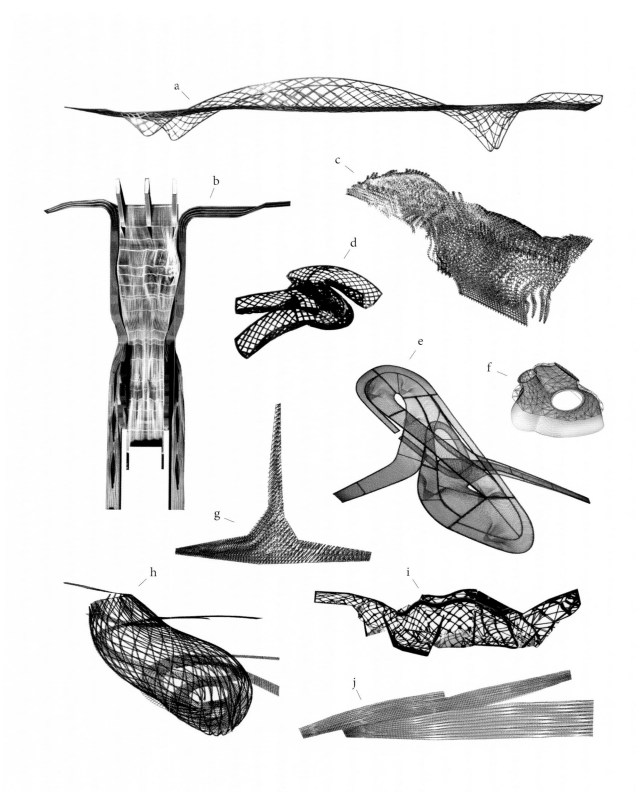

Geodetics

Geodetics

a Alishan Tourist Routes
b West Side Convergence
c Graz Music Hall
d Bridge in Tenafly
e BMW Event and Delivery Center
f World Health Organization
g Three-way Pedestrian Bridge, East River Corridor
h Central Ramp, Kansai Kan National Diet Library
i Cardiff Bay Opera House
j Indoor Sporting Facility, East River Corridor

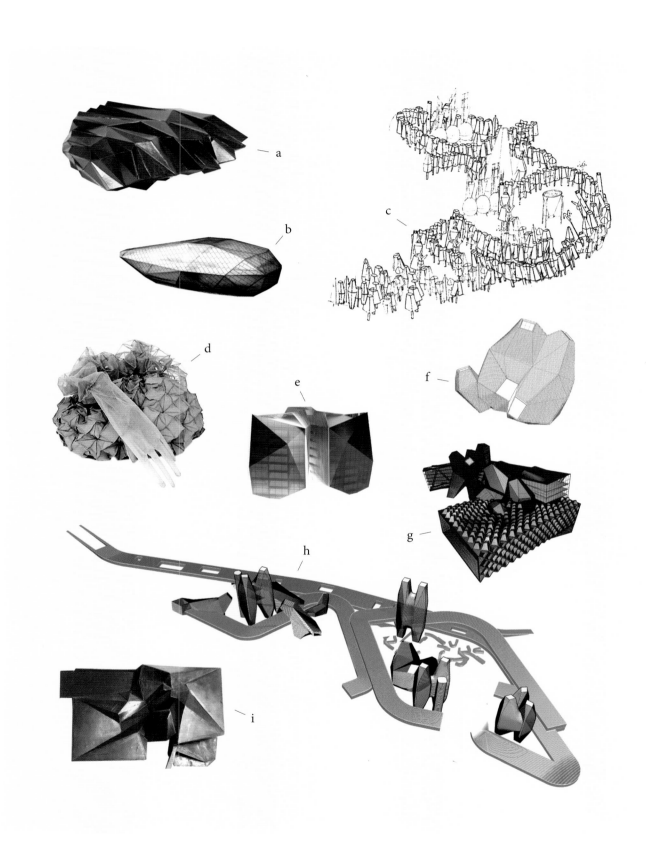

a

b

c

d

e

f

g

h

i

Aggolmerates

Agglomerates

a Main Hall, Taipei Pop Music Center
b Industry Shell, Taipei Pop Music Center
c Villa Farsetti
d Architecture for Dogs
e Katara Hospitality Development
f Pingshan Cultural Cluster
g Taichung City Cultural Center
h Umekita Culture Park
i Osaka New Museum

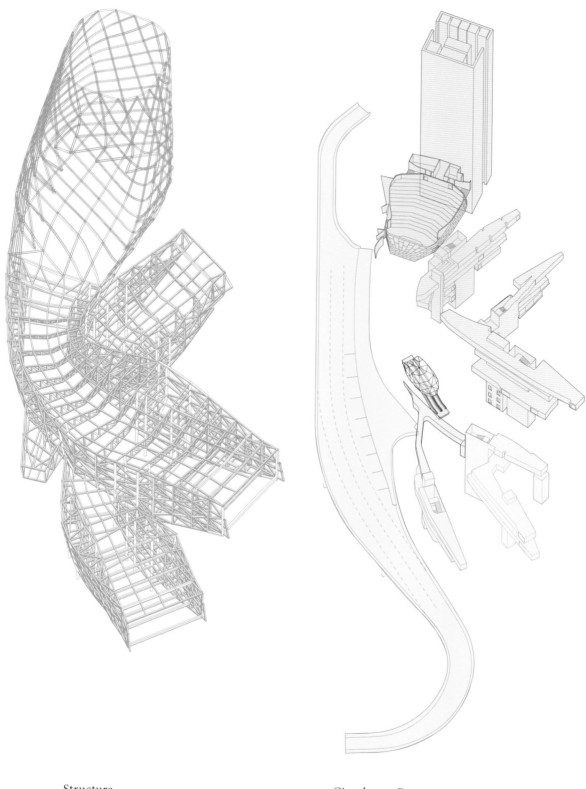

Structure

▬ Steel Framework

Circulatory Program

▭ Tower Core   ▭ Auditorium   ▭ Lobe C Northeast Core
▭ Path   ▭ Lobe A Northwest Core   ▭ Lobe B North Core
▬ Internal Escalator   ▭ Car Path   ▭ Lobe B South Core
▭ Lobe C Southwest Core   ▭ Lobe A Southeast Core

Drawing Matter

Farshid Moussavi's brilliant call to display architectural working drawings as art in this year's Royal Academy Summer Show is about as canny a cultural move, vis-à-vis architecture exhibitions, as any in recent memory—and it could only come from an architect. At a stroke she presents architectural drawing at its most superficial and its most profound. A cursory interpretation would hold that she is merely showcasing the artistic surplus of technical drawings by architects in the context of other art on display in the RA galleries. This view is not entirely wrong, but it is incomplete.

As Farshid is well aware, construction drawings (documents) occupy a peculiar middle ground in relation to meaning and use, quite unique to the discipline of architecture. Understanding a document depends upon the role, knowledge, and intentions of its audience. Construction documents necessarily traffic between what must be communicated by the architect as technical and legal information and, more profoundly, what can be seen and what can be known. Is the technical a cause or a consequence? Should it be expressed or suppressed? The Centre Pompidou, a canonical example of British High Tech, was already visible, to the discipline at least, in the legacy of building-system drawings, which up to that point were deliberately part of the unseen—the between-the-walls, as it were—of architecture. Renzo Piano and Richard Rogers's epiphany, however, went way beyond merely stripping away the skin of the walls to reveal the heretofore hidden. In raising those systems to primary expression as architecture, they brought to bear a level of invention, editing, and deep stylization. Consider, for example, the immense challenges—expressive, cultural, political, technical— of turning "bones and guts" into a viable envelope for a museum! The skin inevitably had to come back but in a way that would not compromise the salient expression. That was the achievement. It might be argued that any technical documentation from any architect could generate enough residual dazzle to be interesting and "artistic." This is not merely a problem of specialist authors versus nonspecialist audiences. (I confess to both modes, production and reception—in fact, it is essential to the way we design.) If the documents Farshid chose to show have any common denominator, it is the peculiar ways these architects wrestle with reason and expression via the technical.

At some basic level our design for the Kaohsiung Port Terminal (opposite) was a response to a challenge laid down by our teacher John Hejduk more than thirty years ago, when he assigned the "musical instrument problem" to our thesis class. Emerging, no doubt, out of Hejduk's abiding interest in the guitars of cubism and Purism, through Juan

Gris and Le Corbusier, Hejduk's later masque work, among other things, sought to join the abstraction of his earlier Purist-inspired project with the more tangible materiality of preindustrial mechanisms. Musical instruments provided the perfect vehicle, being both figurative and mechanical, mediating and extending the human body's mechanism through sound. Moreover, musical instruments embody an intimate proximity between mechanical components and a sounding vessel. Such intensive intermeshing of systems wrought strange and marvelous conformal responses in each—a kind of information exchange. To this day the technical records of musical instruments are among the most transcendently beautiful drawings to come out of the Cooper Union. Interestingly, since the instruments were described through the architect's conventions of plan, section, and elevation, their actual function was less evident than the artifactual by-products of the conventions themselves. Plan sections, say, of a clarinet, do not so much describe the function of a clarinet as provide a diagram of formal consonance—an economy of relations that could be a clarinet or equally something else—highly specific geometrically, yet indeterminate as to scale and function— that is, until the architect sets the scale and function. Hejduk would call them "pregnant with architecture."

The consequences of that exercise, to us at least, were both irresistible and bedeviling—not least because they suggested that a simple technical operation, a section or plan cut, could yield such fantastic graphical results. In the event, the exercise, which was meant to inform the students' subsequent thesis designs, would not yield up very much new architectural material to the immediate efforts of the students. Most every student could hyperdescribe conventional building systems in conventional or nonconventional buildings (I remember a hyperdescribed roof ventilator); one could make buildings that looked like musical instruments; and finally, one could extract geometric motifs from instruments in the manner of Le Corbusier's Purist derivations from cubism. Hejduk and his cohort had thoroughly mined and re-mined the latter territory in the 1960s and 1970s. But by 1981, when he assigned the exercise, he was after something else, inchoate to him and, at the time, most certainly to us.

Across the space of thirty-five years, the tantalizing promise of the musical instrument drawings hovered around our work like a phantom flame—sometimes flaring up, sometimes quiet, but always there. It took a while to realize that a certain literalness in addressing function got closer in principle than the route of appearance mimesis. The building must perform as an instrument, not look like one.

In reversing the typical direction of representation from a preexisting model—that is, musical instrument to building—only a logic of relations conveyed by geometric traits of instruments and similar bodies is advanced. Geometric traits imbue new information: structure, skin, building systems, et cetera. As such, they regenerate the logic of musical instruments into buildings without mimicking them or reducing the information to emblematic lines—projected as in, for example, guitar-shaped walls. Rather, the Kaohsiung Port Terminal becomes both a spatial and optical manifold.

Like the reversibility of light, the space of the Terminal distributes and delivers people to and from ships as it directs their passage visually. A single point of view encompasses diverging routes from ticketing to ship. It is as much an organ for concentrating and channeling people and things as it is an optical device for concentrating attention. This design approach connects to building technology in a way that is very different from the High Tech of Piano and Rogers. Space, skin, structure, and building systems (guts) are still the elements in play but with different consequences.

High Tech's buildings largely stay true to the equilibrating grid of modernism. Their aesthetics of orderly rationalizing follow modernism's equipoise and a human's place in it. Walls are selectively dematerialized to reveal and emphasize color-coded building systems and circulation, calling attention to their rational disposition by how connections are made with machine-shop details drawn from precise fabrication and aerospace. All building systems extend uninflected by one another in the ordinate system of the grid. It is a humanism for the space age. Yet, the space and systems remain defined by modernism's unaffected and uninflected grid.

This typical modernist hierarchy is reversed as seen in the grid of cladding of the Terminal—continuously inflected by the changing form of the envelope. Panels must change position and angle to accommodate the changing geometry. There are sutures at junctions because the overall building form—since it is not grid based—resists a direct mapping of panels. Hence, there are boundaries that are unmapped by standard panels. These marginal areas, in effect, reveal another system. Sutures edge gores on a pattern, similar to those on clothing patterns. A printed pattern on fabric is either continuous or discontinuous across the garment, depending on the continuity of the fabric across regions of the cut pattern, or the intrusion of a seam or suture connections. Unlike in High Tech, fastenings do not call for attention but are matter-of-fact, as in earlier modernism.

In short, the Terminal becomes a kind of vessel under pressure. More specifically, the inward pressure of the outer skin and the outward pressure of the inner skin constrain the structure, circulation, and building systems. These pressures consequently induce conformal responses across the building's systems, from skin to structure to ductwork to circulation. Legible scale evinced by railings and stair treads is suppressed; vertical circulation is hidden between the walls. The vast interior space is inside a large branching vessel—a strange, white space without features or consoling measures.

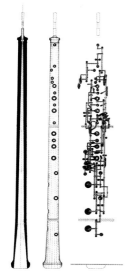

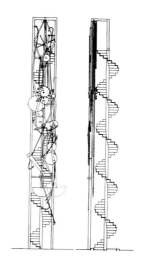

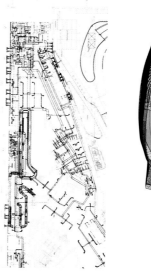

The Inspiration
Oboe Drawing
Cooper Union
Stephen Isola, 1980–81

THE MUSICAL INSTRUMENT PROBLEM: A THIRTY-YEAR QUEST

Our Dysfunctional Emulation
Clock Tower
Reiser + Umemoto, 1984

Our Functional Instrument
Musical instrument logic of the Terminal puts pressure on ductwork organization designed by engineers, such that it is analogous to the logic of an oboe.
Kaohsiung Port Terminal
Reiser + Umemoto, 2017

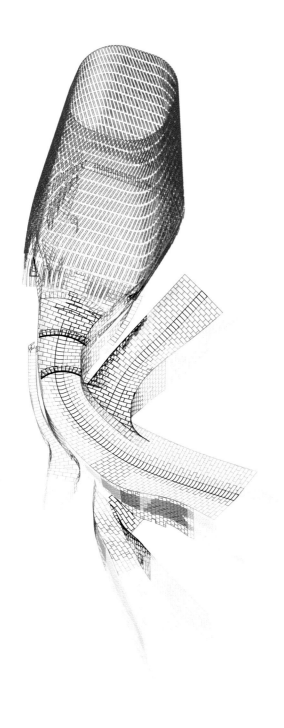
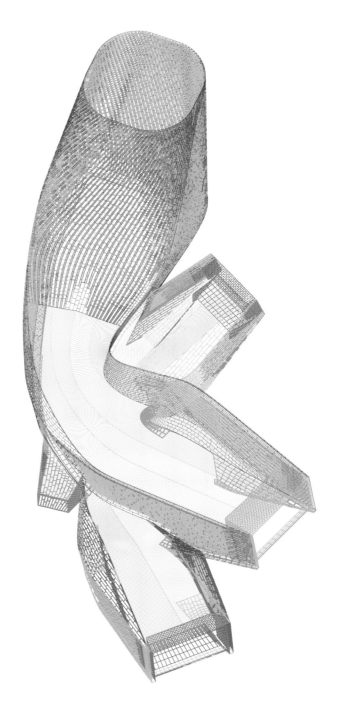

Internal Panels

Flat Panel   Flat/Bent-in-Place Panel

Single Curved Panel   Double Curved Panel

External Panels

Lobe A Under Panel	Standing Seam Panel	Lobe B Under Panel
Curved Glass Panel	Double Curved Panel	Lobe A Updated Panel
Lobe A Inner Panel	Lobe A Inner Single Curved Panel	Glass Panel
Lobe A Under Single Curved Panel	Lobe A Tower Panel	Ferrari Panel
Normal Side Panel	Lobe A Divided Panel	Lobe C Updated Panel
Lobe B Under Double Curved Panel	Twist Side Panel	Glass Panel
Lobe C Updated RUR Panel	Lobe B Panel	Lobe C Under Panel
Lobe C Inner Single Curved Panel	Lobe C Inner Panel	Lobe C Panel
Dark Metallic Panel	New Developable Ferrari Panel	Lobe D Panel
Lobe A Panel	Lobe B Updated Panel	Lobe B Inner Panel

Jesse Reiser on Aldo Rossi

In the spring of 1979, John Hejduk invited Aldo Rossi to teach at Cooper Union. I'm not certain when he met Rossi, but Rossi was crucial, I would say, to John's last major shift in his work. He saw something in Rossi's analogical project that would allow him to transition from his Purist work, which he was doing in relation to Bob Slutzky and others, to his metaphysical late projects. That is my intuition as to why he wanted Rossi.

He invited Rossi originally to teach the thesis group, but John was unhappy with their work, so he shifted Rossi to the third-year studio, where I happened to be a student. So it was really a chance thing. It was Rossi's second trip to America, and travel abroad was still a big deal. Back then, to be international was more significant for architects than it is today. I think Rossi was also trying to find an analogous architecture in America, to extend his own project. So he assigned us Thomas Jefferson's Academical Village because it was fundamentally a European Enlightenment vision about an architecture that would form the new American— more an idea than a thing. We were to do a new version or interpretation of the Academical Village on any site we wanted.

My first talk with Rossi, however, was not about architecture. He came by and saw two models on my desk, a Battle of Britain tableau with a German Heinkel being closely pursued by a Spitfire. I'd done model making since I was four. Anyway, my friend John Nambu and I were always building models and had the two highly detailed— I mean really very carefully detailed—models on the desk.

Rossi came by and was immediately attracted to the scene and the detail: the German aircraft kits had complete markings, including swastikas, and the paintwork on the Heinkel entailed precisely applied splinter camouflage in 1940 RLM colors. It was all really precise realism, which was part of the discussion I had with Rossi. First, he admired the two aircraft—he loved the duck-egg underside of the Spitfire—and then started talking about his favorite Italian bomber from the period, the Savoia-Marchetti. He said it was unlikely that they ever operated over the British Isles but that they did account for a lot of British shipping in the Mediterranean. The plane was nicknamed "the hunchback."

Hejduk came by and had more of an aesthetic reaction to the whole thing. Overall, he admired the form and camouflage patterns on both planes, the colors and so forth. Rossi and I then got into a discussion of realism and atmospheric perspective: since model planes are miniatures, you can never use the actual colors. To make them look real you need to add atmosphere, which meant lightening the color, thereby making them look like scaled things seen from a distance—not toys. It was an issue of realism, which was a part of his ideological position.

And then Slutzky came by—didn't look at the Spitfire, looked only at the Heinkel, and while he was impressed with it, he indicated that it was also a clear sign of where the school was going: there was a common misperception that associated Rossi's work with fascism. I am not entirely convinced Slutzky actually held this view; his quip may have simply reflected his anger and dismay that his and Hejduk's projects were diverging and that Rossi was somehow implicated.

So the Battle of Britain tableau was a flashpoint. My later conversations with Rossi shifted to the question of how to find a model in America. I found an indirect route to the model question in relation to the Academical Village through painting. We were talking about Edward Hopper (this is discussed in Rossi's *Scientific Autobiography*); I was interested in Hopper and had done copies of his paintings in high school. He grew up in Nyack, across the river from where I grew up, and his work resonated with me. There was something about the everyday subject matter, but there was also something really interesting in that the major oils—this is something I did discuss with Rossi—were never, or very rarely, of actual places. The watercolors were, but the major oils were composites and distillations of a lot of different locations, so they appear to be everywhere and nowhere. There is a strange quality to them; everybody is convinced they know, for example, where *Nighthawks* was, but in fact, it's nowhere. It is similar to the film *Eraserhead*. Everybody is convinced they know the places it depicts—Baltimore, Detroit, Cincinnati—but it was filmed, confected, in Los Angeles, which is the opposite of what one would expect. It was a distilled realism in Hopper—a realism of no-place, an unreal realism. Detail was strategically removed. It wasn't really classical, but at the same time it was not really avant-garde. Rossi was always very ambivalent about the avant-garde himself. Hopper resonated with a modern sensibility while being a realist—resonated even with the abstract painters. The only realist that Mark Rothko tolerated was Hopper, because of the compositional and painterly structure of his canvases. Ultimately, Hopper's genius lies in the fact that once you see one of his paintings, the whole world starts to look like a Hopper painting. This, of course, was not lost on Rossi. And really this discussion about Hopper, and the work I did afterward, derived from that.

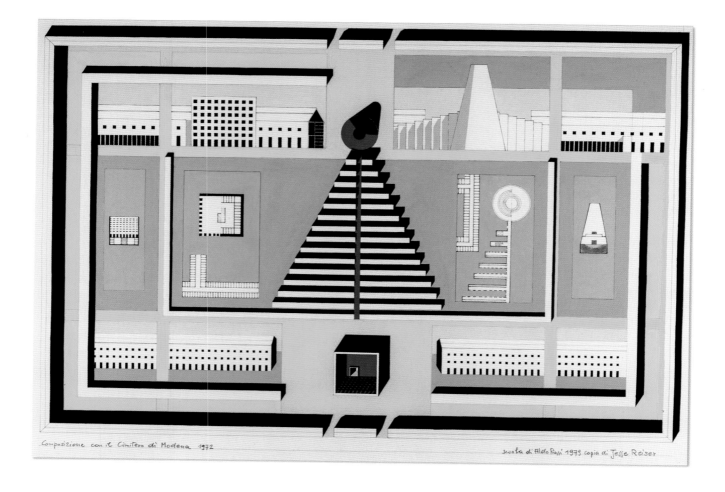

Composizione con il Cimitero di Modena 1972   *scuola di Aldo Rossi 1979 copia di Jesse Reiser*

My third-year project was well received, so Rossi invited me and Frank Gerard, who was also in the class, to intern over the summer. It was a very small office—a total of only six or seven people—in a bourgeois apartment in Milan. It was actually not even an office but more a case of desks set up in a domestic space—Via Maddalena Uno. He sat in the living room and worked on a big wooden board on trestles. He had a manual American typewriter, either an Underwood or a Remington—not an Olivetti, which was important to his position vis-à-vis design in Milan. It was a room with nothing to suggest high design.

He would spend the morning writing—he had a very structured day—and then look at projects in the afternoon, and then spend one day a week drawing on his own, maybe on the weekend. He would do one of two things: either hand drawing, or he would have film positives of drafted drawings that he would run through the blueprint machine, on which he would then use oil pastels and something called *trielina*, a solvent that would melt the pastel to produce more painterly effects and tints. He would apply this solvent with a rag, so he could either build up the surfaces manually and keep the strokes or dissolve the strokes with the rag and produce washes. His drawings, then, fell into two rough categories: completely freehand drawings and illuminated blueprints.

He wanted me because he liked the drawings I did at Cooper, and he had an idea: the drawings I would do that summer would be the beginning of a whole new portfolio. (I was supposed to keep doing them even when I got back to the States, and I never did. I only did a few.) It was not about his design of the Modena Cemetery. That had been done in 1972. This was about Rossi creating a school, in two senses: connecting to the old schools of painting, but also helping to move his architecture out of the Italian scene.

It was part, I think, of his ambition to internationalize his project. It also connected to the Academical Village idea. It was part of the analogical architecture project, I think—or this is what I am projecting onto it.

He gave me one of the large film positives of Modena that he used to run blueprints from. In retrospect, it's actually really sad what I did: to transfer the drawing, I put the film directly on the Arches paper, then used a pin to produce points, and then connected the points in pencil. There was nothing created by me. It was a transfer of an existing drawing, and using the film was a practical expedient. The blueprints were large, but he wanted everything I did to be on rag paper, so the film positive scaled it down to fit the dimensions of the paper. I basically ruined the film: I was taking pins and pushing them through it. It was a brutal and direct transfer of the drawing and it made the film useless to run future blueprints from. I still feel guilty about it. I was twenty-one years old and otherwise a very dutiful student.

I was carefully looking at the previous iterations of the Modena Cemetery, of which there were many, and I was going to base the coloration on what I saw in them. But Rossi had something really specific in mind about what the colors would be. He took me to the art supply store and started pulling gouache tubes out, and I was completely shocked because they didn't match the other drawings of Modena in terms of coloration or palette. It was a strange combination of colors that I was convinced wouldn't work. It was a mixture of beiges and tans in the background. This was a drawing for America—or that is how I saw it. This was a way of being specific yet general enough to transcend site or place, sort of like a Hopper. Then he would have a strange abstraction of what he saw as local color, a weird mixture. It seemed like combinations from *Good Housekeeping* or *Ladies' Home Journal*, or like in the Bird Cage restaurant at Lord & Taylor. I mean, you would see this palette in what were then called "restaurants for ladies," which, ironically, were an attempt by American designers to be European in a tasteful way—or what they thought was European.

He had his signature red, which was basically unchanged, then cadmium, and then black. Then he pulled out—this was the surprising part—these intense Day-Glo yellow-greens, which were like the black-light posters that my sister had on her walls in the 1960s. Or Peter Max, or pop. It was this incredible, counterintuitive palette that he wanted for the drawing. I was totally flabbergasted—but I went along with it, of course. I was convinced it wasn't going to work, but it did. It worked really, really well.

I did the pencil transfer, and then he would come by every day and we would do tests—*fare una test-a, fare una test-a*—so it was constant. Color location wasn't completely preordained. We would do tests on samples to decide where the colors should be. All the colors were to be applied straight from the tube. No mixing. Totally flat graphics, like silkscreen. It was important to him, obviously. It took a long time to do each drawing, so he invested a lot of effort in every one, taking me to the store and monitoring my progress. And when he finally signed it, it was: "School of Aldo Rossi, drawn by Jesse Reiser."

It related to classicism. It had a universality, or was attempting a kind of universality, which would be counter to that of the modern movement. It was a cosmopolitan project different from that of modernism or the International Style of Philip Johnson and Henry-Russell Hitchcock—he was always ambivalent about both. But he had to somehow move his model from Italy, and he did this with color. There is an ideality to the drawing, but then it's localized in terms of color. Rossi, like one of his favorite writers, Jorge Luis Borges, always went back to language, even in relation to color. Recalling Borges's essay "The Argentine Writer and Tradition," there is a famous argument that goes something like this: no camels are mentioned in the Koran, which is proof of its authenticity—the camel being too ubiquitous to mention. Only a regionalist, one who consciously resorts to local color, would commit that error. Rossi's fictive palette swerved around that problem, being contradictory, everywhere and nowhere, authentically inauthentic— essentially American. He didn't think I was an American because I was a Jewish New Yorker. The real Americans were Texans. I was too tragic and cosmopolitan in background. When he went to Texas: "These are real Americans." The color choices were totally improbable— how could you get all those colors to work?—and there was no precedent for it in the office.

TEXTUAL PROJECTS

———

NARRATIVE

VILLA FARSETTI
1984

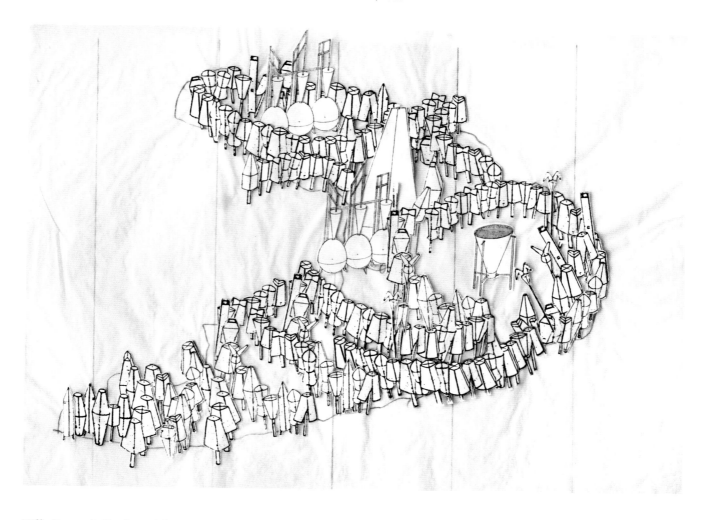

Villa Farsetti: Garden of the Heteroclite

Located northwest of Venice, in a state of neglect, the gardens of the Villa Farsetti were chosen by Aldo Rossi, the director of the 1985 Venice Biennale, as one of the exhibition's project sites. Originally boasting one of the most famous gardens in the region, the villa now sits on an empty plot of ground, bordered on all sides by a canal that follows the centuriations laid down by the Romans in antiquity, effectively isolating the site from its surrounds. The program, essentially open, called for a new design of the once-extensive garden.

In our proposal, the idea of a historical reconstruction or a utopian scheme was discarded in favor of a mechanical garden for the yearly Venetian rite of Carnival. Upon entering the site by way of the entrance gate, the revelers, obeying the laws of Dionysian abandon, interact with a series of architectural-mechanical constructions (*thaumata*) reenacting the inevitable temporal sequence engendered by the Phallic rite. Thus the garden is divided into three major zones corresponding to the sequence: the Agon (Contest), the Marriage, and the Komos (Triumphal Procession).

Rossi searched for sites with dense historical narratives that no longer possess any material traces of their past. Existing now only as text, the humanist gardens of the Villa Farsetti once featured architectural elements, including a miniature model of Rome and various allegorical objects, that instructed Venetians in the wonders of classical antiquity. Thought of as a kind of theater, the site of the garden acts as a generative space that visitors enter as both observers and participants. It echoes the comedic structure evolved from a pre-Christian fertility rite that entails the ritualistic death (or contest) of the old king, which leads to the birth or resurrection of a new king—a period of chaos that is supplanted by a celebratory reestablishment of order.

PREVIOUS: Detail of the Garden of the Heteroclite proposed for the Villa Farsetti gardens, one of the sites for the 1985 Venice Biennale. The participants in the festivities are depicted as abstracted geometric figures.

ABOVE: Collage of the figures in the Garden of the Heteroclite, which appears in the third panel of the final image. Each grouping is arranged through a process of photocopying and collage on tracing paper.

OPPOSITE: Assemblage #8 appears slightly to the right of the center in the final Villa Farsetti collage.

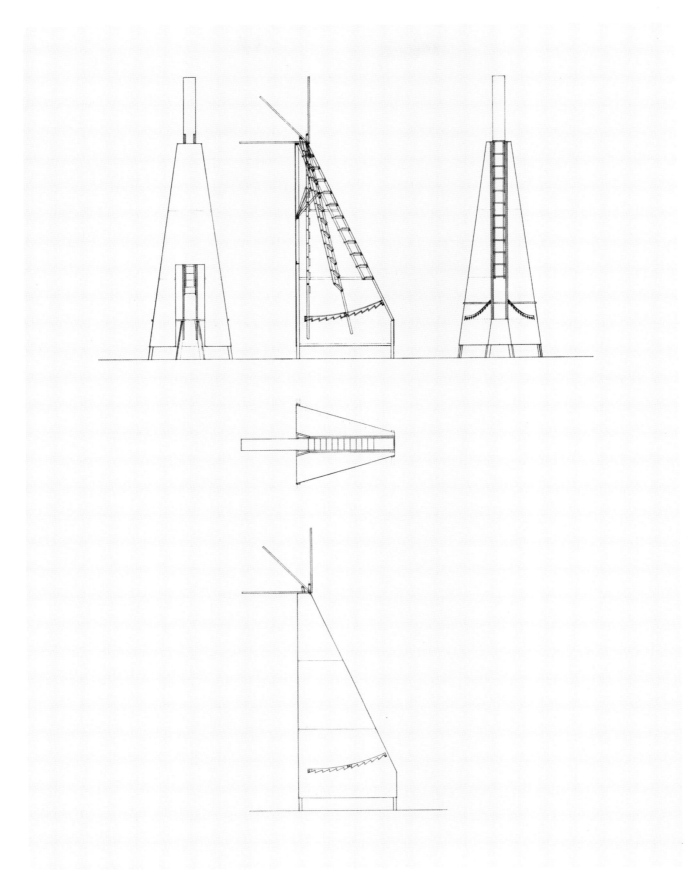

Jacob's Ladder was built at full scale at the Yeshiva Museum in New York in 1984.

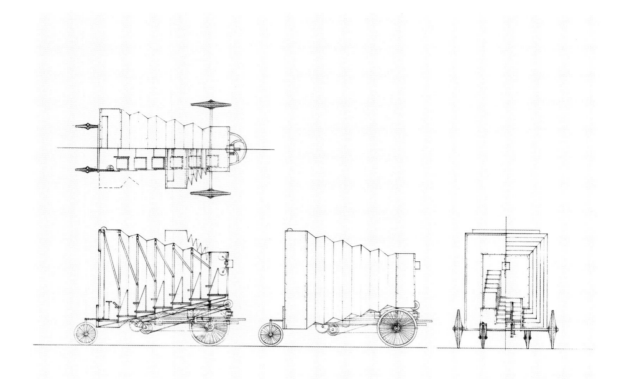

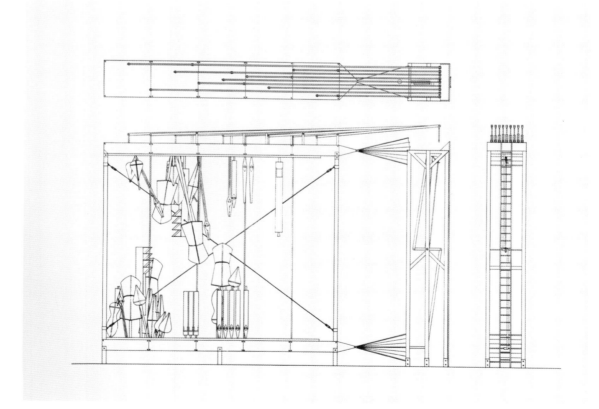

TOP: Camera Theater
BOTTOM: Wind Organ

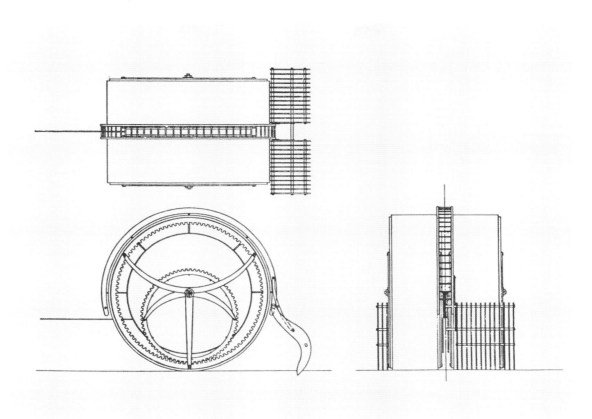

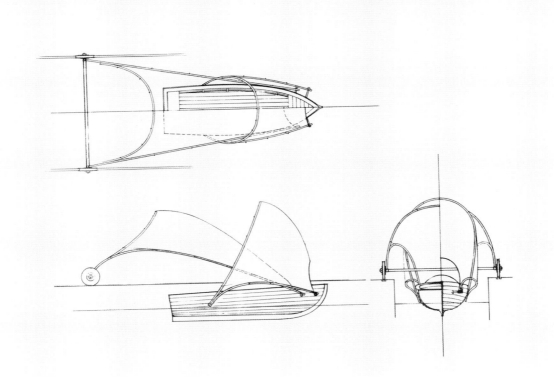

TOP: Harrow, which has a single tooth that scores the earth as it moves

BOTTOM: Floating in the narrow canal surrounding the garden, the sailboat (Sloth) is pushed slowly by the wind.

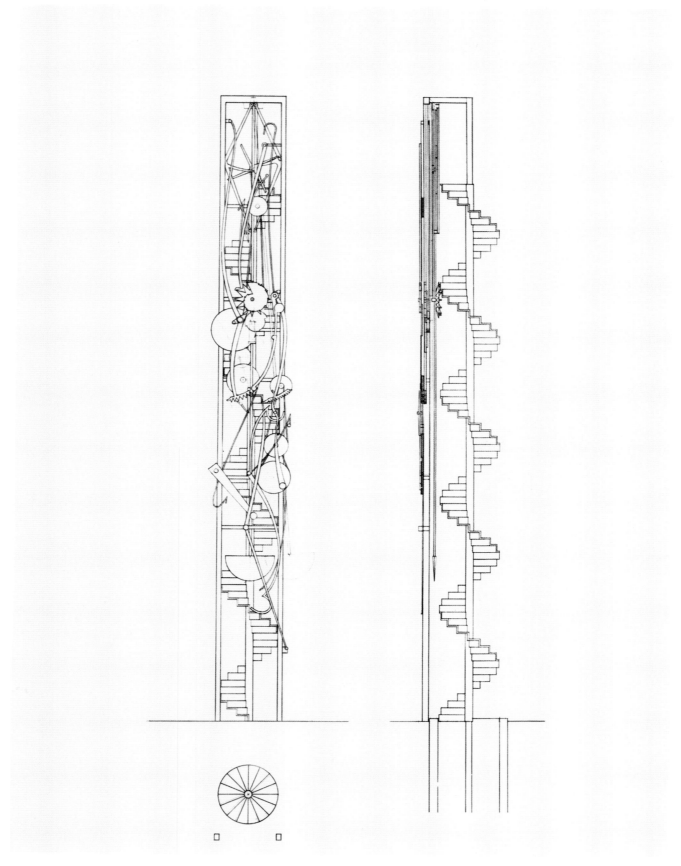

The Clocktower occupies the corner of the garden and takes its form from the exploded interior of a clock.

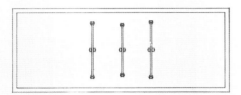

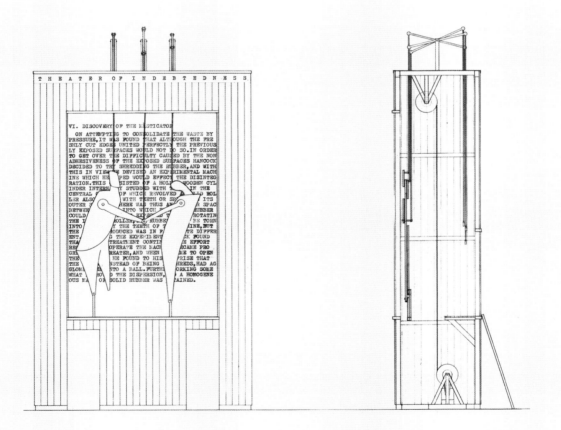

In the Theater of Indebtedness, marionettes perpetually shake hands and alternately bow their heads.

MNEMONIC
THEATER
1983–1986

Architectural elements from the *Mnemonic Theater* in the Otis Elevator Factory courtyard, 1986
Torso, Jacob's Ladder, Shield, Bride, and Bull (from left to right)

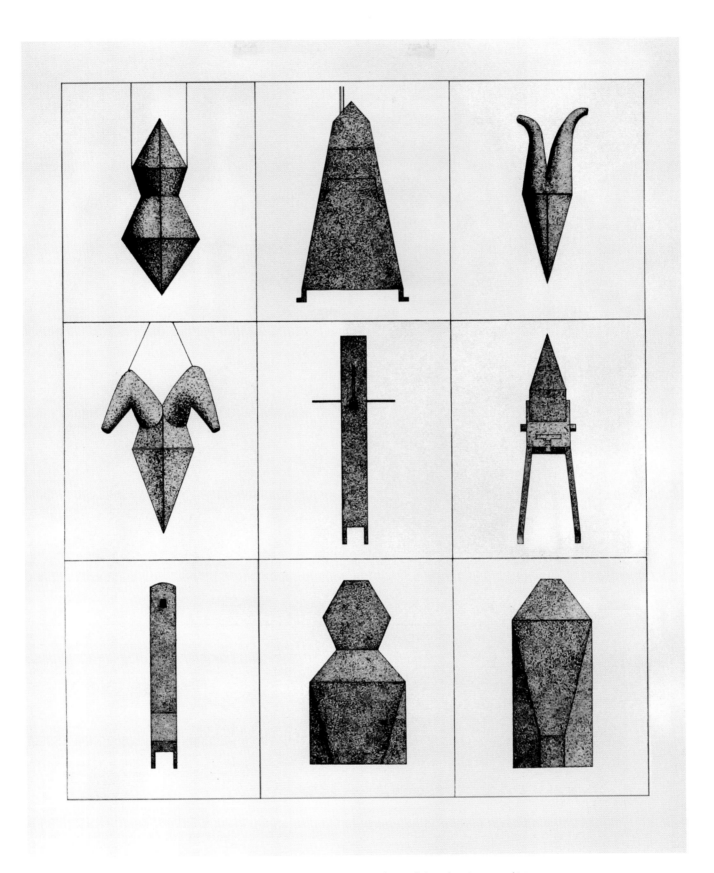

The Nine Decan Figures, intaglio etching depicting architectural objects later incorporated into
the Villa Farsetti project and built full-scale for a private client, 1983

Bull, bronze, 1986

Torso, bronze, 1986

Theater of the Occupations of Saturn with the Decan Figures, bronze, 1984

Marionette Theater, 1982

Walls of the Second Theater, bronze triptych, 1983

Dancer, cardboard, papier-mâché, and black paint, 1988

THE LONDON PROJECT: GLOBE THEATER
1988

The London Project: Theatrum Mundi

Discussions of the London Project began in 1986 between Leslie Gill and Marek Walczak, who conceived of a collaboration centered on the mythological and material dimensions of specific sites across London, based on Wenceslaus Hollar's 1647 perspective engravings of the city. Unlike New York (with its regular grid laid out in the early nineteenth century) and Paris (with its grand avenues slashed by Georges-Eugène Haussmann), London presents a networked, irregular urban fabric unified by its refusal to adhere to any rigid system of organization. Medieval structures stand next to newer buildings spread along meandering streets, thus providing sites that were sufficiently textured with layers of history and topological irregularity for the project's objectives. Culminating in 1988 as a group exhibition at Artists Space in New York, the London Project generated a diverse body of work among its various participants, each of whom was assigned a specific site rich in historical and cultural significance. Our assigned location was the historical site of the Globe Theater in Bankside.

> To the cosmic meanings of the ancient theater, with its plan based on the triangulations within the Zodiac, was added the religious meanings of theater as temple, and the related religious and cosmic meanings of the Renaissance Church. The Globe Theater was a magical theater, a cosmic theater, a religious theater, an actors' theater, designed to give fullest support to the voices and gestures of the players as they enacted the drama of the life of man within the theater of the world.... His theater would have been for Shakespeare the pattern of the universe, the idea of the macrocosm, the world stage on which the microcosm acted his parts.
> —Frances A. Yates, Theatre of the World, 1969[1]

This conception of the Globe Theater, which has its roots in the magico-religious tradition of the Renaissance, envisioned a theater designed according to the precepts of universal harmony, which would act as a divine mediator between the microcosm—man—and the macrocosm—the universe—as set forth in the celestial hierarchies leading ultimately to God. Premised on the idea of universal sympathies, the theater operated as an effective talisman that not only served locally as a place for the enactment of drama but also exerted a reciprocal influence on the "greater spheres" of the world, attracting favor from the heavens. Thus the Globe existed first and foremost in the realm of ideas—tied neither to any particular locality nor to the material stuff of building.

It is perhaps ironic that the contemporary descendant of the Globe Theater is the mass media, whose occult origins are masked by the sophistries of technique and whose use as a universal medium of control and persuasion by the state is enough to make "the angels weep," to borrow William Shakespeare's own phrasing. A direct translation of the Renaissance theater—an attempt, in other words, to create a modern equivalent in line with contemporary technique—seemed of questionable value. We believed it not only possible, but essential, in proposing a new theater, to exchange the real estate of Bankside, the site of the original Globe, for a site both ubiquitous and universal. Living "in the absence of gods" and lacking any credible "idea of the world," it seemed reasonable to regard the detritus of postindustrial society, the seemingly endless flow of printed matter, as a suitable ground for the project, for it fulfilled the requirement of being both placeless yet at home everywhere. The chaos of discarded language would, in effect, serve as the site for the theater, acting as a kind of profane liturgical text—a Borgesian "mirror of enigmas."

Approaching the site on Bankside where the Globe Theater once stood, we were drawn to the Renaissance notion of the Globe as a space that mediated between microcosm and macrocosm. Following the construction of the Rose Theater, built in 1587, and the Swan, built in 1595, the Globe was completed in 1599 as a public playhouse for the masses. It has been suggested that its circular structure was modeled after the Roman amphitheaters of antiquity, many

Detail of Wenceslaus Hollar's 1647 engraving *Long View of London from Bankside*, which shows the location of the Globe Theater. Hollar's panoramic impression of seventeenth-century London was used to establish the sites of the London Project, all of which are visible in the complete image.

of which were likewise constructed out of timber. Perceived by Protestants as spaces of immorality, theaters in the early modern period were not permitted within city boundaries and were thus constructed in areas of London such as Shoreditch and Southwark that were notorious for crime and debauchery.

Instead of designing a new theater for the empty site of the Globe, we proposed a collection of structures invested in textual production. As the initial utterance orders elements in space, unmuddling the murky expanse of chaos in the Judeo-Christian creation myth, the written word in turn fixes speech onto the two-dimensional plane of the page, locking thought into specific spatial organizations. For some without a traditionally fixed place, the printed word becomes sacred, functioning as a mobile locus. This translation of physical place into the form of a book provides a site of localization, of portable emplacement, a wandering center around which to gather. The structures in our project were not intended to be site specific but instead to serve as discrete, self-contained sites of textual proliferation set up in relation to one another. They thus functioned on multiple registers as physical objects, as self-contained sites, and as static textual artifacts open to interpretation.

> *The idea that the sacred scriptures have (aside from their literal value) a symbolic value is ancient and not irrational: it is found in Philo of Alexandria, in the cabalists, in Swedenborg. Since the events related in the scriptures are true (God is truth, truth cannot lie, etc.), we should admit that men, in acting out those events, blindly represent a secret drama determined and premeditated by God. Going from this to the thought that the history of the universe—and in it our lives and the most tenuous detail of our lives—has an incalculable, symbolic value, is a reasonable step.*
> —*Jorge Luis Borges*, "Mirror of Enigmas," 1964[2]

> *Even the articulate or brutal sounds of the globe must be all so many languages and ciphers that somewhere have their corresponding keys—have their own grammar and syntax; and thus the least things in the universe must be secret mirrors to the greatest.*
> —*Thomas De Quincey*, Autobiographical Sketches, 1853[3]

> *History is an immense liturgical text where the iotas and the dots are worth no less than the entire verses or chapters, but the importance of one and the other is indeterminable and profoundly hidden.*
> —*Léon Bloy*, L'âme de Napoléon, 1912[4]

Detail of the language loom, Métier à Aubes, 1986

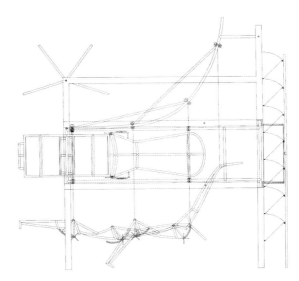

Métier à Aubes drawing, pencil on paper, 1986

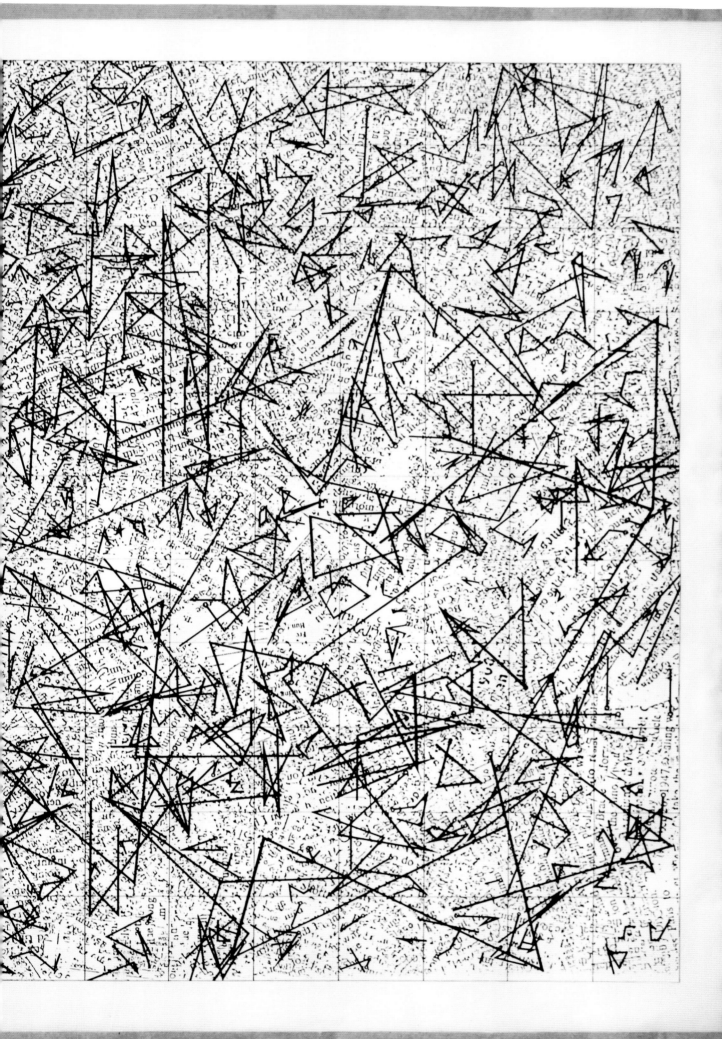

Engendering Plate

The idea for the Engendering Plate came about as a result of a project I had been working on several years before, requiring the construction of a number of papier-mâché hemispheres. Many charming masks were made in the eighteenth century employing papier-mâché, the methodical and repetitive technique of building up numerous uniform layers of torn and pasted paper. The papier-mâché form would be allowed to dry, then would be sanded smooth, sealed, and gessoed before a final coat of paint or gold leaf was applied.

What fascinated me about the hull of pasted paper I had created came about accidentally. I had built up the papier-mâché hemisphere from alternating layers of telephone Yellow Pages and newsprint. As I began sanding the inevitable irregularities that covered the surface of the newly made form, I noticed an unusual phenomenon: the higher areas on the surface naturally sanded off first,

obliterating the language from that layer and revealing the language on the underlying layers. The resulting surface, crisscrossed with miscellaneous bits of language and fortuitous conjunctions, had the appearance of a terrestrial globe. The similarity was even more striking after I applied a coat of varnish—ordinarily, of course, only a sealer before the gesso coat. The technique I had stumbled upon was compelling, but it would be three years before I understood its possibilities.

I began to play with the idea that the act of sanding was in some way analogous to the action of a catalyst that promotes a reaction but itself remains unchanged and indifferent. New combinations of word fragments likewise emerged only as long as the sanding action continued. When the sanding ceased, the configurations would be fixed, just as live bacteria are fixed on slides before viewing.

In the finished Engendering Plate, such allusions to antique maps or globes would have been troubling, as they would suggest sensual or tactile qualities associated with a superficial aestheticism, or a carnality, and we intended the coupling of language to be of a dry or siccative nature— the conjunctions were to remain strictly in the realm of language and not present a material aspect. It was therefore necessary to transfer the fixed language photographically. The nature of the photographic process immediately rendered the image as a shadow, cleansed of all incidental qualities and possessing the proper degree of aridity.

PREVIOUS: The Engendering Plate, over which a grid divides the selections of textual fragments into legible "signatures." Photocopy on vellum, 1987

ABOVE: The photographic reproduction of the Engendering Plate "fixes" language production, consequently "drying out" the materiality of the plate. Collage and varnish on plywood, 44.5 x 68.6 cm (17.5 x 27 in.), 1988

OPPOSITE: The square A8 from the Engendering Plate (left), from which language fragments are selected to produce three distinct signatures. The process that generated the Book of Sigils is derived from a Kabbalistic numerological technique. From square A8, three legible signatures emerged (right). The signatures read: "lurses arc," "cijry," and "eiuir."

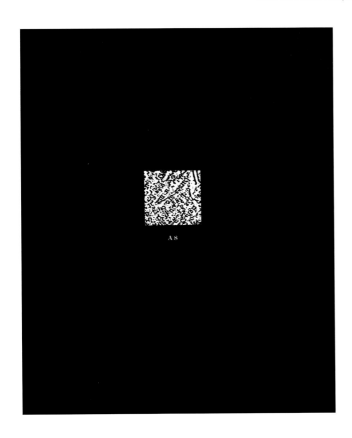

A 8

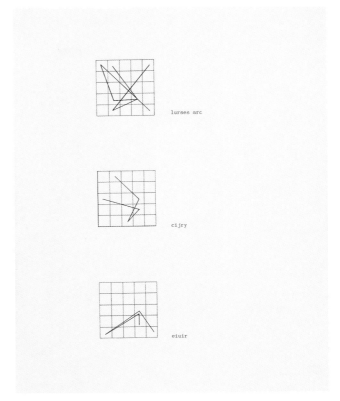

lurses arc

cijry

eiuir

Book of Sigils

An eleven-by-seventeen-inch portion of the Engendering Plate was enlarged photographically to enhance its readability. The enlarged portion, measuring sixteen and a half by twenty-five and a half inches, was then gridded out in one-and-a-half-inch squares, as in a Mercator projection, with the vertical axis lettered from A to K and the horizontal axis numbered from one to seventeen. Thus the field was broken down into 187 squares, or "views." Subsequent operations on each view were performed in isolation from adjacent views. Most views would yield three legible bits of language (words, phrases, or word fragments). These were recorded in a book set up for this purpose, cataloging each view and the salient pieces of language, or "residents." The next series of operations used a five-by-five-inch square matrix (the "martial gridiron") containing twenty-five letters of the alphabet (all but the letter Z). The letters were shuffled, then each was chosen at random to be affixed within a square of the gridiron. Then the letter Z was dropped to land by chance somewhere outside of the grid (as a foil to the grid's determinacy). The letters of the residents were then plotted onto their places in the grid and their positions connected with lines, starting with the first letter of the resident and continuing to the last.

Thus, the martial grid laid open as with a sword the language of the resident, revealing an internal sign or signature. Each signature was duly recorded in the book alongside its corresponding resident, a total of 561.

Enlarged Section of Engendering Plate with Sigils

The signatures developed in the book were methodically redrawn in nine proportional grids and replotted at their origins; that is, the starting point of each signature coincides with the first letter of its corresponding resident. The signature originates from the initial point (indicated with a circle) according to the amplitude of its "voice." In certain instances the voice is so weak that the signature remains a congested blot, almost illegible. In others, the emanations extend beyond the boundaries set by the views, crossing or perhaps recrossing neighboring signatures, forming larger constellate groupings. The points of fortuitous overlap among signatures (generated as they were in isolation and in the chaste dryness of language: rigor mortis) signified a kind of blind coupling: each in its own space, overlapping but indifferent.

In its entirety, the image represents the index of three successive extractions, or "fixings," from the flux of the Engendering Plate: the first is the fixing of the language on the plate at the cessation of sanding; the second, the transformation of that language through the breaking up of the plate into views; and the third was effected in the random alphabet plotting in the martial grid. Therefore, a third-degree condition of suspension is achieved, wherein the unstable products of operations governed by chance unite in a song of stasis.

Book of Sigils, 1988

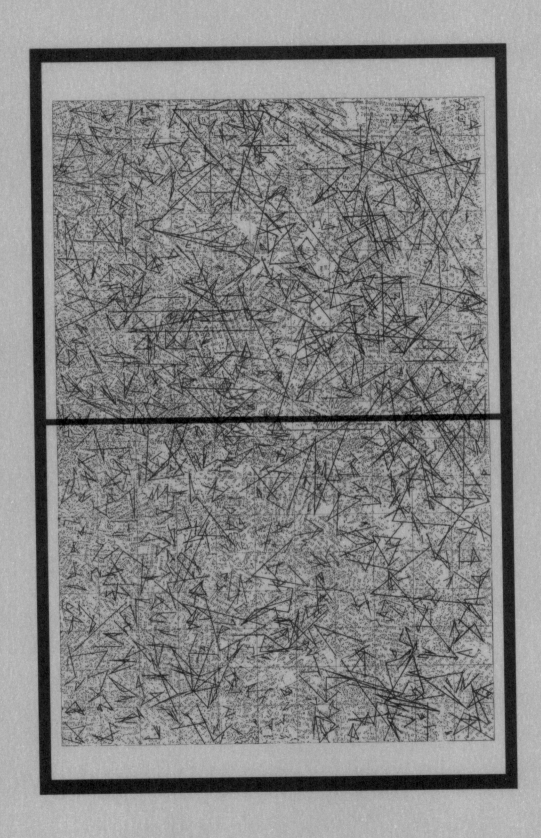

Shadow Theater, 1988

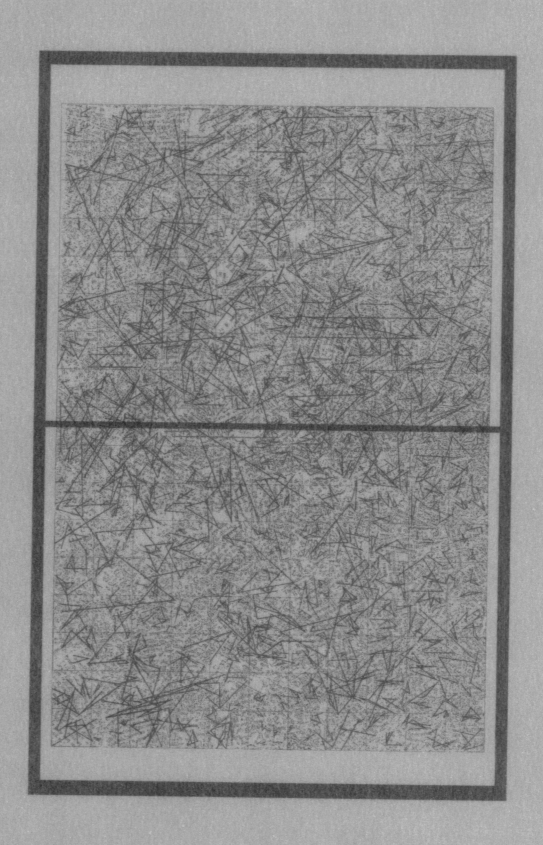

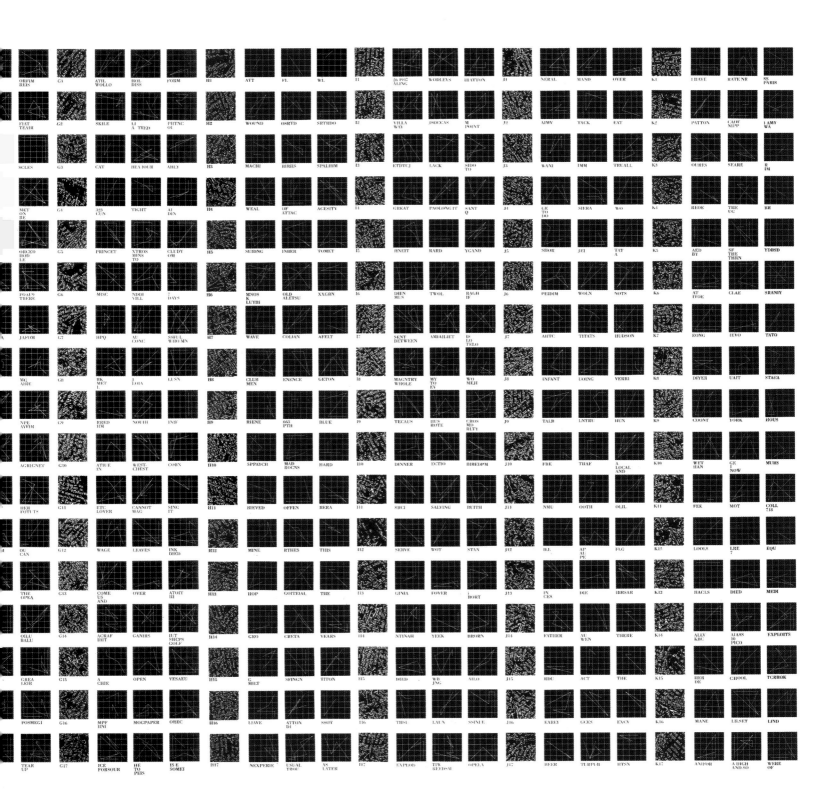

The complete Book of Sigils, 1988, showing the squares from the grid of the Engendering Plate
alongside their three corresponding sigils

105

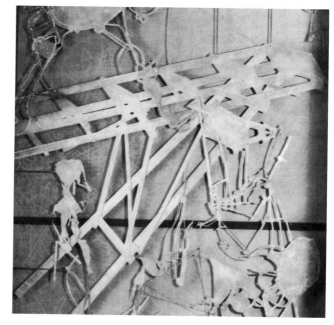

The Shadow Theater

The Shadow Theater came about in a rather haphazard manner, and in retrospect (although it is perhaps anachronistic to look back on something that begs the deferment of its own completion) provided the most satisfactory way of bringing into proximity two disparate aspects of the previous work: the Engendering Plate with Sigils and the Cameo (Root) Plate. The fissures or gaps inherent, yet invisible, in both plates were only manifest in the process of their making, or in a close reading of that process. In other words, the instability of the ground they establish is understood only by the knowing observer; their outward aspects, regardless of the accidents of pattern and design, present an appearance of unbroken continuity. A synthesis of the two plates was neither possible nor desirable. Instead, a kind of double mirror would be inserted between the two faces of the work, which would serve to expose the instability of both.

This mirror-like interface first suggested itself during an unsuccessful effort to break down and list the characters, objects, and actions described in the Cameo (Root) Plate, in the naive hope that this list would serve as a program for the design of a mechanism and figures (puppets) that would possess the order and mutability of language. The attempt to construct such a mechanism failed, paradoxically, because the classical hierarchies always latent in the project would simply reassert themselves in a closed or seamless manner. It was therefore necessary to provide some means of access, a window, between the Cameo (Root) Plate and the Engendering Plate. The shadow elements provided this means, for while they do partake of certain parts of the initial Cameo (Root) listing, they do so in a way that would foil any merely synthetic reading. Instead they participate in that process which,

in the words of Alfred Jarry, "symbolically attributes the properties of objects, described by their virtuality, to their lineaments."[5]

The shadows themselves pointed the way, for they operated as a kind of cue-card-cum-blocking (for those actors who always forget what to say and where to say it). They are the trace of everyday objects suspended between the Cameo (Root) and the Engendering Plate (now a screen door: every window needs a screen), serving the double purpose of revealing and concealing that which we find closest to us and is yet withheld from our grasp.

> Since what we see in the sky, and what we find in the depths of our hearts are both equally removed from our actions, with the one shining far above our undertakings, and the other existing far beneath our expressions, a kind of relationship is formed between the thought we give to the most distant things and our most intimate introspections. They seem to be the extremes of our expectation which echo one another and resemble each other in hoping for some decisive event in the heavens or in the heart.
> —Paul Valéry, Variations on an Idea of Pascal, 1950[6]

PREVIOUS: The Cameo (Root) Plate, 1988

ABOVE LEFT: The flattened zinc structure casts a shadow through the screen of the Shadow Theater, creating the illusion of objects with depth suspended behind it. The yellow writing scripted in paint along the edges of the zinc cutouts is drawn from the text in the Cameo (Root) Plate.

ABOVE RIGHT: A detail of the Shadow Theater reveals shadows cast on the screen on which the Static Song of the Sigils has been printed.

OPPOSITE: The Theater of Operation attempts to establish a set of possible actions (or gestures) available to featured mechanisms and figures.

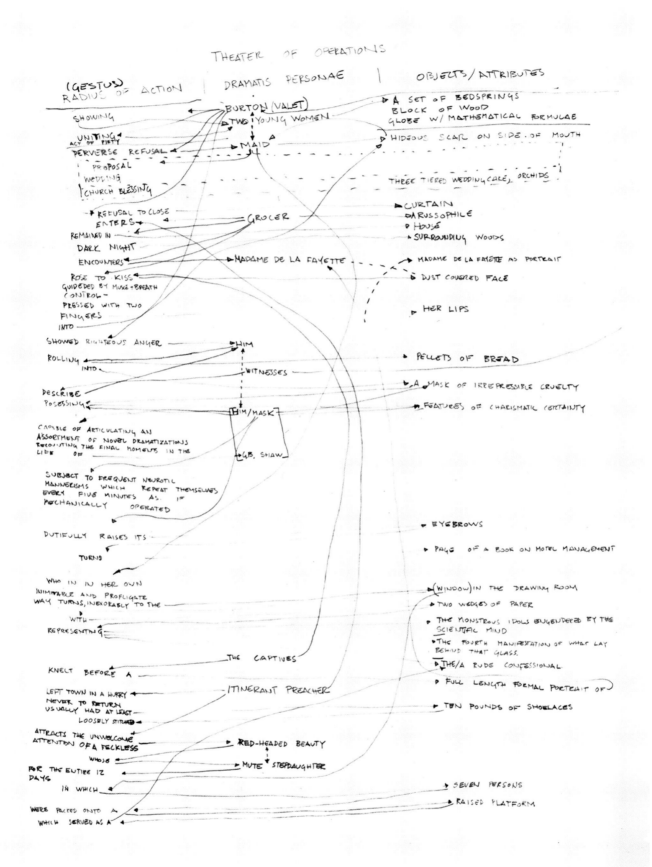

THEATER OF OPERATIONS

(GESTUS) RADIUS OF ACTION	DRAMATIS PERSONAE	OBJECTS/ATTRIBUTES

BURTON (VALET)
TWO YOUNG WOMEN

SHOWING

A SET OF BEDSPRINGS
BLOCK OF WOOD
GLOBE W/ MATHEMATICAL FORMULAE

UNITING
ACT OF PIETY
PERVERSE REFUSAL
PROPOSAL
WEDDING
CHURCH BLESSING

MAID

HIDEOUS SCAR ON SIDE OF MOUTH

THREE TIERED WEDDING CAKE, ORCHIDS

REFUSAL TO CLOSE
ENTERS
REMAINED IN
DARK NIGHT
ENCOUNTERS
ROSE TO KISS
GUIDED BY MUSE + BREATH
CONTROL
PRESSED WITH TWO
FINGERS
INTO

GROCER

MADAME DE LA FAYETTE

CURTAIN
A RUSSOPHILE
HOUSE
SURROUNDING WOODS

MADAME DE LA FAYETTE AS PORTRAIT

DUST COVERED FACE

HER LIPS

SHOWED RIGHTEOUS ANGER
ROLLING
INTO
DESCRIBE
POSESSING

HIM

WITNESSES

HIM/MASK

PELLETS OF BREAD

A MASK OF IRREPRESSIBLE CRUELTY

FEATURES OF CHARISMATIC CERTAINTY

CAPABLE OF ARTICULATING AN
ASSORTMENT OF NOVEL DRAMATIZATIONS
RECOUNTING THE FINAL MOMENTS IN THE
LIFE OF

G.B. SHAW

SUBJECT TO FREQUENT NEUROTIC
MANNERISMS WHICH REPEAT THEMSELVES
EVERY FIVE MINUTES AS IF
MECHANICALLY OPERATED

EYEBROWS

DUTIFULLY RAISES ITS

TURNS

PAGE OF A BOOK ON MOTEL MANAGEMENT

WHO IN IN HER OWN
INIMITABLE AND PROFLIGATE
WAY TURNS, INEXORABLY TO THE
WITH
REPRESENTING

THE CAPTIVES

(WINDOW) IN THE DRAWING ROOM
TWO WEDGES OF PAPER
THE MONSTROUS IDOLS ENGENDERED BY THE
SCIENTIFIC MIND
THE FOURTH MANIFESTATION OF WHAT LAY
BEHIND THAT GLASS
THE/A RUDE CONFESSIONAL

KNELT BEFORE A
LEFT TOWN IN A HURRY
NEVER TO RETURN
USUALLY HAD AT LEAST
LOOSELY STRUNG
ATTRACTS THE UNWELCOME
ATTENTION OF A FECKLESS
WHOSE
FOR THE ENTIRE 12
DAYS
IN WHICH
WERE PACKED ONTO A
WHICH SERVED AS A

ITINERANT PREACHER

RED-HEADED BEAUTY
MUTE STEPDAUGHTER

FULL LENGTH FORMAL PORTRAIT OF

TEN POUNDS OF SHOELACES

SEVEN PERSONS
RAISED PLATFORM

The Shadow Theater, 1988. Stretched on an aluminum door frame, a screen on which the engendering plate is printed obscures the view of zinc shadow puppets, whose silhouette produces the perception of depth behind the screen.

Métier à Aubes

The construction Métier à Aubes, which takes its name from a fragment of Raymond Roussel's novel *Impressions of Africa*, is an artifact derived from the ongoing Globe Theater project. The project seeks to illuminate the currently obscured yet ancient and venerable relationship between language and architecture. This relationship, though generally excluded from current definitions, is clearly articulated in preclassical Greek literature as *diadala*, and more recognizably in the language of Rome. The Latin verb *textus* (according to classical Roman rhetoricians) indicates the (de)composition of both a literary and an architectural work, and is the root of the word *textile*, thus leading back to Roussel's pregnant *jeu de mot*, whose twofold meanings fortuitously encompass the antique definitions: "Métier [work/loom] à Aubes [dawn/paddle wheel]. I thought of a profession which required getting up at the crack of dawn."[7]

The construction may be divided into two mutually informing mechanisms suspended in a framework: the upper, a language loom consisting of a series of prescribed metal plates, and the lower, an adjustable reclining chaise (*figura*) from which the plates can be read. The entire apparatus may be viewed as a kind of protestant mechanism, whose resistance may be explained ethically or historically but whose possibility of functioning effectively is scarcely attainable—or attainable only after a willing suspension of disbelief.

1 Frances A. Yates, *Theatre of the World* (London: Routledge and Kegan Paul, 1969), 189.
2 Jorge Luis Borges, "Mirror of Enigmas" (1964), in *Other Inquisitions* (Austin: University of Texas Press, 1964), 125.
3 Thomas De Quincey, *Autobiographical Sketches* (1853), in *Writings*, vol. 1 (London: A & C Black, 1896), 129.
4 Léon Bloy, *L'âme de Napoléon* (Paris: Mercure de France, 1912).
5 Alfred Jarry, *Exploits and Opinions of Doctor Faustroll, Pataphysician*, trans. Simon Watson Taylor (Boston: Exact Change, 1996), 21.
6 Paul Valéry, *Variations on an Idea of Pascal* (New York: New Directions Publishing, 1950), 202.
7 Quoted in Michel Foucault, *Death and the Labyrinth: The World of Raymond Roussel* (Berkeley: University of California Press, 1987), 37.

ABOVE: Métier à Aubes is composed of T6 aluminum alloy, magnesium, and stainless steel. The rotating language loom on the upper left consists of five metal plates and can be read from the chaise below.

OPPOSITE: Plan and elevation views of the chaise

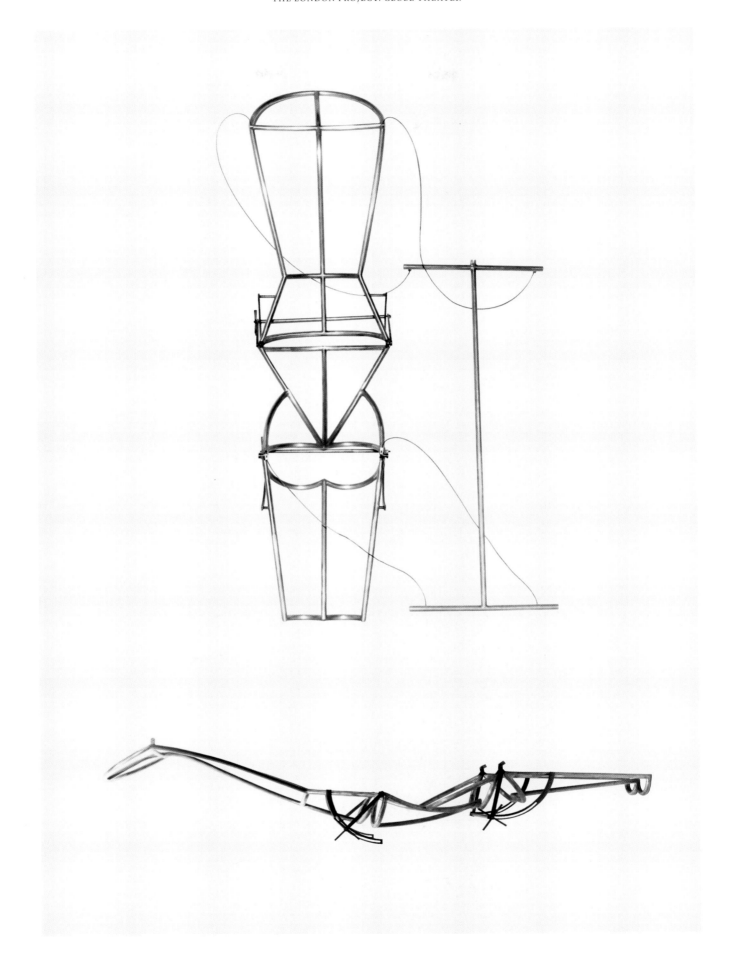

ERO/MACHIA/HYPNIA HOUSE
1988

*The dreamer of a golden age in this brazen time must
realize that his way has already been paved with the bodies
of the now nameless dead. The price of longing means
treading this mire that is unavoidable, however one may
wish to travel light.*
—*Anonymous*

Aktion Poliphile: Hyperotomachia—
Ero/Machia/Hypniahouse

A competition brief that would have led us to situate a
domestic project at once in the mazes of Renaissance
allegory and on the banks of the lately suburbanized Rhine
suggests either a pastoral escapism born of historical
indifference or, more insidiously, a project that would
unavoidably (and perhaps unintentionally) affiliate the
work with that disease of the soul that, to paraphrase the
literary critic George Steiner, gave hell a native tongue.

The domestic realm and its attendant associations of
the private and the personal threaten to cast a veil of
innocence over—to domesticate, in other words—what
would in the public realm more easily reveal its true
face. We are speaking of events barely fifty years old. The
house, paradoxically, becomes the forum for these issues.
Paradoxically because, as Daniel Libeskind points out,
"After all, the kitchen and the backyard and all those sorts
of small things are ultimately extendable right into the right
or left and into the center of power."[8]

This project seeks to negotiate that dangerous terrain
(of projections, fabrications, representations) by fixing
a steely gaze on a recent sleepwalking prot/ant(agon)ist
(here I refer to Adolf Hitler) for whom the Italian monk
Francesco Colonna's dream of the "strife of love" (when
viewed in light of its present public consequences) becomes
the "love of strife." As Walter Benjamin asserts in his
censure of the Futurists, "The logical result of fascism is
the introduction of aesthetics into political life" and "all
efforts to render politics aesthetic culminate in one thing:
war."[9] Dis-ease permeates the very fabric of domesticity,
from the most trivial household objects to the apparently
inviolate precincts of grass, trees, and even the horizon
against which they are seen. The house penetrates these
conventionally perceived realms, seeking to interrogate
them not merely as categories of space but as the
unquestioned emblems of domestic well-being.

The house was conceived as a chain of linked yet discrete
spaces tied together by a series of discontinuous paths
that enable one to traverse the various emblematic rooms
independent of the vagaries of their inhabitants. The rooms
of the house can be seen, then, as a kind of additive picture
script, whose parts are read like the words and sentences of
a discursive language. Thus, a working method unfolded
that uses images of undigested (hence identifiable)
historical minutiae, disposed within and among the
program requirements of the competition brief. The result
is an apparently seamless photomechanical mosaic.

A description of the living room may serve to clarify this
idea. The room is bounded on four sides by the following:
the library/study on whose walls hangs a map depicting
the routes of certain aircraft on the night of Saturday,
October 14, 1944; the facade wall, or Lancasteromachia,
founded on the joining of 1:1 molds of aircraft parts
(Lancaster Mk. 1 and Junker 88A4) and depicting (rather in
the method of now-discredited historical paintings) a brief
encounter in the skies over Düsseldorf; the storage wall
(which requires no explanation); and the concrete living-
room floor, which is inscribed with a branching text.

The text on the floor of the living room is assembled
through the methodical coupling of sentence fragments
gleaned from various daily newspapers and tabloids.
The laws of syntax are rigorously obeyed to produce
a continuously bifurcating text; short-lived dramatis
personae make their sudden appearance, proceed along a
probable course of action, then exit abruptly as the possible

PREVIOUS: Roof Plan of the Ero/Machia/Hypniahouse

OPPOSITE: Landscape collage, "Thus We See a Diseased View of Nature," 1987

So schauten kranke Geister die Natur __

syntactical routes are exhausted. In certain locations on the floor the sentences rejoin, resulting in an onanistic circularity of action (but these are merely instances). Within each possible route the narrative seeks to attain an artificially attenuated existence. Thus the narrative is sustained and proliferates only as long as the syntactical mechanism is supplied with language.

These abject concretions within the fabric of the domestic program form a kind of clew[10] against which the conventional program of the house might be read and through which views of the Rhine meadow offer testimony. In this way, apparently neutral views of "nature" are filtered through a historical matrix that is both pneumatic and critical.

When read through *Hypnerotomachia Poliphili* and its labyrinthine discourses, the seemingly innocent competition brief acquired various sinister qualities. Filtered through the text's wide-ranging paranoia, the anodyne aspects of the house suddenly appeared uncanny, as if a traumatic past lay buried beneath a shallow cover of domesticity, threatening to resurface. The *Hypnerotomachia*, with its invented language, ambiguous imagery, and potentially grave subtexts, encouraged a critical look at the competition's normative program requirements and the role that Poliphilo's distant dreams might play when transplanted to suburban Wiesbaden. Drawing from famously incomplete or manufactured histories, the *Hypnerotomachia* composites fragments and traces into a chain of novel associations. Unlike the author's contemporaries, who presumed an authority and rationality in their transformation of ancient materials into novel treatises, Colonna did not consider his sources definitive and instead favored a process of syncretic combination that was as open as it was impenetrable.

Just as the remnant objects of Rome were used to reconstruct an entire culture, the material surrounding this project proposed a disinterment of recently suppressed histories. The *Hypnerotomachia*'s unique aggrandizement of Roman antiquity thus served as a framework for a radical interpretation of social and cultural history through an immanent material substrate.

The upheaval of the Second World War, with cultural and material impositions that had been so emphatically forced into the household, could not be erased from the territory or the proposition. The apparently mute aesthetics of suburban domesticity could not be divorced from the politics at the heart of such an insidious history. The house thus developed into its own *Hypnerotomachia*, upended in the context of postwar Germany to become a contemporary nocturne rather than a reference to classical antiquity. Enabled to represent new internal hierarchies, the project incorporated outside sources without consideration of obsolete notions of progress and continuity. A life could be read through the domestic fixtures of the house—between one object and the next, a whole world could be excavated from layered fragments and debris. As traces of the past could not be reduced to private matters, the inhabitants' personal domains would become subject to reinterpretation, drawing the weight of political history into daily affairs.

Set in sheet metal and military-industrial production, historical texts and popular slogans, notices, object descriptions, and commands were rendered inaccessible upon the surface of the domestic stage. Once read against a body of resonant imagery, fragments unidentifiable on their own assumed a spatial valence, revealing associations that were interrogated through collage and recomposition. This process of re-membering enabled a high degree of specificity to emerge from an otherwise indeterminate

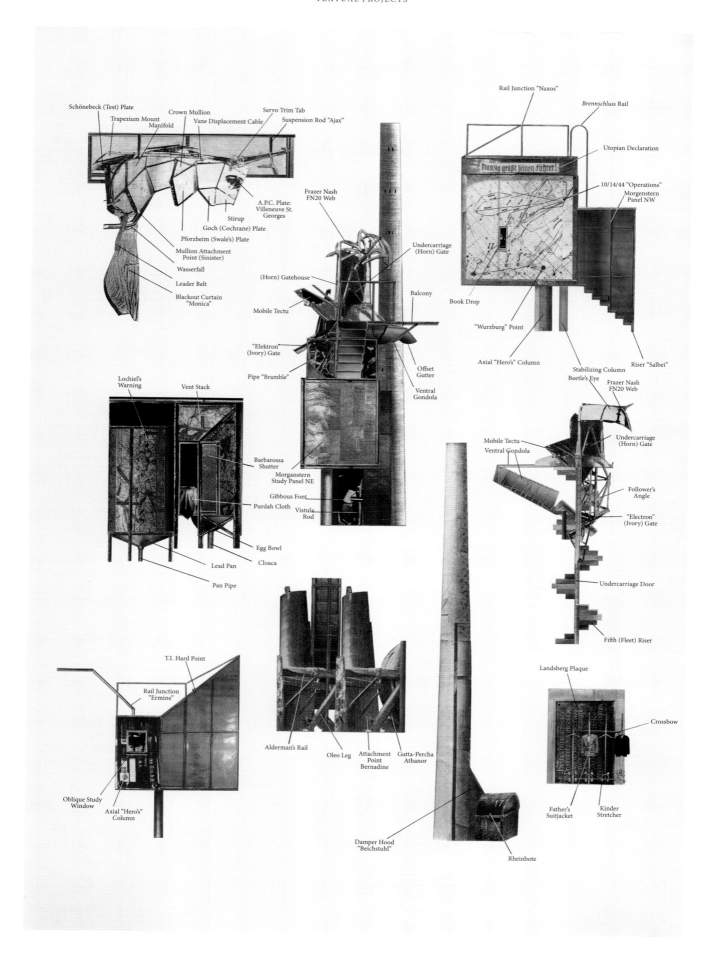

Schönebeck (Test) Plate
Trapezium Mount Manifold
Crown Mullion
Vane Displacement Cable
Servo Trim Tab
Suspension Rod "Ajax"

A.P.C. Plate: Villeneuve St. Georges
Stirup
Goch (Cochrane) Plate
Pforzheim (Swale's) Plate
Mullion Attachment Point (Sinister)
Wasserfall
Leader Belt
Blackout Curtain "Monica"

Frazer Nash FN20 Web
(Horn) Gatehouse
Mobile Tectu
"Elektron" (Ivory) Gate
Pipe "Bramble"

Undercarriage (Horn) Gate
Balcony
Offset Gutter
Ventral Gondola

Rail Junction "Naxos"
Brennschluss Rail
Utopian Declaration
10/14/44 "Operations"
Morgenstern Panel NW

Dan;ig grüßt seinen Führer!

Book Drop
"Wurzburg" Point
Axial "Hero's" Column
Riser "Salbei"
Stabilizing Column
Beetle's Eye
Frazer Nash FN20 Web

Lochiel's Warning
Vent Stack

Barbarossa Shutter
Morganstern Study Panel NE
Gibbous Font
Purdah Cloth
Vistula Rod
Egg Bowl
Lead Pan
Cloaca
Pan Pipe

Mobile Tectu
Ventral Gondola
Undercarriage (Horn) Gate
Follower's Angle
"Electron" (Ivory) Gate
Undercarriage Door
Fifth (Fleet) Riser

T.I. Hard Point
Rail Junction "Ermine"
Oblique Study Window
Axial "Hero's" Column

Alderman's Rail
Oleo Leg
Attachment Point Bernadine
Gutta-Percha Athanor

Damper Hood "Beichstuhl"
Rheinbote

Landsberg Plaque
Crossbow
Father's Suitjacket
Kinder Stretcher

118

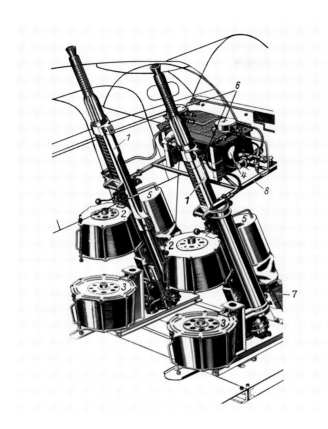

set of relationships between the program and the subject matter. It became possible to represent affinities between household objects and industrial regimes, between technological developments and culturally biased narratives, between power structures of the home and power structures of the nation.

Historical photographs, specimen plates, texts, and numerous other images collapsed with the imaginary of technological catastrophe, latent in their popular dissemination. Treated as textual artifacts, the fragments were broken apart and recombined, revealing recurring themes that brought an idiosyncratic syntax to surfaces and spaces. Positing architecture not as a symbol of renewal but as a mobile archaeology for cultural, generational reflection, the house articulated our objective—a conclusive note for the larger textual project—to draw the myths of an aestheticized past into an immediate present.

The project's investment in techno-industrial ephemera emerged from our own interest in the aircraft technologies refined over the course of bombing operations in Western Germany. These technologies, with their corollary instruments and artifacts, not only resonated with the ruins that constituted the project's antiquarian dimension but possessed a discursive instability, allowing unexpected outcomes to emerge from a variety of domestic narratives. The technologies of war offered systems and organizations that could be recomposed into precise architectural objects

but would not be reduced to them. The aircraft possessed an intense ideological significance within the context of the war, despite the portrayal of its primary use value and design priorities as strictly confined to material terms. Just as the scope of Roman cultural history was fundamentally inaccessible to Renaissance surveyors, these armaments presented ruins whose comprehensive reconstruction was impossible, leaving gaps to be filled with projections of a potentially fabricated nature.

The stories recounted by former bombers opened the project to a mythic dimension as dense as any in the *Hypnerotomachia*'s ekphrases. The mythologized figure of the bomber spawned an endless array of characters, settings, and objects that preoccupied audiences long after the war's end. This type of memorialization cast events as legendary efforts, each one bearing the responsibility for victory but not for individual acts of violence. The simplification of complex histories into imprecise and digestible narratives could also be channeled into an ambiguity of similar economy. In an episode of the

OPPOSITE: Ero/Machia/Hypniahouse Fragment Plate

ABOVE LEFT: Two MG FF/M 20mm Schrage Musik vertical cannons mounted in the cockpit of a Messerschmitt Bf 110 G-4/R Night Fighter

ABOVE RIGHT: *Take Off*, Dame Laura Knight, 1943. Interior of the Stirling Mk. 3, with four-man crew preparing for a night bombing mission

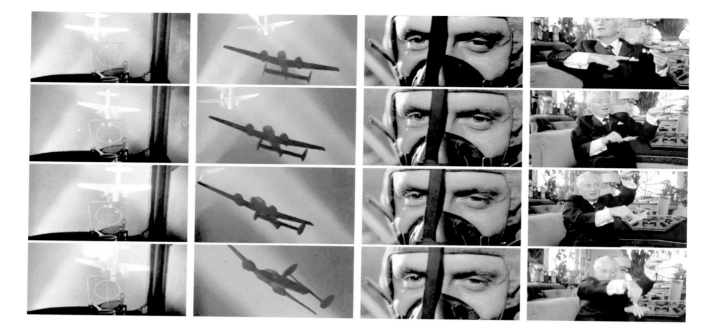

1973 British television documentary *The World at War*, the recollections of a German night fighter pilot—communicated more clearly through his gestures with a model airplane than through words—demonstrate the dissonance between personal memory and supposedly objective historical accounts. The pilot, looking through the gunsights of his aircraft, remembers shooting at a plane but not at a person. The plane, as an extension of the pilot, causes a disassociation between an action and its consequence, such that the pilot does not assume complete agency for his act of violence. Wholly circumscribed by technology, the coordination among fighters, bombers, radar, searchlights, and guns obscured any semblance of the contest between heroic individuals that had preceded the war. Len Deighton's 1970 novel *Bomber* bears this weight with a balance that posits a reciprocity between the agents and technologies of war. The descriptive equivalence of settings, objects, and events employs a precision found through ambiguity, remaining personally ambivalent in the face of disaster.

This quality of ambiguity was elaborated in the Ero/ Machia/Hypniahouse's textual dimension, forming a basis for the collages' narrative uncertainty. Despite the futility of divorcing specific personal histories from wider effects afforded by the technology (or even attempting to recount one without reference to the other), such texts were often steeped in a tone of unquestionable confidence. More than the rigor of their internal consistency, the texts' reluctance to recognize any external influence defined their place within the scope of our work. Two spaces that could apparently coexist—one bounded by the myopia of engineered processes and the other surrounded by cloudy memories—provided a context for bringing together divergent accounts. Competing readings influenced one another without acknowledgment, and when presented

as complementary, fostered the problems of agency and uncertainty that had been carefully excluded by the original rhetoric. These accounts not only describe weapons as remnants of cultural devastation but also subject them to a pervasive analytical impulse that attempts to render them mute technological artifacts. In a constant relay from unwavering faith in numbers to a manic reverence for valiant pilots, the imagery oscillates between parallel narratives of the technical and the heroic.

The project—as a textual document, as a series of images, and as an architectural proposal—could negotiate a discursive territory somewhere between a newsreel and a historical painting. The house was also a house, and so could be received alternately as an impersonal cultural fragment or a dense personal history, shading the surfaces of domesticity outlined in the program. The very same impulses fraying at the edges of the domestic program were reflected in the overt form of wartime sheet metal and glass—a category of cultural production that, unlike the furnishings of the household, is the undeniable product of the politics with which it had been so closely associated.

ABOVE: Film stills from the British documentary *The World at War* of a night fighter operation recalled by flying ace Wilhelm Herget, describing the use of Schrage Musik cannons against an intercepted bomber. Following closely underneath, the attacker could remain in the bomber's blind spot until opening fire.

OPPOSITE TOP: Views of a Short Stirling B. III. Drawn as a specimen in isolation, it is identifiable by its insignia and identification letters. "*The Stirling B.Mk.III of No. 75 'New Zealand' Squadron illustrated…was finished in the standard R.A.F. Bomber Command pattern over the upper surfaces, and matt black over all wing, tail and fuselage under surfaces, extending up the fuselage sides and including the vertical tail surfaces.*"[11]

OPPOSITE BOTTOM: Studies of ground-floor plan and roof plan for transfer

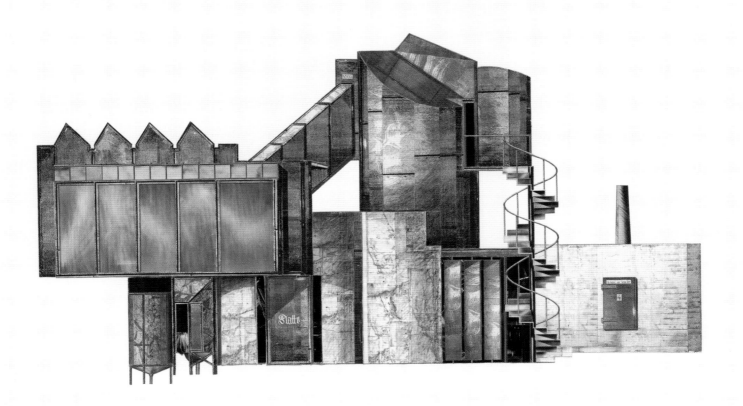

West elevation

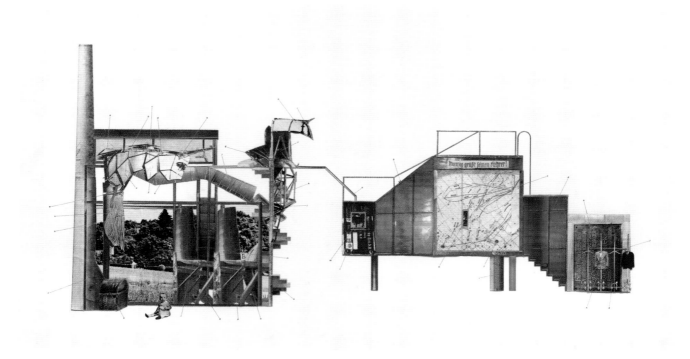

In his essay "Projective Verse," the American poet and literary theorist Charles Olson's notion of an utterance that carries with it a breadth of emotive associations informed our approach to spatial and textual composition. Olson provides a method for poetic, lyrical, and metaphysical invention that, for our purposes, was more attuned to the recomposition of image fragments than to the treatment of strictly historical texts. Olson states that elements "must be taken up as participants in the kinetic of the poem just as solidly as we are accustomed to take what we call the objects of reality" and further, that "these elements are to be seen as creating the tensions of a poem just as totally as do those other objects create what we know as the world."[12] Treating individual memories with the same weight as collective, supposedly objective historical accounts, we leveled them to the same plane as the material debris of history. The Lancaster's undercarriage, the nose of the pursuing Junkers—both existed in a materialized, indexical form on the wall, accumulating household significances. Far from offering a sobering explanation of the artifacts' roles and capabilities, the text expanded the fragments into associations with interminable mythological dimensions.

This approach facilitated a reading of the Facade Writing—a text that refers to the view from the living room through the Lancasteromachia's frame—against the collaged imagery. The subject matter of the text engages the problems of mythologization by following a tendency to generate internal consistencies and interconnections. By deploying the narratives of the War to synthesize the seemingly disparate realms of personal and public histories,

we established a common ground, consequently rendering visible the significance of industrial production. The house showed no disparity between the material of history and the ideas that the material generated, presenting history through a form much more closely related to its content than the misleading neutrality of purely historical text.

Through collage, we approached the more indeterminate architectural consequences of a house built from the War's material and cultural leftovers, of industrial production imported into building practices and the potential of these practices to prefigure domestic life. A tension emerged through our drawing processes, coinciding with two primary and opposing effects of collage. On the one hand, collage encourages the loss of source material and dilutes its original meaning, until it assumes new, potentially aleatory qualities; imagery is treated purely as material, without regard to provenance. On the other hand, the contents of collage are recontextualized yet maintain original identities that are identifiable in varying degrees, according to the viewer.

We sought out precarious moments in the imagery that lay somewhere between these two extremes, selecting compositions that undermined historical narratives while confronting the distortion of radically preexisting interpretations in the presence of uncertain terms. To a degree, the open-endedness of the references facilitated their absorption into an independent formal language. What developed through line drawings and collage only obliquely supported our historical interests.

On a more instrumental level, tending to architectural priorities provided an aspect to work against. Honing in on the role of collage in our design process without being limited to the graphic imprecision of the source imagery, we found that the more developed collages functioned as surface treatments. The process of collage thus served as a means of mediating the various construction systems and material logics that held the forms together.

8 Daniel Libeskind, "Versus the old-established language of architecture," *Daidalos*, no. 1 (Sept. 1981), 97–102.

9 Walter Benjamin, "The Work of Art in the Age of Mechanical Reproduction," in *Illuminations*, trans. Harry Zohn (New York: Schocken, 1969), 241.

10 String used in a labyrinth.

11 William Greene, *Famous Bombers of the Second World War*, vol. 2 (Colchester, England: Book Service, 1975), 146.

12 Charles Olson, "Projective Verse," *Poetry New York*, no. 3 (1950).

OPPOSITE: Ero/Machia/Hypniahouse, interior elevation

ABOVE: Resor House, Jackson Hole, Wyoming, Mies van der Rohe, 1939. Much like Mies van der Rohe's collages for his Resor House, which delineate the space in pencil of interior views from the living room, our approach to working with collage supposed a stable architectural frame in which the contained image was interchangeable, assimilated without upsetting a preexisting order. Although we never would have drawn the contents of the completed collages, drawing allowed us to first establish the organizational and formal elements of the house.

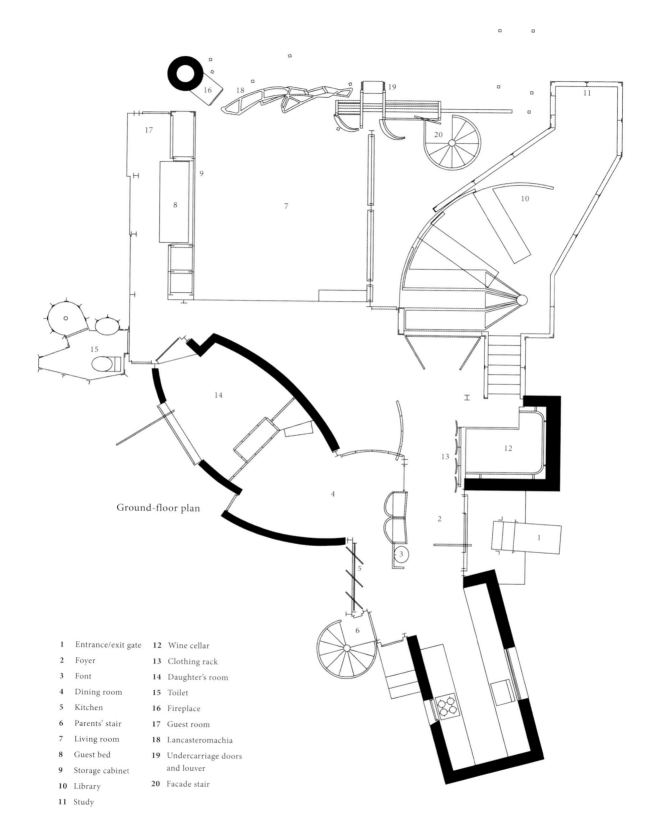

Ground-floor plan

1	Entrance/exit gate	**12**	Wine cellar
2	Foyer	**13**	Clothing rack
3	Font	**14**	Daughter's room
4	Dining room	**15**	Toilet
5	Kitchen	**16**	Fireplace
6	Parents' stair	**17**	Guest room
7	Living room	**18**	Lancasteromachia
8	Guest bed	**19**	Undercarriage doors
9	Storage cabinet		and louver
10	Library	**20**	Facade stair
11	Study		

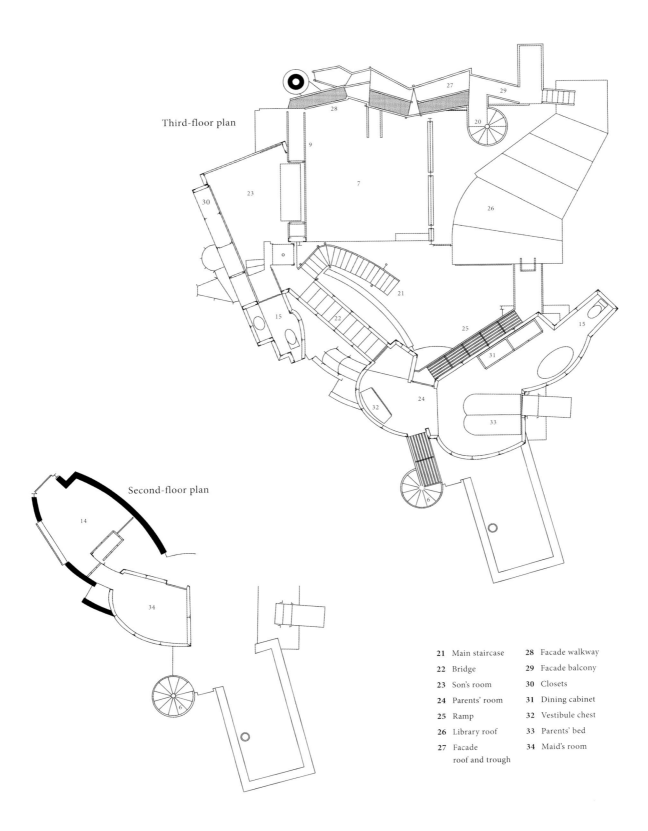

Third-floor plan

Second-floor plan

21 Main staircase
22 Bridge
23 Son's room
24 Parents' room
25 Ramp
26 Library roof
27 Facade
   roof and trough

28 Facade walkway
29 Facade balcony
30 Closets
31 Dining cabinet
32 Vestibule chest
33 Parents' bed
34 Maid's room

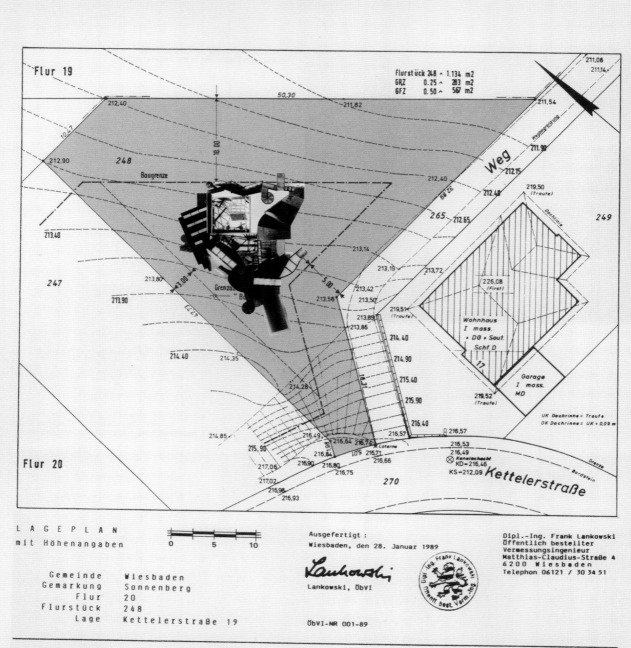

Flur 19

Flurstück 248 ≙ 1.134 m2
GRZ   0.25 ≙ 283 m2
GFZ   0.50 ≙ 567 m2

50,30

248

Baugrenze

247

Grenzo...
"Ba...

Flur 20

Weg

249

Wohnhaus
I mass.
+ DG + Sout.
Schf. D

Garage
I mass.
MD

UK Dachrinne = Traufe
OK Dachrinne = UK + 0,09 m

Kettelerstraße

270

LAGEPLAN
mit Höhenangaben

0   5   10

Ausgefertigt :
Wiesbaden, den 28. Januar 1989

Lankowski, ÖbVI

Gemeinde   Wiesbaden
Gemarkung   Sonnenberg
Flur   20
Flurstück   248
Lage   Kettelerstraße 19

ÖbVI-NR 001-89

Dipl.-Ing. Frank Lankowski
Öffentlich bestellter
Vermessungsingenieur
Matthias-Claudius-Straße 4
6200 Wiesbaden
Telephon 06121 / 30 34 51

Lageplan des Grundstücks

Site plan of the Ero/Machia/Hypniahouse in Wiesbaden, Germany

No Place Like Home: Domesticating Assemblages

Robert E. Somol

Reiser + Umemoto's Koenig House, or Ero/Machia/Hypniahouse, was designed as an entry in a juried exhibition in Frankfurt for a house in Wiesbaden for a family of four. The theme for this domestic competition was supplied by Francesco Colonna's architectural treatise/love story *Hypnerotomachia Poliphili* of 1499, an obscure Renaissance text first partially translated into English a century later as *The Strife of Love in a Dreame*. Reiser + Umemoto rearranged this translated title as "The Love of Strife," which already predicted the final fate of their project by recalling Kurt Schwitters's *Merzbau* in Hanover, Germany, "The Cathedral of Erotic Misery," which was destroyed by Allied bombs in 1943.

Colonna's text, not surprisingly, is almost immediately dismissed as an ornamental decoy in the letter of invitation to the competition: "With the phantastic descriptions of architecture of Francesco Colonna which were mentioned earlier we intend to inspire your phantasy but we do not wish to put a sound plan into question." If it is not already evident from the selection of a fifteenth-century allegory, the competition's sponsors mandate that text not infect structure, program, or enjoyment, and the competition brief explicitly asks for clear structure, high standards of functionality, and appeal to all sensual activities: the Vitruvian triad of firmness, commodity, and delight. The success of Reiser + Umemoto's intervention is the way in which they directly confront the competition brief by rigorously rereading the planning details and program requirements against themselves. Unlike their neo-avant-garde predecessors, Reiser + Umemoto refuse to deny or suppress the fiction of function. Instead, they push it to the extreme and take it deadly seriously, as all good blasphemers must. By engaging function critically and not repressing it or accepting it as given, they can open the discipline from within to what are traditionally construed as outside references, thus avoiding the alternatives of a purely formal manipulation or an iconic appliqué. Thinking consistently through the desires of function (the love of strife?) permits the other choices in the scheme to be informed imaginatively.

Among other requisites, the Poliphile program calls for a wood stove, a room with a shower, visual contact between the kitchen and entrance, a wardrobe and storage room, and shafts connecting the bedrooms with the laundry room for the efficient disposition of dirty clothes. With this "innocent" information, Reiser + Umemoto reinterpret the pastoral ideal of the clients—their "dream of living in a bright residence near the woods"—as a nightmare renunciation of history unconsciously replayed within the specific requirements of the domestic program. The house, with its conflicting indications of scale, emerges variously as a bunker, a concentration camp, a munitions factory, and a stalag (the number 17 readily visible on both sides of the entrance facade). A private residence in an affluent spa town on the Rhine becomes the site for the reinscription of a fifty-year-old episode in world history, for the exchange of the personal and political implicit in the microfascism of domestic living arrangements.

Like the interior dining scene of John Heartfield's *Hurrah, die Butter ist alle!* (Hurrah, there's no butter left!, 1935), the Poliphile project investigates the politics of the home front, where guns and iron become the preferred butter substitute. The elevations and plans invoke weaponry, machine housings, and shells, which also serve as a reference to the effect of ballistics that Walter Benjamin attributed to Dada collage. Most disturbingly, on one side of the windowless kitchen/

The Merzbau, the Cathedral of Erotic Misery, Kurt Schwitters, 1933

Sixteenth-century woodcut after Francesco Colonna's *Hypnerotomachia Polophili*

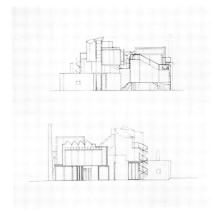

Initial drawings of southeast (top) and west (bottom) elevations over which collage was applied, pencil on paper, 1988

Hurrah, die Butter ist alle! (Hurrah, there's
no butter left!), John Heartfield, Prague, 1935

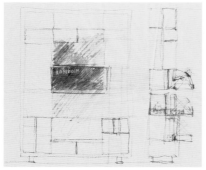

Study of storage cabinet for guests, 1988

OPPOSITE: The house design supports two opposing
tendencies that are fully articulated in the storage
wall and the branching text on the floor. Whereas
the storage wall is a rectilinear structure that
features in Fraktur script a series of German labels
and commands, inscribed on the floor's surface is
a branching, rhizomatic text composed through
the reassembling of text fragments from various
newspapers and tabloids.

13 Benjamin, "Work of Art in the Age of Mechanical
 Reproduction," 233, 241.
14 K. Michael Hays, "Reproduction and Negation:
 The Cognitive Project of the Avant-Garde," in
 Architectureproduction, ed. Beatriz Colomina and Joan
 Ockman (New York: Princeton Architectural Press,
 1988), 176. For an instance of historico-theoretical
 recycling parallel to that of the designers discussed
 here, compare the text of this essay by Hays on Hannes
 Meyer to two of his other essays, "Photomontage and
 Its Audiences, Berlin, Circa 1922," *Harvard Architecture
 Review* 6 (1987) on Raoul Hausmann, and "Critical
 Architecture: Between Culture and Form," *Perspecta* 21
 (1984) on Mies. Curiously, the latter discusses design
 choice and precise architectural intention in terms
 similar to those of Nicholson.

incineration chamber there is a vault door with the number 4 that opens onto the
stove with its four burners, directly above which the smaller of two smokestacks
begins. In fact, the doubled smokestack/chimneys—symbols more of Holocaust
than hearth and home—frame two ends of the scheme and define the desired
line of sight between the kitchen and road. Their placement also serves to suggest
the inevitable funneling from the relatively open entry facade and living room
to the final destination of the closed and claustrophobic kitchen. Opposite the
oven there is a sink, registered on the outside elevation by a pair of metal panels
or shutters, beneath which the wall is stained with fluids from other domestic
experiments. For Monteurs Reiser + Umemoto, domestic architecture becomes
war conducted by other means.

Through a creative realignment of text, program, and site, Reiser + Umemoto
adduce a related content and technique: specifically, the montage tactics of the
Berlin Dadaists. They replay (which one does with a *Platte*, a record) the critique
of Weimar and the Reich performed by the Dadaists against the contemporary
backdrop of a recently united but still amnesiac Germany. While the overall
design process is based on montage, specific instances in the scheme more
directly allude to the images and themes of the Dadaists, as in the framed and
diagonally split collage mural to the right of the "east end room" on the exterior
elevation. Directly behind this panel on the interior wall is the text of a Nazi
memorial from Landsberg, the Bavarian prison where Adolf Hitler ("Germany's
greatest son") was imprisoned in 1924, during which time he recorded his own
totalizing desires of and for strife, *Mein Kampf*. In front of this commemorative
plaque four wardrobe valets (two of which impale formally attired torsos) stand
guard and pay homage like the republican automata of George Grosz or the
dummies and mannequins of Raoul Hausmann. To the left of these truncated
ciphers or prosthetic war cripples, a tactical aircraft map depicting bombing
runs serves as wallpaper for the exterior of the library/study, beneath a headline
that declares "Danzig greets its führer!" Continuing around to the left, the
entry wall is framed by the twisted fuselages of an Allied bomber and German
fighter, through which the natural beauty of the landscape can be glimpsed: truly
Benjamin's "orchid in the land of technology," but equally a reflection on Filippo
Tommaso Marinetti's celebration of the beautifying potential of war, which can
enrich "a flowering meadow with the fiery orchids of machine guns."[13]

Throughout their episodic design, Reiser + Umemoto appropriate and redeploy
the Fraktur script extensively used by the Nazis for propaganda. In addition
to critically reframing the documents of Nazi ideology, this lettering, by
emphasizing the linear form of the characters, reduces the symbolic function of
the integrated linguistic sign. It breaks up and empties the content of words and
recasts them in their physical materiality, as gouged scars, as the all-too-graphic
marks of brute power. The Fraktur type enables Reiser + Umemoto to attain the
effect sought earlier in their Globe Theater project in London, for which a much
more elaborate system had to be developed, a mechanism that would eliminate
the hand (and choice) and translate words into mere lines and graphs.

Scripted in Fraktur, "*Platte*" signs the Poliphile project while referring to the
Engendering and Cameo (Root) Plates produced by the architects as part of the
London Project. In fact, the text collage that covers the living-room floor of the
Poliphile project is the second iteration of the Cameo (Root) Plate used for the
Globe Theater; Reiser + Umemoto simply reproduced the entire descriptive
passage from the earlier project to explain its new situation. It is precisely aspects
of sampling and recycling like this that unite the designers, and the critics, of
the new architectural art of assemblage. Here K. Michael Hays's comments on
Ludwig Hilberseimer's Vorschlag zur City-Bebauung can be applied equally to
the work of Reiser + Umemoto or Ben Nicholson, as well as to the writings of
Hays himself: "His project summarizes other projects, only the most obvious of
which is his own."[14]

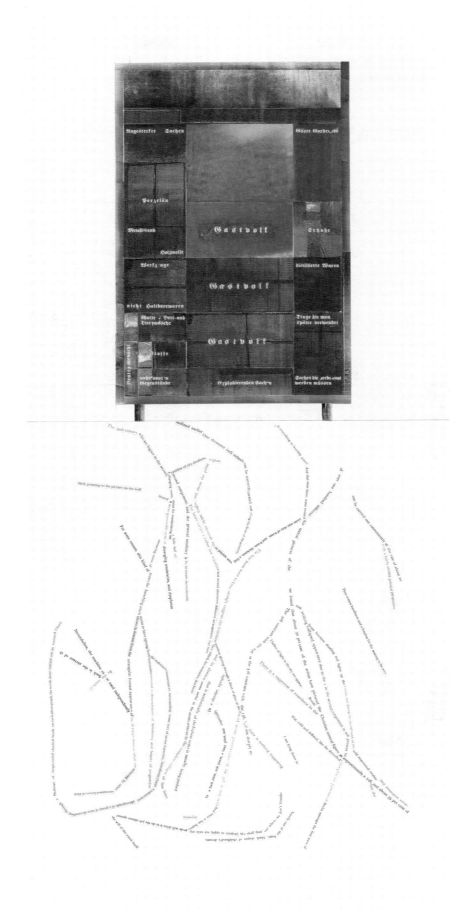

SEMIOTEXT(E) ARCHITECTURE: NAUSEA, CRISIS, A WAY FORWARD

One cannot overstate the importance of the journal *Semiotext(e)* to a generation of artists, writers, and thinkers interested in forging culture anew through the lens of structuralism and post-structuralism. Almost a whole generation of speculative architects was invited to contribute to this issue of *Semiotext(e)*, its first and only issue devoted to architecture. It was to be the summation of a generation of work on the intersection of architecture and language.

When we received the book with our and everyone's work, we were horrified. Some have accused the architects in the issue of attempting to annex the radicality of the *Semiotext(e)* project without understanding its deeper concerns. Our anxiety, however, focused on the consistent disciplinary aporia revealed in the projects themselves. For in truth, the issue, though containing projects of varying quality and depth, did deliver a fairly comprehensive survey on what interested architects at that time could do within the theoretical framework of that moment. What the issue brought home to us was the absence of avenues of development beyond what we had already done; there remained an unbridgeable gap between words and things. And since we were not content to persist with more commentary around things or with parallel projects on the materiality of language—or worse allegory—then we had to look elsewhere. Seeing the gap as a useful limit rather than an end, we shifted our focus to the possibilities of matter itself, viewing it as inherent in the discipline. Later we learned that the issue was not produced by *Semiotext(e)*'s own editors but by others in the spirit of experiementation, which in this case went terribly wrong. In any case, there was consensus that it was the end of a period of work in architecture.

This occurred during a period of economic downturn and with the birth of a child. We no longer could sustain our own studio doing only occasional work. It signaled the moment I had to go out and teach to earn a living. Because of that, we had more active exchange with young colleagues, which we hadn't expected. We started to do competitions where site, program, and other constraints were external. We realized that our architecture needed to work within objective circumstances yet remain at some level independent of them. How would we advance a project in architecture where site, program, and client weren't under our control? While the textually based project ended for us, the materio-formal project embedded in that textual work would continue. There may still be a hermetic element in our work, but it's no longer the sole basis, rather an abiding substratum of an otherwise exoteric set of conditions.

MATERIAL DIAGRAM

———

SCAPES

YOKOHAMA PORT
TERMINAL
1995

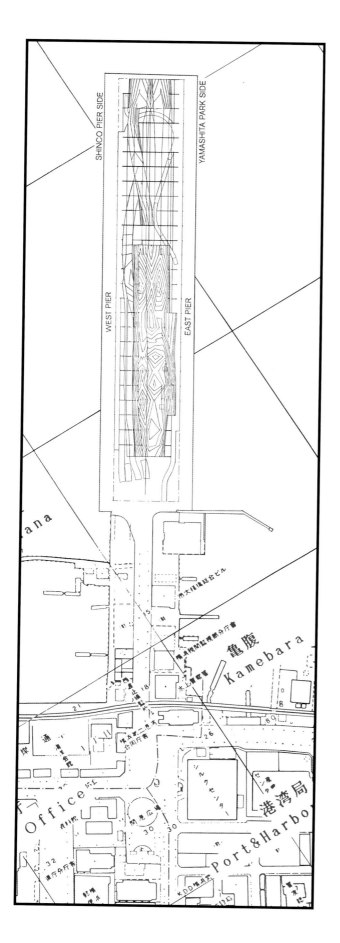

We formulated our proposal for the Yokohama Port Terminal competition in response to what we perceived as the inherent duality between global systems of transport and exchange and the condition of the specific sites through which such systems cross. These conditions are exemplified by the port of Yokohama and specifically encoded within the program of the port terminal proper.

This liminal condition prompted us to develop our proposal to encompass the general functional imperatives of the cruise terminal (as a smoothly functioning link between land and water transport) and the specific civic possibilities suggested by the pier configuration itself. We thus conceived our proposal as an incomplete or partial building—partial both conceptually and formally—in recognition of the fact that such programs frame thresholds in two distinct yet overlapping continua: in the cruise terminal's cycle of embarkation and disembarkation and, at the civic level, as a place of rest and recreation in the course of an excursion. Consequently, completion, both physically and virtually, is effected only periodically—in the linkage of terminal to cruise ship or in the closure of the completed urban event.

Affiliated with its nineteenth-century antecedents, the large shed structure of the Yokohama Port Terminal evolved in part from our previous landscape projects that involved a series of awnings constructed from steel trusses and fabric. Whereas the nineteenth-century airship shed type is characterized by a totalizing conception that employs uniform and repetitive structural units enclosing a single homogeneous space, the structure of the proposed terminal engenders heterogeneity through selective perturbations and extensions of the structural frames. Each successive truss undergoes a transformation, such that the shed is composed of a variable unit repeated along a single trajectory. Not in service of an ideal geometry, the truss system manifests a progressive differentiation, yielding a complex of spaces that smoothly integrate multiple terminal, civic, and garden programs within and below the port terminal's span.

OPPOSITE: Site plan of the Yokohama Port Terminal and map of the surrounding harbor area

BELOW: Basic airship shed under construction (top), and Goddard rocket internals (bottom). Drawing inspiration from rocket engine construction, in which the constraints of the envelope organize the rocket engine, the port terminal's surface integrates structure and program.

RIGHT: The Yokohama Port Terminal's truss system emerged from a hybrid airship shed structure and was developed with a branching truss system. The section guidelines determining spans were provided by the competition organizers (bottom).

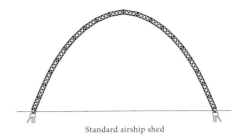

Standard airship shed

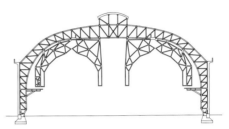

Airship shed with branching trusses

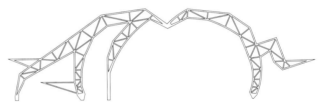

Yokohama Port Terminal truss #26

Yokohama Port Terminal elevation

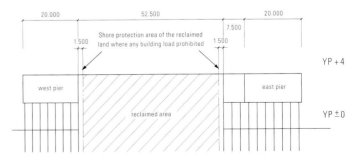

Sectional rules for Yokohama Port Terminal

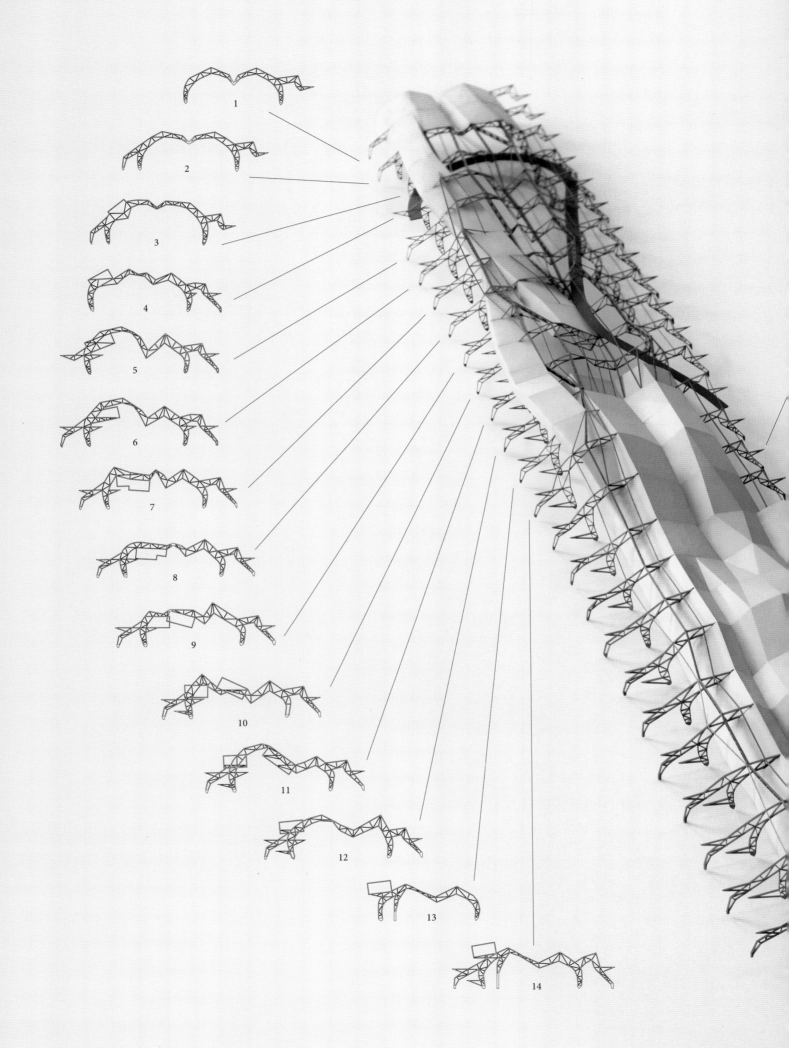

Truss System

The proposed terminal is a shed building measuring 412 meters (1,352 feet) in length, comprising three hinged steel trussed arches of 42.5 meters (139 feet) average span placed at 16-meter (53-foot) intervals. These arches are joined longitudinally by trussed members of conventional configuration and purling carrying either metal cladding or extensive glazing. The steel shed structure springs from hinges placed at the surface of the main level. The hinges are carried on concrete piers extending from the basement parking level through the apron to the surface of the main level. Tension rods connecting opposing arch hinges counteract horizontal thrust from the arches. These tension rods also serve as partial support for the main floor slab. The variations of the trusses throughout the Yokohama Port Terminal enable topological transformations along the structure's outer shell.

The initial stages of development for the shed building's formal dimensions involved the translation of hand drawings and models into AutoCAD. After building a volumetric wax model, we then scanned the profiles of the model with a contour gauge to generate elevations. These profiles were drawn and traced over in AutoCAD to produce the series of trusses. Another volumetric model was produced to further develop the general form of the port terminal's outer shell.

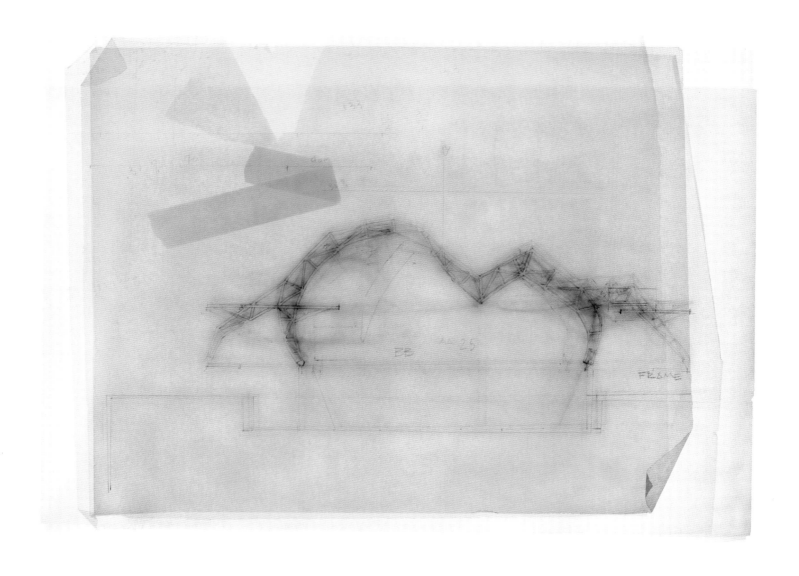

Layered sketches of trusses on tracing paper

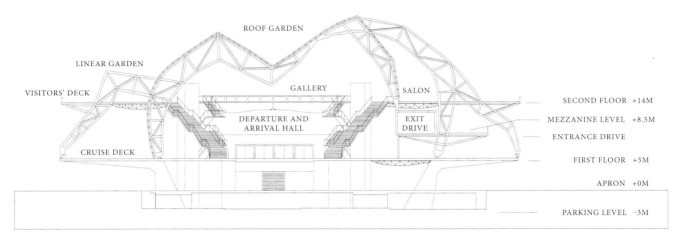

ROOF GARDEN

LINEAR GARDEN

VISITORS' DECK

GALLERY

SALON

SECOND FLOOR +14M

MEZZANINE LEVEL +8.5M

DEPARTURE AND
ARRIVAL HALL

EXIT
DRIVE

ENTRANCE DRIVE

CRUISE DECK

FIRST FLOOR +5M

APRON +0M

PARKING LEVEL -3M

Section at departure and arrival hall

Niwaminato

The concept of *niwaminato* (庭港, garden port) is addressed in the overall formation of the shed. The proposal synthesizes a garden element, which functions as a public landscape, with the port terminal's convoluted surface, which is developed to generate a series of urban/landscape effects. These effects include the production of an artificial terrain within the overall configuration and silhouette of the building envelope as well as the deployment of a series of interconnected garden programs and promenades on and within the thickness of the roof terrain. Broken down, these urban/landscape elements include linear garden promenades along and adjacent to the visitors' deck, exposed deck gardens, vertically negotiable roof terrain, and enclosed year-round greenhouse gardens located within the depth of the arched roof trusses.

Model of Yokohama Port Terminal with docked cruise ship

Circulation

Two routes offer vehicular access into the port terminal. A ramped two-lane drive is accessed from the root of the pier, rising 18 meters (59 feet) above grade, traversing the length of the major programmatic elements of the terminal along their periphery and terminating in the loop of the traffic plaza. This route enables one to pass through the trussed outriggers of the arches while experiencing the view unfolding from the Shinco side of the pier. The traffic plaza combines functions for the cruise terminal with those for citizens' use, providing direct access into the departure and arrival hall as well as ramp access to below-grade parking. In addition, a two-lane access road descends from the pier root to below-grade parking for six hundred cars. Access from the parking level to the departure and arrival hall and citizens'-use facilities above is provided by banks of elevators.

The main level, which is 5 meters (16 feet) above grade, contains the principal spaces related to cruise ship embarkation and disembarkation. They are disposed in a linear, symmetric composition along the longitudinal axis of the pier. From the traffic plaza curbside drop-off, one may enter the departure and arrival hall directly. This hall leads directly into the China Inspection and Quarantine (CIQ) facility, providing access to the visitors' deck, citizens'-use facilities, and gardens via two symmetrical staircases and associated elevators. Beyond the CIQ facilities lies the departure and arrival lobby, which provides the principal access to cruise decks on both the east and west sides of the space. Staircases to the apron are also provided for occasional embarkation and disembarkation from that level.

OPPOSITE: Circulation model

RIGHT: Roof circulation plan

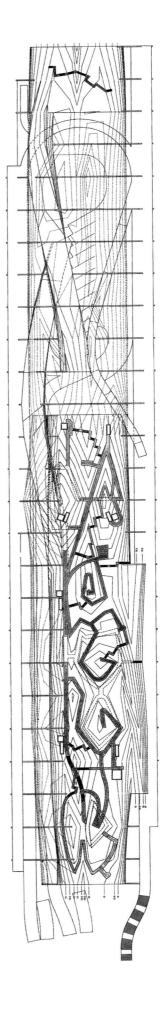

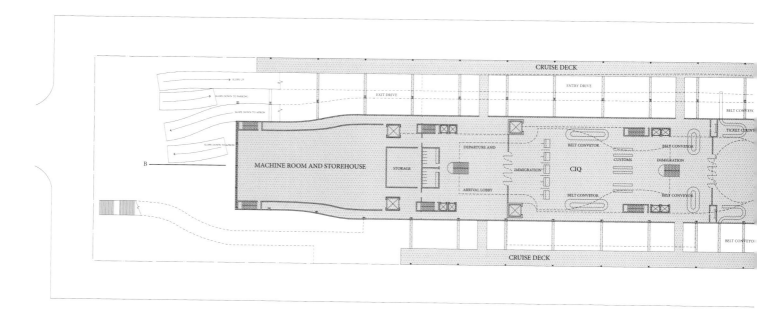

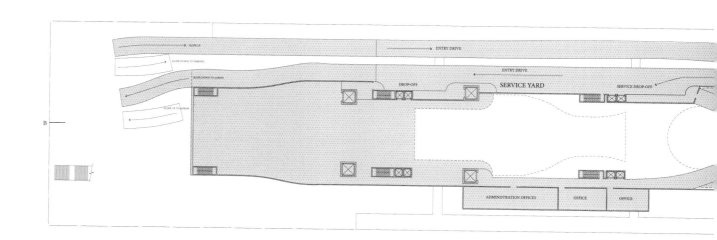

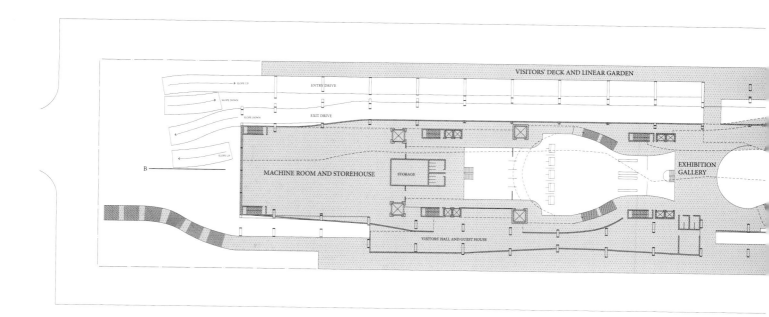

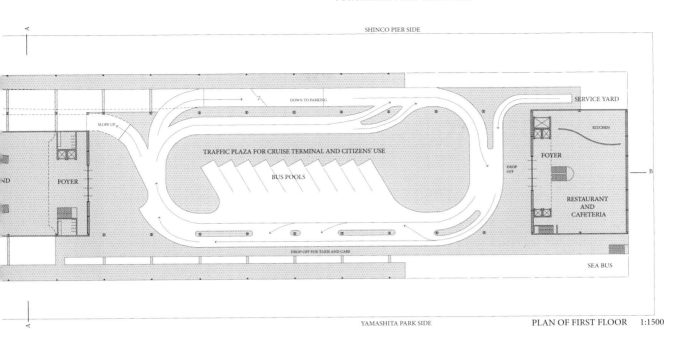

PLAN OF FIRST FLOOR   1:1500

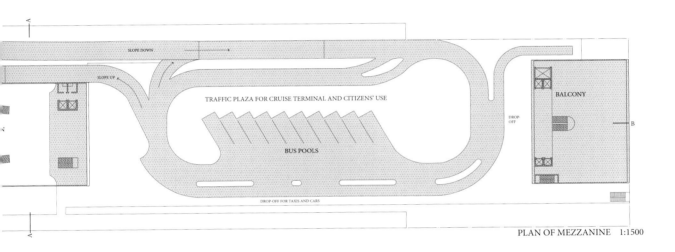

PLAN OF MEZZANINE   1:1500

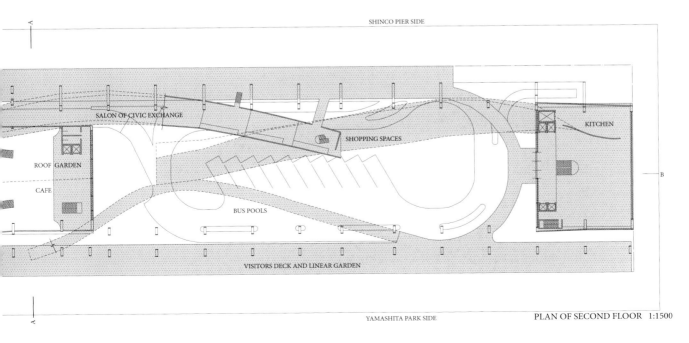

PLAN OF SECOND FLOOR   1:1500

MATERIAL DIAGRAM

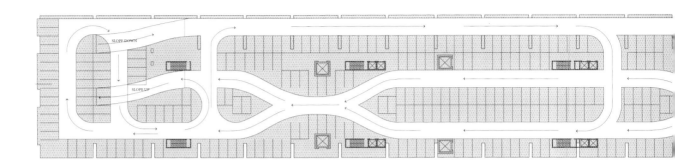

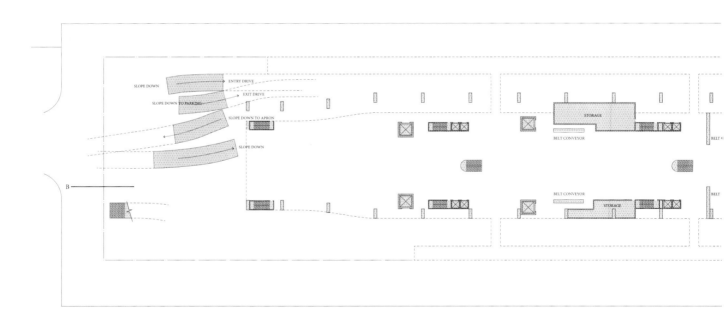

154

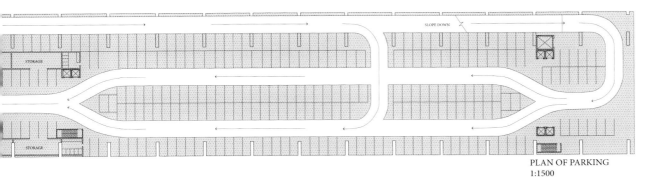

SLOPE DOWN

STORAGE

STORAGE

PLAN OF PARKING
1:1500

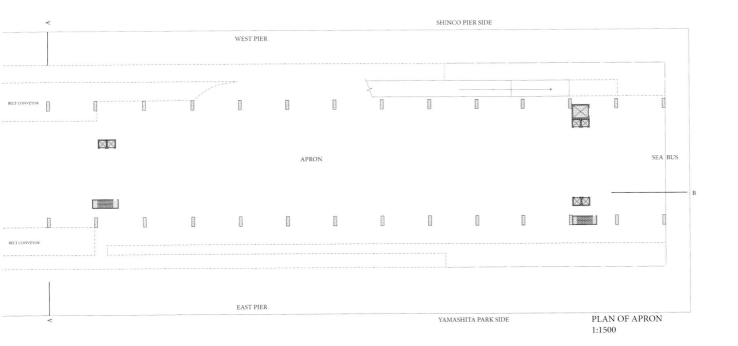

SHINCO PIER SIDE

WEST PIER

BELT CONVEYOR

APRON

SEA BUS

BELT CONVEYOR

EAST PIER

YAMASHITA PARK SIDE

PLAN OF APRON
1:1500

Preliminary model of Yokohama Port Terminal

The "chocolate bar" model of Yokohama Port Terminal

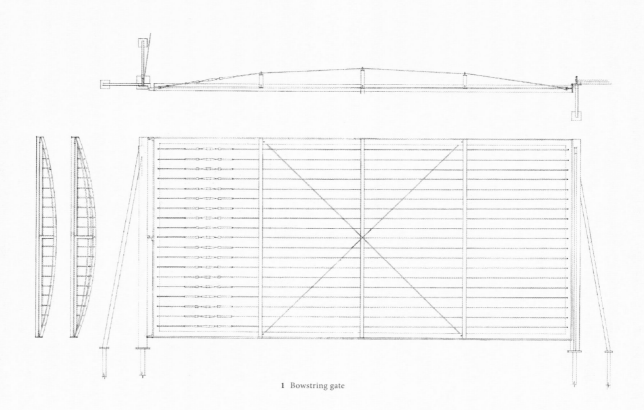

1 Bowstring gate

SECTIONAL STRUCTURES

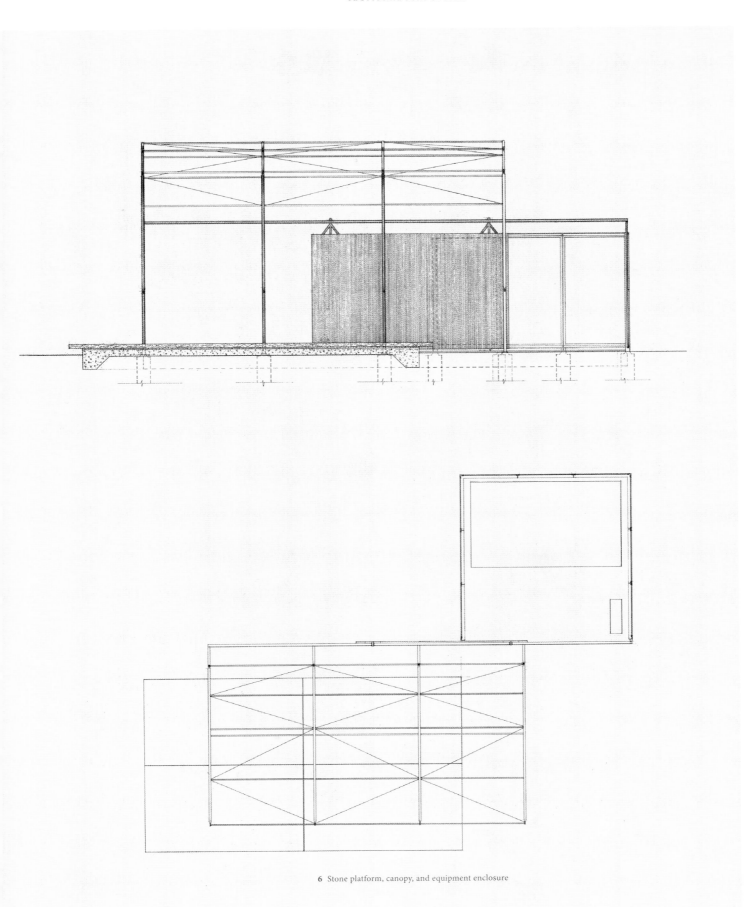

6 Stone platform, canopy, and equipment enclosure

1 Bowstring gate

2 Bowstring fence

3 Swing canopy

4 Pergola

5 Pool and spa

6 Stone platform, canopy, and equipment enclosure

Co-idle bridge

Co-idle bridge, silver soldered bronze, 1993

Pergola with cantilevering benches

Spa/submerged living room

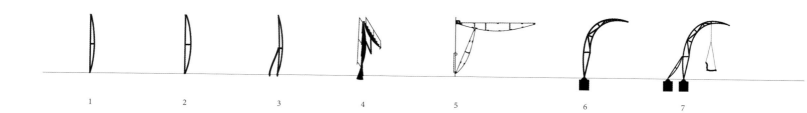

1   2   3   4   5   6   7

8   9   10   11

Structural Genealogy

1 Gate section A

2 Gate section B

3 Bowstring fence post

4 Co-idle bridge

5 Folding dining table

6 Canopy

7 Canopy with swing

8 Pergola

9 Canopy with sliding door

10 Métier à Aubes

11 Yokohama Port Terminal

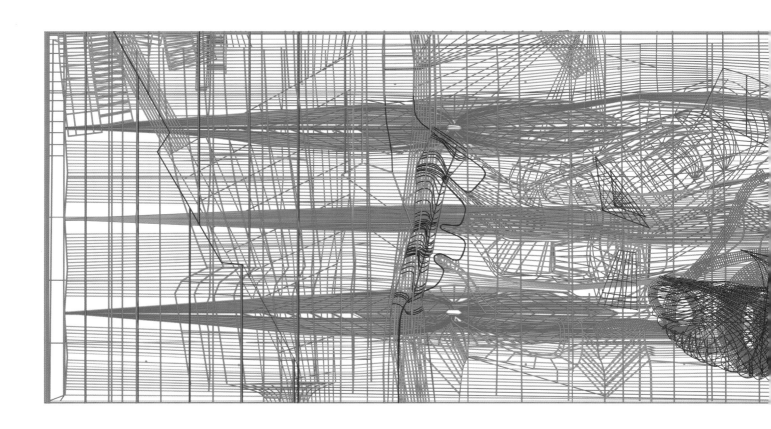

KANSAI LIBRARY
1996

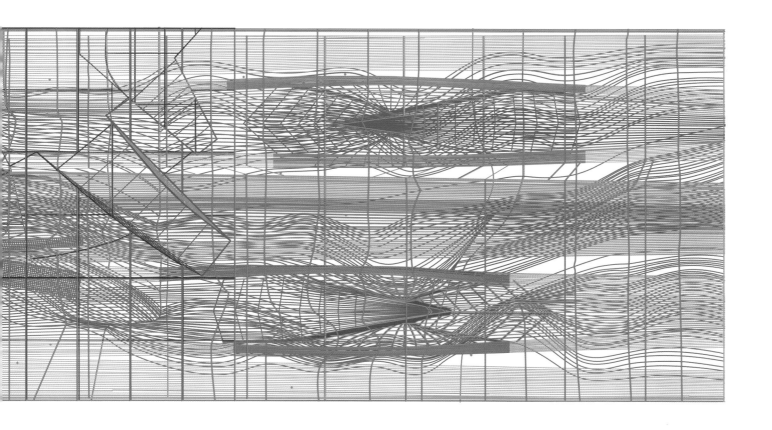

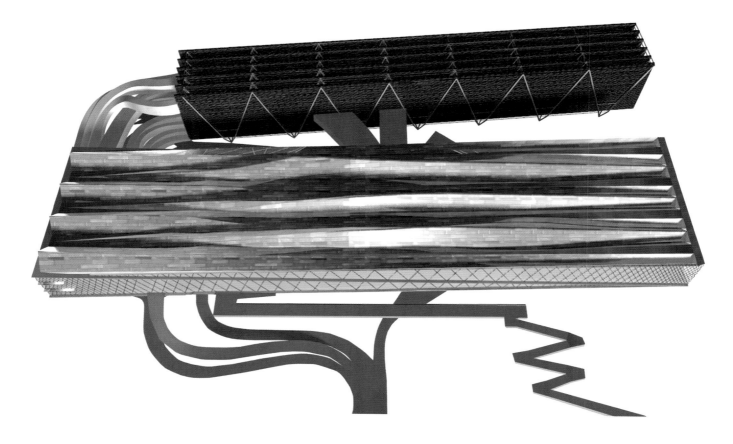

Kansai National Diet Library

Our proposal for the Kansai Kan of Japan's National Diet Library has sought to address the apparent paradox surrounding the universal proliferation of data, the presumed placelessness of information, and the persistent necessity, nevertheless, to find a definition for this condition in architecture. Beyond the admittedly important legal and archival necessity of preserving hard copies of documents, the persistence of the library may be ascribed to less recognized processes of globalization.

The general phenomena of decentralization and dispersion of institutions made possible by new technologies overshadow a correspondingly specific trend toward centralization and agglomeration, both within and appended to major urban centers in global economies. Japan's principal cities (where most of the country's data is produced and consumed) have seen the advent of information zones: agglomerations of buildings and public spaces relatively small in scale whose organization promotes mutual interests and information exchange through direct communication. A new form of public space thus arises out of the interaction of two logics: first, the close proximity of major institutions and corporations, and

second, the consequent influx of smaller institutions and services that are sustained by the presence of their larger neighbors. The success of such codependent organizations is predicated not simply on the major institutions that initiate the information zone but on their capacity to act as catalysts for new programs and uses. Our proposal, therefore, embodies two distinct yet related imperatives: to fulfill the explicit programmatic criteria of the library while developing implicit spatialities that would foster the new and unforeseen irruptions of program brought about by an information zone.

ABOVE: Rendering of the Kansai Kan National Diet Library showing an aerial view of the main Library Building and Stack Building

OPPOSITE LEFT: Exploded structure of the Library Building. The floor slabs are suspended from the roof structure by a rod-net system.

OPPOSITE RIGHT: Exploded structure of the Stack Building

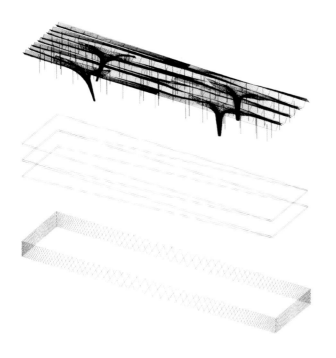

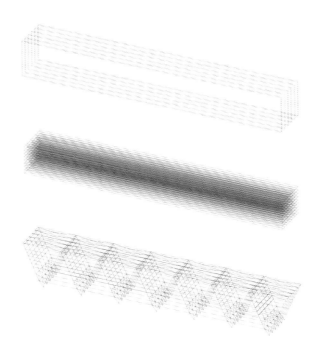

The Library Building

The Library Building comprises three ramped, two-way prestressed-concrete slabs 20 centimeters (8 inches) thick, the whole of which is suspended from a prestressed-steel roof of 6-meter (20-foot) maximum depth by a 9-meter (29.5-foot) grid of suspension cables 5 centimeters (2 inches) in diameter passing through the ramped slabs. The roof is carried on four integral steel piers. The large plan dimension of the slabs and roof necessitate distinct responses to lateral forces (thermal, seismic, and wind). Each concrete slab is divided in two across the long dimension by a thermal expansion joint with mechanical dampers to absorb any lateral dynamic movement. The prestressed-steel roof requires no expansion joint; it transmits its relatively large lateral thermal expansion to its four piers, two of which are fixed to footings. The opposing pair are allowed to slide freely on Teflon pads. The perimeter of the entire Library Building is enclosed by a lattice truss of 20-centimeter (8-inch) welded steel tubes. The ramp-roof assembly thus forms a rigid box that resists lateral earthquake forces. Further, vertical seismic movement is effectively damped by the relative flexibility of roof and slab assemblies.

The Stack Building

The Stack Building is a bar 182 meters long, 25 meters wide, and 25 meters high (597 by 82 by 82 feet). It is composed of steel truss walls oriented vertically, acting as gigantic storage units for automated, compact, and fixed stacks. Books and documents are accessed via catwalks and the automated conveyor system, which efficiently routes library materials to and from the reading rooms and Operational System Department for shipping to and receiving from the outside. Since the Stack Building is organized around the concept of the storage wall, stacks are categorized sectionally in layers as automated, compact, or fixed. There are no horizontal slabs or floors as such in the Stack Building. Horizontal movement is accomplished along the catwalks and automated conveyor system. The spaces between the storage walls are narrow, open wells from ground to roof, with skylights that allow filtered natural illumination to enter the entire section of the building.

+ 15m

The Public Spaces

The slabs of the 220-by-55-meter (722-by-180-foot) Library Building are formed to maximize continuity and interconnections among the public spaces and levels. Topological deformations—cuts, mounds, ramps, ripples, and stairs—render the library a landscape with smoothly functioning major programs and also foster the emergence of new and unanticipated configurations of social space. Visitors enter the library from two locations. Pedestrians and those arriving by bus gain access via a pedestrian road in front of the building at Seika main street. A ramp leads up to the second level and joins an automobile drop-off in front of the main entrance. Entry into the lobby is also possible from the parking level via ramps. The lobby space provides direct entry into a restaurant, a store, lockers, and an auditorium above. Controlled access into the library's main reading room is possible through five ramps.

Programming in the library is based on the notion of precincts rather than dividing walls. Consequently, the main reading room's programs bleed into both the floor below and an Asian document and information center farther up the ramp.

ABOVE: Interior rendering of the Kansai Library
OPPOSITE: Rendered elevation view of the Kansai Library

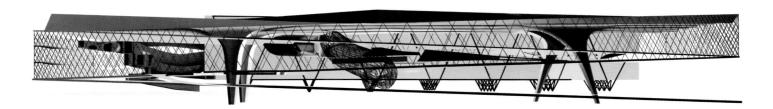

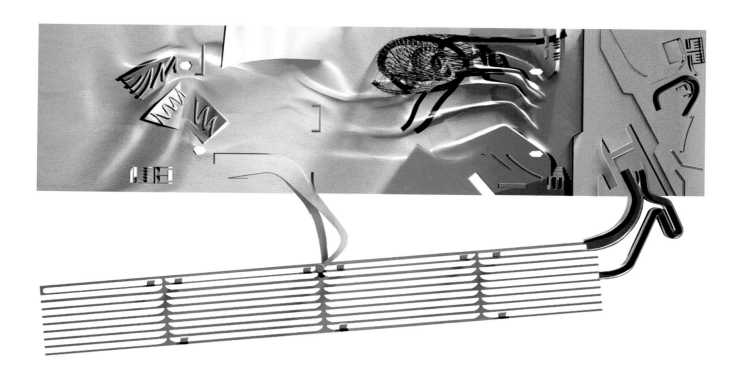

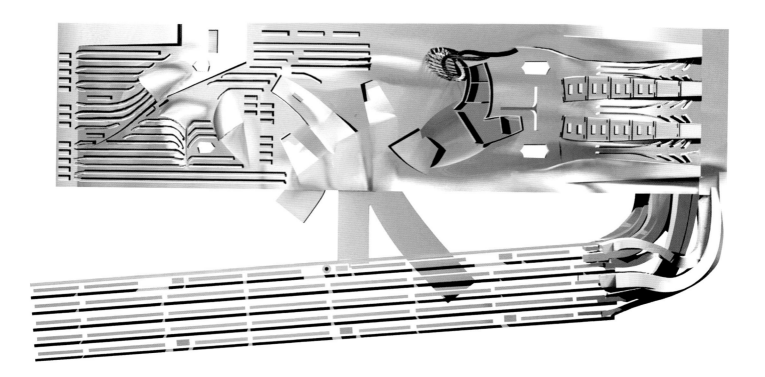

Renderings of the floor plates in relief

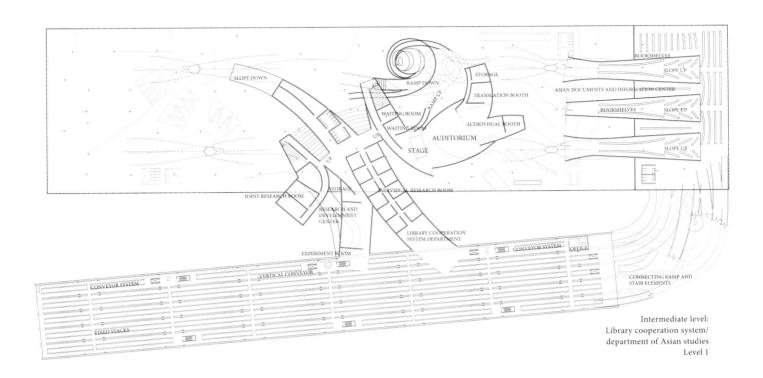

Intermediate level:
Library cooperation system/
department of Asian studies
Level 1

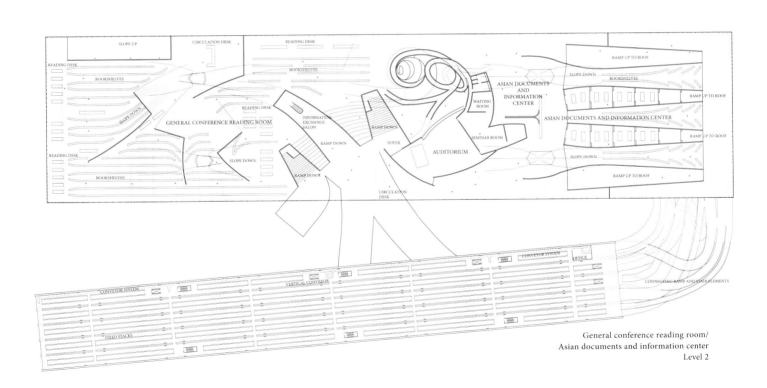

General conference reading room/
Asian documents and information center
Level 2

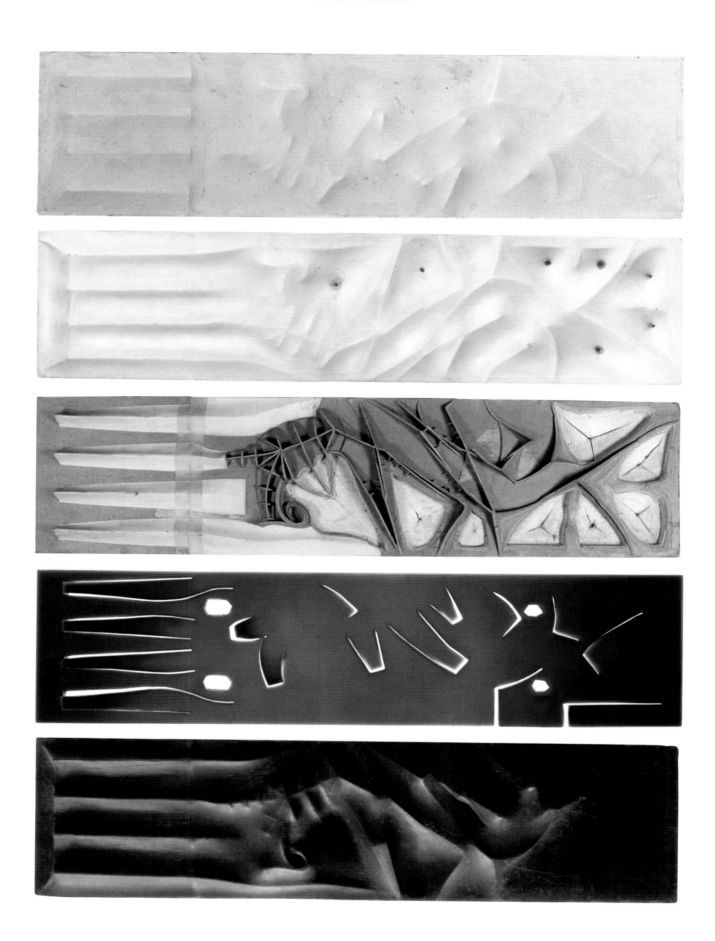

Various form-finding models composed of plaster, cardboard, and wax
aided the development of the Library Building's undulating floor plates.

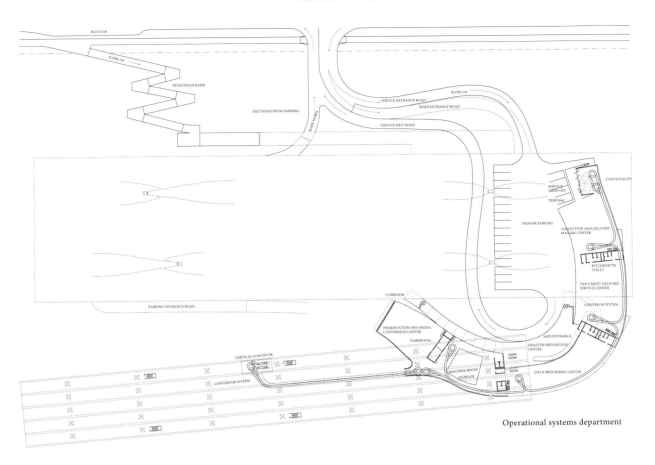

Operational systems department

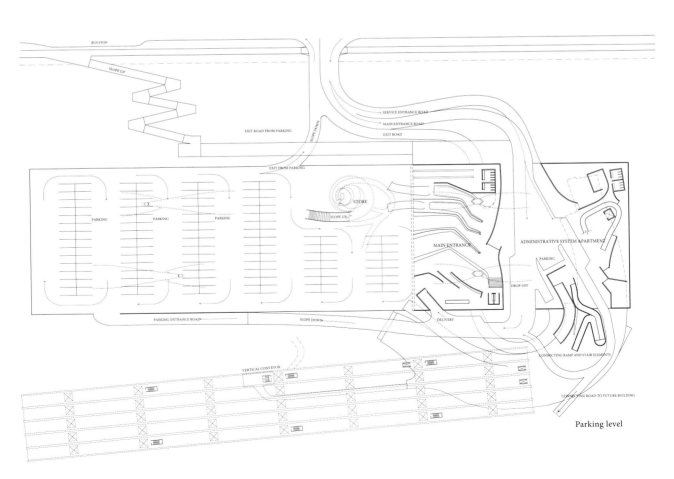

Parking level

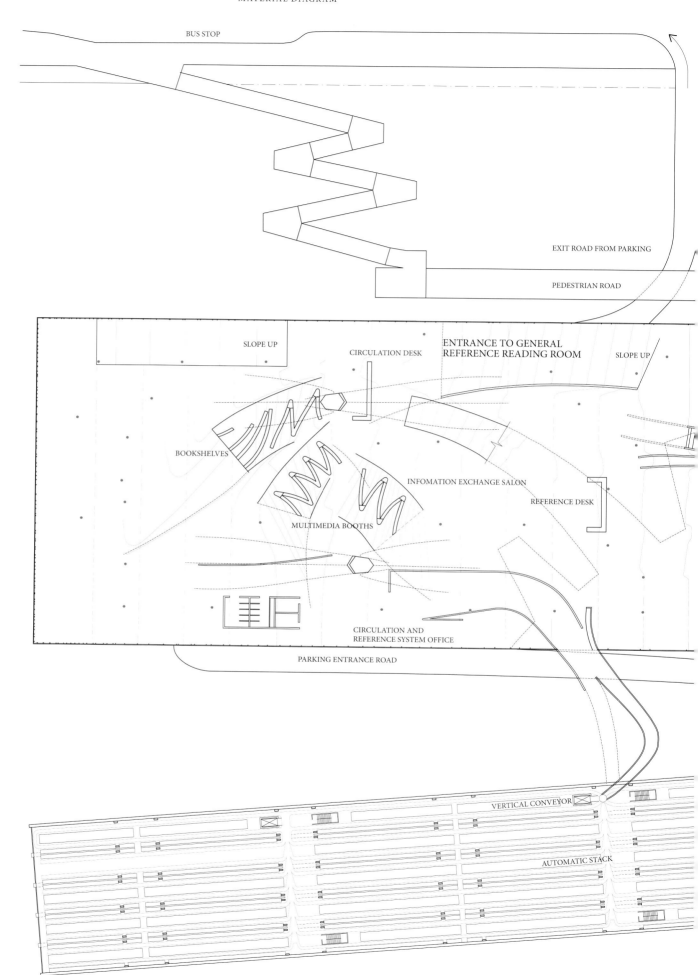

BUS STOP

EXIT ROAD FROM PARKING

PEDESTRIAN ROAD

SLOPE UP

CIRCULATION DESK

ENTRANCE TO GENERAL
REFERENCE READING ROOM

SLOPE UP

BOOKSHELVES

INFOMATION EXCHANGE SALON

REFERENCE DESK

MULTIMEDIA BOOTHS

CIRCULATION AND
REFERENCE SYSTEM OFFICE

PARKING ENTRANCE ROAD

VERTICAL CONVEYOR

AUTOMATIC STACK

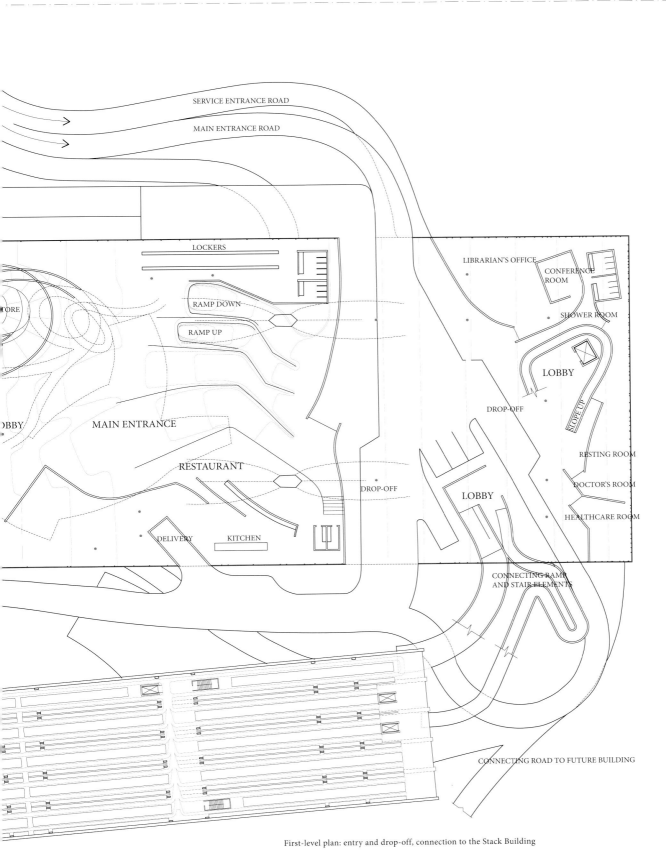

SERVICE ENTRANCE ROAD

MAIN ENTRANCE ROAD

LOCKERS

LIBRARIAN'S OFFICE

CONFERENCE
ROOM

RAMP DOWN

SHOWER ROOM

RAMP UP

ORE

LOBBY

LOBBY

SLOPE UP

MAIN ENTRANCE

DROP-OFF

RESTING ROOM

RESTAURANT

DOCTOR'S ROOM

DROP-OFF

LOBBY

HEALTHCARE ROOM

DELIVERY

KITCHEN

CONNECTING RAMP
AND STAIR ELEMENTS

CONNECTING ROAD TO FUTURE BUILDING

First-level plan: entry and drop-off, connection to the Stack Building

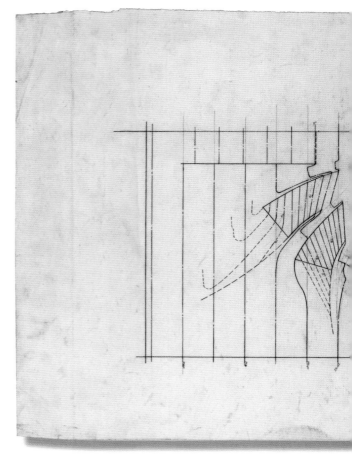

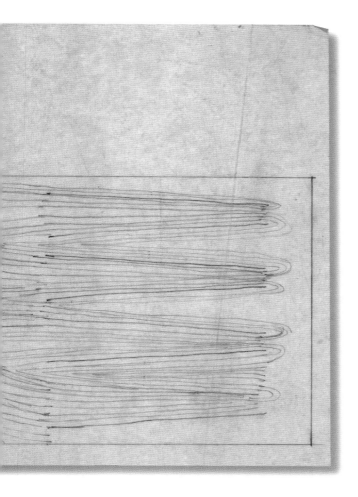

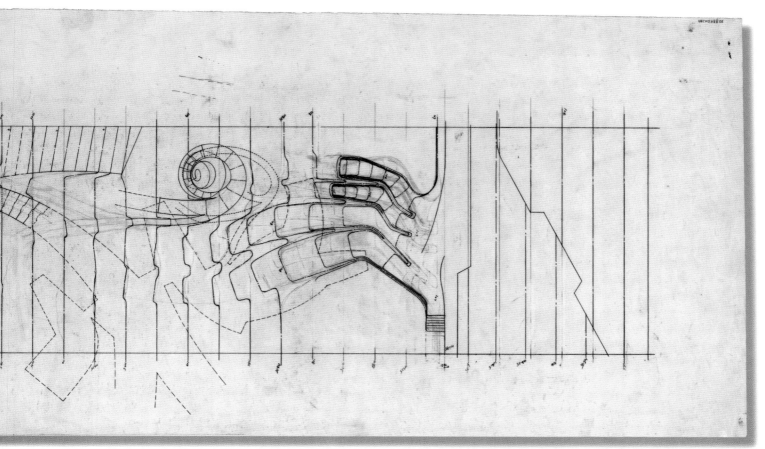

TOP: Topographic sketch of Kansai Library second-floor plate BOTTOM: Drawn topolines of Kansai Library first-floor plate

Smoothly Striated

Brett Steele

Plan and Plan(e)

What interests us in operations of striation and smoothing are precisely the passages or combinations: how the forces at work within space continually striate it, and how in the course of its striation it develops other forces and emits new smooth spaces.

—*Gilles Deleuze and Félix Guattari,* A Thousand Plateaus, *1980*

View of entrance ramps and Geodetic Store, Kansai Library

Jesse Reiser and Nanako Umemoto's 1996 competition entry for the Kansai branch of the National Diet Library appears—especially at first glance, given its programmatic bifurcation—to instantiate certain paradoxes of Deleuze and Guattari's notion of smooth versus striated space.[15] The liquefying effect of their distinction between a nomadic, unbounded, continuous space and the sedentary, delimited space of rigid systems and institutions (like the difference between felt and woven fabric), nearly twenty years after the essay's writing and ten years after its now widely available English translation, remains (almost fatally) attractive to architects these days, thanks in no small part to a frequent misapprehension: that the text privileges (in the authors' concept of smooth space) an almost unbounded spatial fluidity and connectivity at once material—an arrangement of the *stuff* of the world—and virtual—the resulting patterns of our occupation of that world. Read in this way, Deleuze and Guattari's notion of smooth space represents for many architects a model that is doubly compelling, both a (deep) fetishization of space itself, as if a pure concept, and a (shallow) recognition of its end-of-century realities. Undeniably, an image of smooth, mobile (in the terminology of Deleuze and Guattari, *nomadological*) space is wholly consistent, whatever else its implications, with our suddenly *wired* world, whose principal and overwhelming characteristic is an endless stream of networked, deeply interconnected products, images, and interfaces. That a theory of space could itself rely on such an image (given especially the accelerating status of space itself as a product whose patterns of consumption hardly distinguish it from those of any other niche-market categories of the everyday) and not merely serve as a backdrop to this reality is one of the lasting legacies, to architects at least, of the "working of matters" and "exteriority of relations" materialized in the texts of Deleuze and Guattari.[16]

Reiser + Umemoto's design undoubtedly aligns itself with users whose identities extend to the laptops and cell phones that are used to negotiate any interface of today—whether a library building or a database. But that's not the point here. The achievements of the project lie elsewhere, in the ways it goes beyond merely accommodating either the accessories of the information age or its consequent and overwhelming demand for document and record storage (which serves as the programmatic justification for the new Kansai library). Instead, the project explicitly addresses the consequences of conceiving of buildings themselves as information structures, storing information relating to the potentials contained within their own material organization, including the diverse programmatic, circulatory, and structural forces they both constrain and are shaped by. Reiser notes the important distinction Deleuze draws between Friedrich Nietzsche's term *puissance* and Michel Foucault's *pouvoir* as the basis for understanding this potential; both terms are translated as "power," but while *pouvoir* refers to a conventional image of the "powers that be," *puissance* suggests the power to act—new possibilities and capacities.[17] As the architects have written of the Kansai project:

> *The minor ramps that punctuate the overall sloped-slab organization are deliberately made steeper than those that would normally occur in direct path systems. A finer-scaled linear organisation (the reference stacks) then must take the form of switchbacks in order to climb and descend. Thus the excessive slope (while not directly negotiable) enables the development of a range of switchback typologies deployed on the surface. . . . In this way a certain degree of determinacy (slope potential) suggests a range of possible itineraries (like a field of moguls on a ski slope) that in turn may induce a wide range of possible negotiations.*[18]

Reiser + Umemoto have resisted the temptation to pursue diagrams of a singular, totalizing space of limitless interconnection, an abstract image, which is encountered as frequently today in the advertising slogans of the digital age as it was in modernist architects' manifestos. It is architects, interestingly, who throughout the twentieth century have fetishized images of the seamless connectivity, fluidity, and freedom of movement supposedly made possible by their projects, long before the arrival of *Wired* magazine and the everyday remarketing of the world in an attempt to instill (if not install) the need to interconnect its constituent objects/subjects.[19] Architects' strong attachment to images of the liberating aspects of circulation in their buildings in some way registers a deeply repressed recognition of the material reality their discipline routinely, inevitably constructs—ruthless separations and divisions constituting an unavoidable aspect of social life. The accelerating social stratification resulting from today's explosion of digital tectonics/technologies (evident in growing disparities in access to everything from cable television to high-speed ISDN lines or the latest release of Form•Z) confirms, in a much more pedestrian example, a key aspect of what Reiser and Umemoto refer to as their solid-state approach to architecture: the need for an awareness that whatever is taken to constitute virtual systems (whether it be information or media) must necessarily be embedded in material realities.[20]

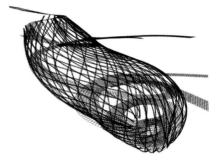

The Geodetic Store is a central ramp that allows circulation between the Library Building's floor plates.

> *When we speak of "information," we should use the word "form." The scalar measures of information (e.g., energy and entropy in thermodynamics) should be geometrically interpreted as the topological complexity of a form.*
> —René Thom, Structural Stability and Morphogenesis, 1975[21]

Reiser + Umemoto go well beyond the sort of slippery-smooth fascination with images of unbounded connectivity that have led many to misinterpret Deleuze and Guattari's text. Their Kansai design registers a much more complex dialectic, identified by Deleuze and Guattari:

> *No sooner do we note a simple opposition between the two kinds of space than we must indicate a much more complex difference. . . . We must remind ourselves that the two spaces in fact exist only in mixture: smooth space is constantly being translated, transversed into a striated space; striated space is constantly being reversed, returned to a smooth space.*[22]

Key aspects of Kansai register and reassert architecture's inevitably dual reliance on (sedentary) regulating systems and on other more flexible and less calculable fields of (nomadic) continuous deformation. This is the reality, perhaps, of all forms of architecture, but, as Reiser and Umemoto themselves suggest, an awareness of this condition was actively brought to bear on the making of the Kansai project. The key to collapsing the inherent differences of the two conditions is the use of what Reiser refers to as dynamic diagrams: diagrams that are able to register flows in time and thus the mediating aspect of material structures.[23] The project can therefore be read as a catalogue of interactions (or "mixtures," in Deleuze and Guattari's abovementioned description) between the smooth and the striated.

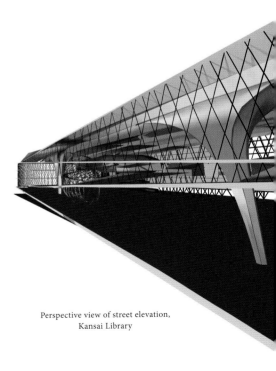

Perspective view of street elevation,
Kansai Library

The project's basic division into two interconnected buildings is a first clue and serves as the basis for the installation of subsequent infrastructural information potentials in the project. The linear Stack Building, measuring 182 meters long by 25 meters wide by 25 meters high (597 by 82 by 82 feet), is ordered by a vertically oriented structural system of high truss walls acting as storage units for automated fixed book/document stacks. The spatial structure and orthographic logic of the building contrasts with that of the adjacent Library Building, which measures 220 by 55 meters (722 by 180 feet) and comprises three sloped floor slabs, which are linked in such a way as to provide maximum connectivity between levels and multiple interconnections among the public spaces. The Stack Building, with its vertical strata, stands in complete contrast to the smooth, horizontal continuities of the Library Building.

But within this overall binary framework subtle deformations—some Euclidean, others more topologically complex—break down and undermine such a reading: the serial regularity of the Stack Building is hyperextended by document conveyors and circulation systems that equalize connections to the adjacent structure, while at the same time this connective tissue is brought into the otherwise continuous field of the Library Building in a way that deliberately territorializes, and so institutionally structures (or striates) the otherwise fluid surfaces of the building. The interpenetrations occur in numerous locations and in various ways; the uniform, two-way structural systems of the Library floor slabs are contained within and suspended from a system of deformed steel roof trusses supported on four massive piers, which, despite its formal flexibility, is a rigid three-dimensional structure able to resolve the lateral forces on the entire building. In contrast, the vertically uniform system of the Stack Building performs structurally: independent wall elements support completely independent catwalks used for document access and retrieval. Just as the potential smoothness of a repetitive vertical structure in the Stack Building is canceled out by the deliberate installation of discontinuous access walkways, the striated roof-truss structure of the Library Building is counterbalanced by its suspension of tilted floor slabs offering smooth three-dimensional paths; what begins as vertically continuous in one building eventually becomes sectionally striated, while the structural discontinuity of the other is overcome by the insertion of repetitive, purely horizontal or vertical movement systems.

Information and Infrastructure

One of the notable aspects of the Kansai project is that the contrasting plans (planar configurations) contribute to this series of reversals (the dense, orthogonal bias of the Stack Building versus the expansive, organic configuration of the Library Building: random access versus read-only). It is a strategy that denies a strict correspondence between the notion of (fluid) smooth space versus (delimited) striated space and that of the distinction between classical, Euclidean geometries and other seemingly organic—and, as many architects suppose, smoother—systems, respectively. Importantly, both coexist in the project and must be understood in terms of a (topological) difference of degree rather than of kind. Some of the systems (such as document storage) describe relatively simple geometric configurations, while others (such as the pedestrian movement through the Library spaces) reflect more indeterminate arrangements. This approach, depending crucially on an information-based description of form (which sees such differences as only the degree of complexity required for their description), is a key to understanding the Kansai project. Embracing and actively installing the potential of radically differing shapes and geometric configurations, it demonstrates a topological, information-based awareness of form disseminated by such texts as René Thom's *Structural Stability and Morphogenesis*.[24]

Shipping and receiving pods study
for first-floor level

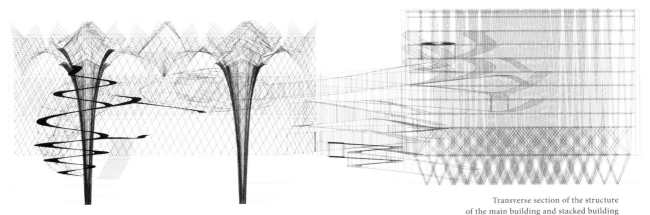

Transverse section of the structure
of the main building and stacked building

As others have written of the ways in which the mathematics of topology can effectively transform everyday notions of such key architectural conceits as form,[25] it is important to recall here that it is through just such an approach that we are returned yet again to Deleuze and Guattari, who cite a key passage from Thom's treatise on topology in their formulation of smooth versus striated space.[26] It is important for architects to recall that Deleuze and Guattari's remarks on opposing conceptions of space form only a small chapter in a (thousand-level) text dedicated to a much larger task: an analysis of the relationship between material appearance (how things look) and virtual descriptions (how things operate) in societies. They convincingly demonstrate the ways in which virtual effects, including information, are not separate from, but always necessarily embedded in, wider *material* conditions. The considerable achievement of Reiser + Umemoto's Kansai project is the ways in which it extends such a thesis to the categories of material reality—able to be understood today as info—no less than as infrastructures—which are conventionally classified as buildings.

From Brett Steele, "Smoothly Striated: Reiser + Umemoto's Kansai Library," *AA Files*, no. 36 (Summer 1998): 14–19.

15 For an extended discussion of the terms, see "1440: The Smooth and the Striated," in Gilles Deleuze and Félix Guattari, *A Thousand Plateaus: Capitalism and Schizophrenia*, trans. Brian Massumi (London: Continuum, 1988), 474–500.

16 This characterization of what constitutes a text, later extended to other material artifacts (such as those under discussion in this article), initiates the reader to the rhizomatic structure of *A Thousand Plateaus* (see page 3).

17 Prepublication draft of Jesse Reiser, "Solid-State Architecture," in *Reiser + Umemoto: Recent Projects* (London: Academy Editions, 1998), 2.

18 Quoted in ibid., 6.

19 Robin Evans discusses architecture's inevitable constraint to "separate and divide" human activity in relation to the rhetoric frequently used by architects to symbolize the "freedom of action" their projects are routinely presented as making possible. Robin Evans, "Towards Anarchitecture," in *Translations from Drawing to Building: The Essays of Robin Evans* (London: AA Publications, 1997), 11–33. Like Reiser + Umemoto, Evans is interested in shifting attention away from what architecture is said to symbolize to how it performs. He suggests a notion of "interference" as more useful than images of unlimited freedom in describing the various ways that buildings constrain (no less than they liberate) human activities (12). In "Solid-State Architecture" Reiser writes: "Consequently, instead of viewing the building in terms of representation or symbolization, what is at stake is its own internal economy and thus its activity as a building" (3).

20 Reiser, "Solid-State Architecture," 1.

21 René Thom, *Structural Stability and Morphogenesis: An Outline of a General Theory of Models*, trans. D. H. Fowler (Reading, MA: W. A. Benjamin, 1975).

22 Deleuze and Guattari, *Thousand Plateaus*, 474.

23 Reiser, "Solid-State Architecture," 9.

24 See "Information and Topological Complexity" and "Form and Information," in Thom, *Structural Stability and Morphogenesis*, 126–30, 144–45.

25 See Greg Lynn, "Blobs: Or Why Tectonics Is Square and Topology Is Groovy," *Any*, no. 14 (1996): 58–61. For a concise review of complexity theory and the mathematics of topology relevant to architectural discourse (also cited by Reiser in "Solid-State Architecture"), see Sanford Kwinter, "Landscapes of Change: Boccioni's *Stati d'animo* as a General Theory of Models," *Assemblage*, no. 19 (1992): 52–65.

26 The passage cited refers to Thom's mathematical formula as one of "retroactive smoothing." Deleuze and Guattari, *Thousand Plateaus*, 481. The portion of Thom's text cited in Deleuze and Guattari is taken from the section titled "The Structure of Societies," near the book's conclusion (318–19); it appears to be a key (perhaps foundational) source for Deleuze and Guattari. In the passage cited, Thom discusses the difference between "military society" and "fluid society"—corresponding not only to crucial aspects (including terminology) of Deleuze and Guattari's distinction between smooth (nomadological) and striated (sedentary) space but, moreover, to larger themes concerning social relations contained within their writings. The same brief passage also discusses flocks, swarms, and other fluid phenomena, revealing Thom's work as a fountainhead of many other current topics in architectural discourse.

An Interview with Jesse Reiser & Nanako Umemoto

Greg Lynn

LYNN: Your project archive contains a really nice blend of digital drawings, physical models, and 3D objects. Had you started to think about using digital technology before Kansai? And when you started the Kansai competition, did you decide to use digital technology in any special way?

REISER: I guess Kansai was the second major competition project where we used digital technology. We had a small brush with it for the Yokohama Port Terminal, just in order to generate the laser-cut model. I think that was the first time we really used the computer, but it wasn't in a generative sense. Before that, we had used Photoshop in the Cardiff Bay Opera House competition.

LYNN: So your first use of the digital was, let's say, documentary—in order to make a laser-cut model.

REISER: Right. We had a physical model and then used a carpenter's copying tool to physically scan the three-dimensional volume. Then that got transferred into profiles, which we drew as trusses, and it finally became a digital problem when we had to laser cut a physical model.

LYNN: When you started Kansai, did you start with the same idea—to use the computer for the model? Or did you also think of using it for drawings?

UMEMOTO: We started everything manually. The design of the Kansai Library looks very simple from the outside, but the inside is very complex. We didn't have a computer at that point, and we were always doing drawings in ink, but Kansai had too many curves. When you drew the wall, you had to draw the double lines, and we couldn't because there were so many curves everywhere. So in the end we had to use computers to generate those curved forms.

REISER: All the deformations of the floor slab started in the wax models. We tried to go as far as we could with either physical modeling in wax or by working back and forth with drawing. But the level of complexity in the drawings required digital modeling. So we brought the

drawings and physical models to David Ruy. He modeled certain portions of the library, which we then reintegrated into the set.

LYNN: I noticed there was some pretty extensive contour cutting of 3D surfaces.

UMEMOTO: Right. But that was generated manually, because once you set the height of the slab, which is quite consistent, you can easily generate the topographic lines on the slab.

REISER: There were still controlling lines that had to be used from David's model, but it was really a back-and-forth process, except for one element, which was the store. We couldn't physically make it, and we couldn't really draw it. So that portion of the project was generated entirely digitally and then brought in.

LYNN: When you were putting things into the computer, what were your specific motivations?

REISER: Well, aside from capturing those areas with precision and being able to define them three-dimensionally, one of the goals was actually representational. The complexity of the project also presented problems in terms of generating renderings. So the digital modeling also had to do with being able to represent the design, even if a lot of it came after the physical modeling and the manual drawing.

LYNN: When you say precision, do you mean it abstractly, as in a 3D, rigorous, controlling geometry, or precision in the plans and sections, or for a model, or for connecting the drawings with the model?

REISER: I think it was mainly to define those areas geometrically.

LYNN: So it was more to have a rigorous 3D document. Is that fair to say?

REISER: Yes. To finally have that kind of document, and then also to be able to manipulate it in various ways—once it was there, once there was some consistency in it. We thought it would be much easier to work with, both for representational purposes and for developing the project.

UMEMOTO: Also, the store has the spiral staircase going up to the roof, and the volume is not surface. It's all a basket-weaving kind of structural system. There's no way we could have drawn that.

REISER: It was very hard to define in any way, given the physical modeling processes and the drawings. The best we could do—and I think this was constantly happening with the project—was to define multiple profiles of those volumes, adjusting the overall profiles as two-dimensional profiles. But to get all the intricacy of that basket weave, we had to wait to model it with David.

LYNN: Once you had the rigorous, three-dimensional geometry, it affected elements in the drawings, right?

REISER: Well, there was a physical model much later that came out of it, but yes, mainly the drawings.

LYNN: And then in terms of representation, did you also test some renderings or wireframes and perspectives?

REISER: We were testing those, but honestly, I think the 3D views were purely representational—for outside consumption, just to communicate the project.

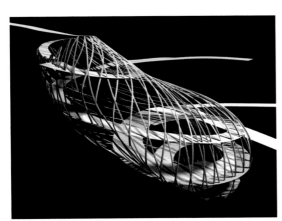

Model of the Geodetic Store, 1996

LYNN: Do you know what David was using in terms of computers and software?

REISER: He had a Silicon Graphics machine, and I think he was running Form·Z and possibly Alias for modeling and also for rendering. We got into some funny things generating texture maps with him.

LYNN: It would be interesting to know how the physical models and the drawings talked to each other. How did digital technology fit into the economy of how you were working?

REISER: In terms of priority, the first things we developed were the physical drawings and the wax model, in parallel. One major thing that happened in the competition was that we brought the wax models to Izzy [Ysrael] Seinuk, the engineer. I would say that a lot of the impetus behind the project was a response to the Yokohama competition. One

Wax floor slab for Kansai Library

The structural problem of wax models

of the things that motivated us was that we saw the kind of surface modeling in the FOA scheme as pretty idealized, and pretty bereft of detail. We were very interested to see how much that kind of surface model could absorb features or organizations outside of the surface model itself. So we decided from the outset that we would make that a theme in our Kansai competition entry.

Anyway, we brought the wax models over to Seinuk with the hope that, as in the FOA scheme, the deformations would be self-supporting. Seinuk looked at the dimensions and the heights and basically said there was no way it would work. The model itself was collapsing in his office. So he suggested that we separate the structure from the surface model—not try to make the surfaces structural—and then make the whole thing a superstructure, basically by hanging the slabs from a very stiff roof.

It actually created an envelope for the building for the first time. It was always that kind of dilemma: how to end a continuous-surface project, how to produce facades, and all the rest of it. That sort of answered the question for us. It started a big shift in the way we worked. We separated the structural dimension of the project from the surface model.

LYNN: And that's because, at the time, you felt like a lot of people were trying to turn digital surface modeling into everything?

REISER: Structure, landscape, everything. We were obviously deeply interested in landscape, but more in the idea that it would not be an idealized landscape—that it could be heavily featured and could absorb a lot of difference. There were even elements in the plan—composite volumes, passages developed through collage—that were kept distinct from the continuous surface. Like rocks in a stream. So that was what really pushed us forward on the project.

LYNN: I remember being tormented by an assumption—I don't know where the assumption came from—that if you used a piece of digital technology, especially a surface modeler, then everything had to be collapsed into one surface and that surface should be 3D-printed with some giant machine in one material. There was an assumption that "digital" meant a totally new, all-encompassing, never-before-seen, supermaterial surface.

REISER: Exactly. Something monolithic and infinitely thin.

LYNN: Can we go back to the wax models and talk a little bit about them as a medium, and their role in the design?

UMEMOTO: We usually make a little wax model, almost like a peanut, and then when we like it, we make it bigger and start to develop it.

REISER: The wax started by accident, when we were at Cranbrook. Carl Milles was a sculptor there at the same time as Saarinen, and it was mainly a bronze-casting foundry. By the time I was there in the early 1980s, there was a garage full of this stuff that the sculptors wanted no part of because they were all doing steel-fabricated sculpture. So the architects took it.

The wax there was cast into sheets, and it had a certain kind of resistance. It wasn't as soft as clay, for example. It was somewhat close to plastic—better than chipboard. One could produce compound curvature that would stay. So it became a great material for generating models relatively quickly. Speed was really important.

LYNN: Were other people at Cranbrook using wax models? Or was it something only you guys did?

REISER: A guy named Mark Loftus, who actually came in second in the Vietnam Veterans Memorial competition, was the one who introduced me to wax.

UMEMOTO: He was a sculptor before he came to architecture school.

LYNN: I thought I knew everyone who went to school with you! Is there anything you want to say about the paperless studios and the people in them and that milieu?

REISER: Well, certainly, Kansai was the product of being in that context with all of you guys. We were involved in competitions—I guess Stan [Allen] did this one, too. But seeing the projects or speculating on the work or getting prank phone calls from you, all of that had a huge impact on how we developed. From Cardiff to Yokohama to this. Our generation was working on the same problems at Columbia. That was super important.

LYNN: I was really into the whole spline language of computers, so I was drafting and modeling, but I never had a rendering engine. It was the David Ruy and Ed Keller generation who pushed the rendering—I don't know if Karl Chu was the one who provoked it or not, but they all went out and bought fifty-thousand-dollar Silicon Graphics machines, which to me seemed not the best use of resources. They were kind of in the middle of things and peripheral at the same time—in my experience, anyway.

REISER: Right. For a lot of the work we did with David, we would go over to his house, he would work on a certain part of it, and then we would bring it back. He was never part of the office.

LYNN: Exactly. And that was always very troubling to me. With Cardiff and Yokohama, that's exactly how Ed Keller was functioning. We would send Ed things, then look at the renderings and be like, "Whoa! That's what it looks like?"

REISER: I remember that there was some comment about your insisting that for Cardiff the building had to look wetter. It wasn't wet enough.

LYNN: [laughs] Well, it was an odd time, but I've always felt an affinity with you guys on that. And it was also something I wanted to get past quickly. I didn't want to have the computer be run by someone who wasn't part of the office.

REISER: David always wanted to maintain his autonomy relative to us and had a real pride in what he did, and in the limits of what he would do or not do, and all of that, which I do understand. He's still like that.

LYNN: Other than rendering, what opportunities in terms of materials, modeling, or fabrication opened up with the move to the digital?

REISER: Maybe less so with material, but in terms of the impact on our design work, it was a huge shift for us. I think we evolved what we set up in the Kansai project in many projects later on. The Children's Museum of Pittsburgh, Eyebeam, Sagaponack, Alishan—all of them

Preliminary sketches of the Geodetic Store's curves, 1996

trace back to Kansai, not only in terms of this extended building thing but also in the way facades are treated, the separation of structure and surface.

We were looking at FOA and Cecil Balmond's collaboration on Yokohama, and early on during the competition phase they had the idea of doing something thin and double-corrugated, like the isoflex system from Robert Le Ricolais. Later, Kunio Watanabe made the project work, but he had to create a superthick origami structure. Looking back on it all, it is really interesting to me how the whole trajectory of the surface-structure idea passed through Columbia, through us, and then moved to Japan, where it's being kept alive by people like Mutsuro Sasaki. He takes great pride in the fact that he can now do these structure projects with much thinner surfaces. He ultimately achieved the topological structure that obsessed so many in the 1990s, but whether it finally is the architectural ideal we imagined is another matter entirely. I think the FOA/Watanabe origami is actually more effective architecturally than the recent smooth projects.

LYNN: Junya Ishigami just gave a talk at UCLA, and his whole mission is building that superthin structural surface—which is very 1990s in the sense of the ambition for digital projects. I don't think there's a direct connection, exactly, but your use of the digital surface and landscape—not always literal landscape but topology and landscape—was significant and influential.

REISER: Thank you.

LYNN: And when you say that about Japan, now I'm realizing—well, take Ishigami, for example. He also has this focus on landscape, with building indoor gardens and thinking of the space between the natural and artificial landscape and these topological surfaces. That's still thriving in Japan.

REISER: That's absolutely true. And they also prefer those landscapes to be relatively unfeatured. They're kept very abstract.

LYNN: Yokohama was like the Rem Koolhaas libraries, where a topological surface would organize flows and movement. With Kansai, there was a lot of movement, but it was more defined with ramps and spirals, and then the surfaces were—to me, anyway—more like landscapes, in the sense that they were shaping rooms and areas and regions.

REISER: We would go into the thickness and try to incorporate space into the slabs.

LYNN: Were there other things going on along those lines at the time? Or did that come from the physical models?

REISER: It was mainly in the physical models. One of the things that pushed all of the secondary features to the surface was a diagram we made of the ramps, of the slabs as ramps that actually connected. We quickly realized working through the section that most of the ramps couldn't be negotiated directly.

UMEMOTO: The slope of the floor plates was so gentle that people would have had to walk to the far end of the building to reach the next level. We introduced much steeper local ramps that in the high-ceilinged zones ended up being too steep to negotiate directly. So we had to introduce a switchback line. I have a background in landscape architecture, so to solve this problem, we realized we could use a lot of techniques landscape architects use.

REISER: But that was mostly postcompetition. A lot of the work that was sent to the CCA on this project was also done postcompetition. It continued on in various physical models. The more elaborate renderings of the slabs happened late, I think—maybe for the show at Columbia. The postcompetition time was even more important in certain respects than the time before the project was submitted.

LYNN: Thinking about that kind of legacy in your work, was there something that came with the digital that didn't exist before? And if so, what was it for you?

REISER: Maybe one of the things that came with it was that the whole process could move more quickly, which was not a trivial thing. We would spend huge amounts of time doing the physical projection and the model making, so the speed that came with the digital meant that one could make changes and intuitively work the model much faster than what was possible with analog tools. The wax sped things up over chipboard, and it had other properties; for instance, one could rapidly generate things like surfaces. But it could never be put together in a coherent, coordinated way with the drawings. Being able even to intuit changes that had to be made got much easier when digital technology became a part of the work.

LYNN: But at the time of Kansai, was that apparent? Or did it seem more like a black hole?

UMEMOTO: I think Kansai was a starting point, so we didn't overthink it. We were doing a small landscape project simultaneously, and we had these complex bridges and things in that project, too. But we made that design with wax and just thought about unfolding it to fabricate it. We knew we could do it, no problem. It's just that you had to convince your client to pay for that, and I thought, forget it. So that was the point where we gave up on that kind of idea. Once we found out the computer could do lots of things—like unfolding very easily and cutting the templates—that really convinced us to move into the digital.

LYNN: After Kansai, how integrated did the digital tools get? Did you ever personally start to model stuff? When did people like David Ruy stop being the "digital people" and just start being designers on the team?

UMEMOTO: Now we always have people who can do everything. After David, everybody was capable of modeling in 3D. We quickly integrated the technique. But it's also become a design tool for us.

REISER: But, honestly, we never really got directly involved, and even now we're feeding them the drawings or sitting alongside them. So I guess we occupy a kind of middle generation in that respect.

LYNN: Well, I don't know if it's generational or not. It's just interesting to see how it gets integrated into teams.

REISER: As things developed, as more people were coming out of school with that equipment, it was just a natural progression.

LYNN: What has changed, if anything, about rendering? Is it still propaganda for you, or do you use it in a different way?

REISER: I still think it's mainly propaganda, honestly. For the most part, the renderings come after most of the design work is done. I think there are very minor ways in which renderings can be used to test things out. But we constantly struggle during digital modeling with the distortions created by the perspective window. We insist on 3D output as a check and typically the first models are surprising—not in a good way! Honestly, most of the formal proportional and aesthetic evaluation takes place in 2D, even on 3D objects—adjusting profiles and silhouette from many aspects. We make literally hundreds of 2D adjustments to create a satisfactory 3D space. Very old school! It's become a studio dictum: never trust anything in the perspective window!

UMEMOTO: Yeah, rendering is definitely minor for us. I know there's a group of people like Bill Mac Donald who push rendering to design things, but our case is different.

LYNN: But I have always thought that your physical models are not just being used spatially; they're also trying to simulate some material properties of structure or envelope—or you try to scale a building idea down to a model in material terms. With Bill and Sulan Kolatan, it's interesting because the O/K Apartment was like a built rendering, in a funny way. It really had the glossy albedo, and it looked like renderings used to look back then. So, for you, who rely on the model to simulate material properties, were you thinking that could also happen with the digital tools? Or is that one of the problems with them—that they're so immaterial?

REISER: You're right, of course, that material properties were and are crucial, but they weren't fully integrated into the design process digitally until the O-14 tower. That is to say, connecting how it looked with how it performed.

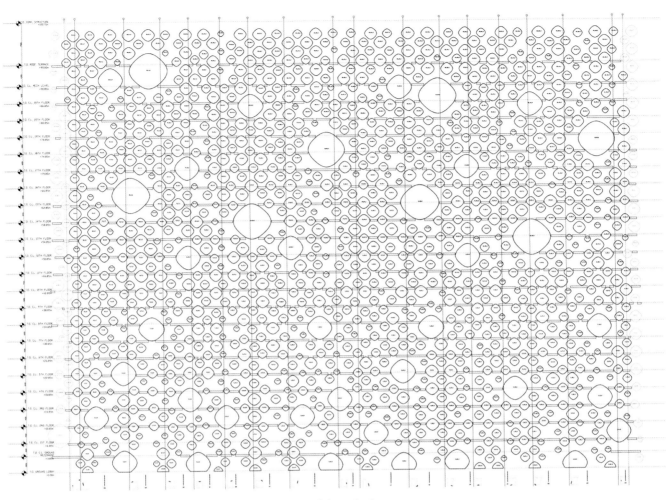

Unrolled O-14 facade

Seinuk gave us limits: on hole size, how close together the holes could get, the amount of allowable drift around grid lines, and so forth. I remember complaining that the first iterations looked too massive. There wasn't enough openness to the shell. Seinuk upped the strength of the concrete so the holes could get larger and closer together. Then everything clicked. People think O-14 is parametric, but that's actually true only to a very limited degree. Roland Snooks very successfully scripted routines to automate updates on the drawing set—no mean feat.

But on the design side, automating the gradients of the holes didn't work for us. The rule-based fields looked obvious and felt dead. We got into a situation where the scripting got so localized—we kept changing the rules—that it was easier to vary the gradients manually. Which is what we ultimately did! I remember Roland remarking that what we were really doing was random and crafted—both pejoratives from his point of view! I felt very vindicated years later when David Byrne observed a similar phenomenon in contemporary music, that rather than mechanically following a metrical rule, a successful expression resides in the sweet spot between order and

entropy: "The emotional center is not the technical center.... Funky grooves are not square."[27]

The immaterial appearance of the O-14 building was a shock to me—how in reality it looks like a rendering, especially before it started aging. I don't think that was necessarily a negative thing, although it wasn't completely within our control, either. But after it happened, it was sort of a shock to see it that way—that it kept those qualities materially, in its built state. That was a more recent realization. And, well, it had to get built. A building had to get built at that scale for us to see it.

From Greg Lynn, "Archaeology of the Digital: Canadian Center for Architecture"(2016).

27 David Byrne, *How Music Works* (San Francisco: McSweeney's, 2012), 45.

Rod-Net Variations 1996–2014

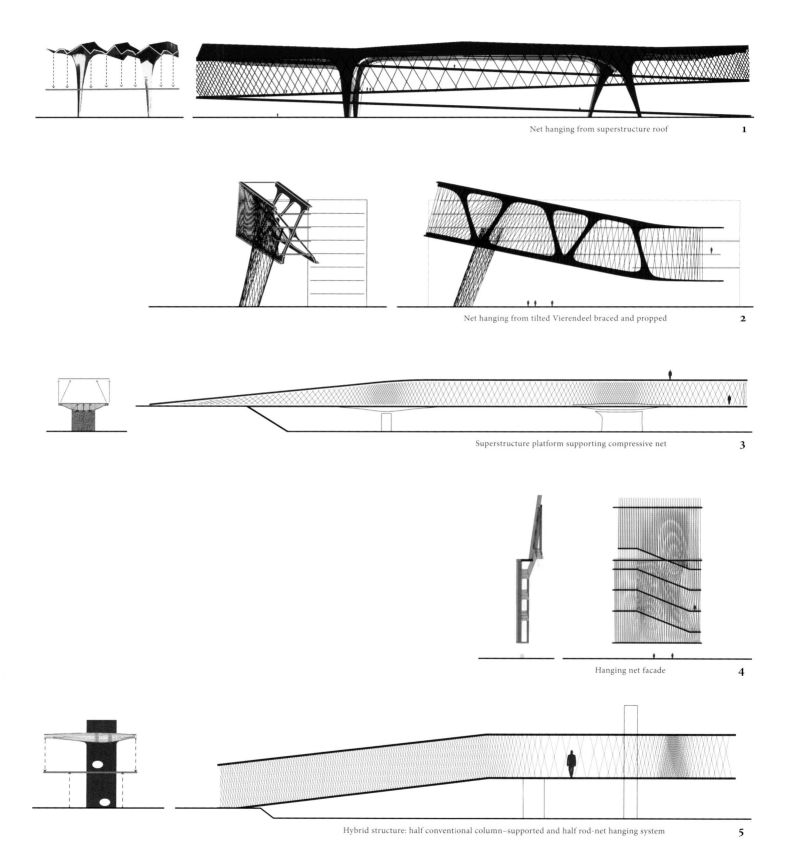

Net hanging from superstructure roof   **1**

Net hanging from tilted Vierendeel braced and propped   **2**

Superstructure platform supporting compressive net   **3**

Hanging net facade   **4**

Hybrid structure: half conventional column–supported and half rod-net hanging system   **5**

WATER GARDEN
1997

Water Garden: Fixed Potentials, Flowing Media

The architecture of the garden, more than that of mere buildings, has historically encompassed a wide range of implications surrounding human engagement with the material environment. A more or less permanent feature of Western architecture (from classicism to the various modernisms) has been the almost ineradicable idea that there exists a permanent and unchanging essence behind the world of appearances and that such essences are universal, taking the form of fixed, simple geometries and timeless typologies.

Time thus makes itself evident within two distinct yet related schemata: first, architecture as a stable and unchanging framework within which, and against which, the temporal unfolds, and second, the extent to which nature's mutability allows the natural to approach or deviate from a certain ideal. In an eighteenth-century French topiary garden, for example, the relative crudity or refinement of simple geometric forms in plant materials serves to establish the norms and limits for their speculation and enjoyment. These schemata are then locked in a perpetual circularity, with permanence set against change and vice versa.

If, however, we shift our focus from static models of nature and architecture to dynamic (essentially time-based) systems, then a new horizon of possibilities emerges. Time is not understood to be prior to, above, or separate from the material world but is engendered by the material and finds its particular incarnations in it.

Nature, then, is less a creation to be speculated on than an inventive and modifiable matrix of material becomings. It might be argued that abandoning the two schemata outlined earlier leads to forms of naturalism—in which nature in some sense is allowed to take its own course (with the assumption that natural development without human intervention will display its own creativity and inherent virtues). However, there exists a fourth possibility that, contrary to a passive naturalism, requires intensive artifice aimed at the production of natural effects.

Nature will of its own inertia tend toward developments of increasing stability and banality. A salient and intensive architecture thus requires the deliberate production of instability in order to produce novelty. Here, it will be necessary to set aside the nature-culture dialectic and focus instead on the processes that establish transverse developments across these regimes.

Machinic phylum refers to the set of self-organizing processes in the universe. These include all processes in which a group of previously disconnected elements (organic and nonorganic) suddenly reach a critical point and begin to cooperate to form a higher-level entity.

Recent advances in experimental mathematics have shown that the onset of any of these processes may be described by the same mathematical model. It is as if the principles that guide the self-assembly of these "machines"—for example chemical clocks, multicellular organisms, or nest-building insect colonies—are at some deep level essentially similar. The notion of a machinic phylum thus blurs the distinction between organic and nonorganic life.

A literal test bed for these conceptions was suggested by Jeff Kipnis, who in the project's formative stages collaborated with us on a design for a water garden at his residence in suburban Columbus, Ohio. The project was then developed in two directions: Kipnis pursued the development of the garden in the earth/substrate as a series of linked pools, and our proposal developed the garden as a grooved laminar

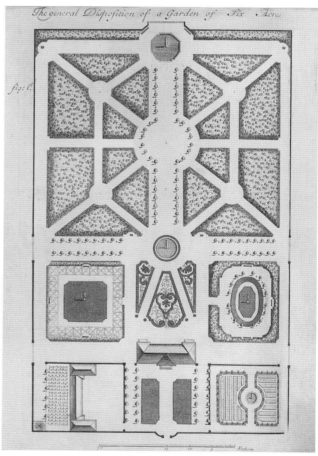

The general Disposition of a Garden of Six Acres, from
Antoine Joseph Dézallier d'Argenville, *La Théorie et la pratique du jardinage*, 1712

Unlike the classical topiary garden (above), which requires constant maintenance and seeks to establish a rigid mastery over the "natural," the Water Garden (opposite) relies on perpetually shifting and irregular forces that gradually alter the garden's form.

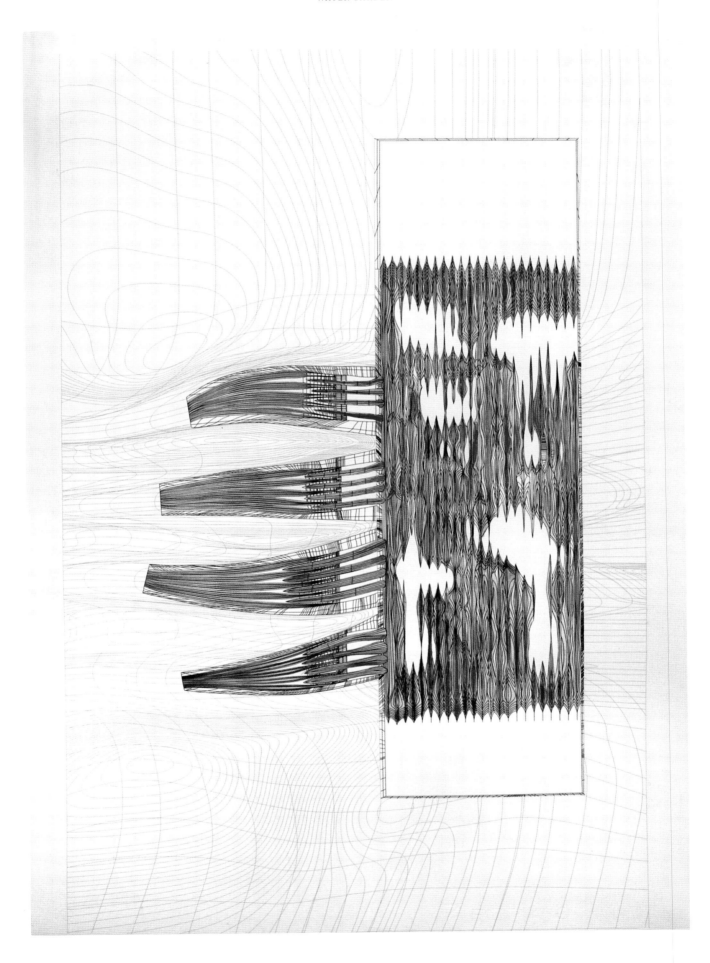

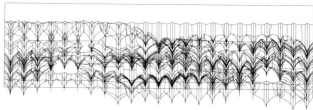

End elevation isometric

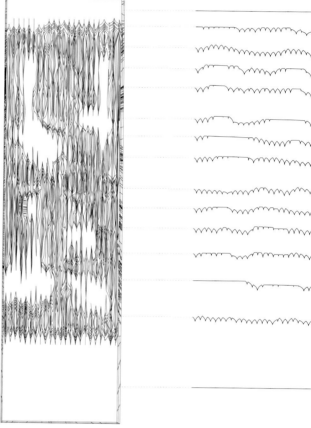

Plan of concrete substrate B

Microgrooves   Cross sections of ogival furrows

system in a concrete slab. In outline the garden consists of a furrowed-concrete slab measuring 7.3 by 21.9 meters (24 by 72 feet), containing a laminar system of twenty-four parallel grooves, each with a variable ogive cross section measuring an average of 45.7 centimeters (18 inches) from point to base. This material geometry constitutes the "primitive" through which a hierarchical series of global and local transformations—warps, dimples, folds—are expressed. Extreme and unstable configurations in the topology are essentially built into the concrete substrate in order to express them in the vital media (water, soil, plant materials, and chemical salts) of the "flow space" above.

The topology of the substrate induces transformational events that disrupt the evolution of the media flowing on it. In such topological manifolds, the characteristics of the mapped media are determined not by the quantitative substrate space below but rather by the specific singularities of the flow space of which they are a part. This means that the "dead" yet intensive geometry of the grooves excites material and/or biological novelty in the media. In literal and instrumental fashion, multiform gradients in the geometry diagram and trigger the gradients of growth inherent in natural systems and yield a prodigious, if only partially manageable, field of blooms.

ABOVE LEFT: Three Google Earth views of the Water Garden depict changes in the vegetation over time and across seasons.

OPPOSITE: The microgrooves of the Water Garden influence, at varied depths, the flow of materials across and through its surface.

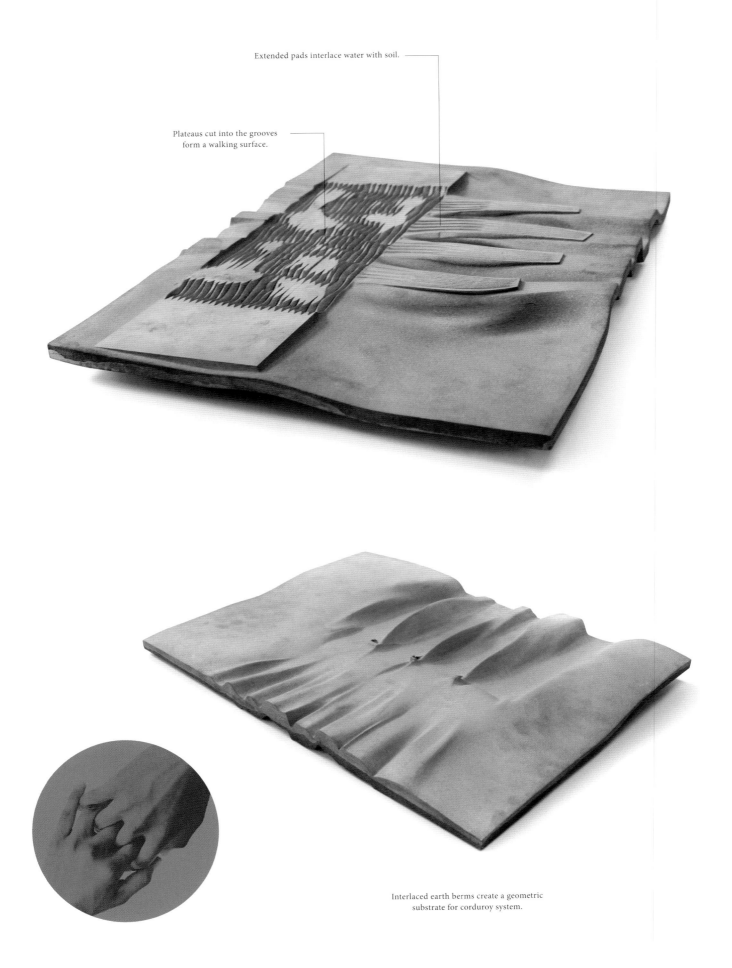

Extended pads interlace water with soil.

Plateaus cut into the grooves
form a walking surface.

Interlaced earth berms create a geometric
substrate for corduroy system.

ABOVE: Plan of Specimen Garden, Wolf Residence, 1988

OPPOSITE: View of Specimen Garden with Long Island Sound preservation beyond

LANDSCAPES

Métier à Aubes in situ

Landscape, Jadow Residence, Mill River, Massachusetts

INFRASTRUCTURE

———

TERRITORIES

On Infrastructural Urbanism

Jesse Reiser and Nanako Umemoto

New York, 1998

The city is the nexus of material and informational flows, developed within multiple infrastructures of transportation, distribution, culture, and knowledge. The increasingly interconnected world has produced cities where global systems are intermeshed in local environments and scale shifts rapidly from the local to the regional and international. As the locus of intense economic, social, and idea exchanges and connections at all levels, the city of the twenty-first century must support these vital urban interactions and design new meeting, working, and entertainment environments.

The past thirty years have seen a wholesale devaluation in the force traditionally accorded to the discipline of architecture. The perceived failure of modernism has given rise to a variety of tendencies, all of which would deny the efficacy of architectural design. It is especially disheartening to witness the general reluctance to assert an architectural will, given this country's very open potential for expression and the creation of the new. We do not accept these arguments for the end of modernism but rather work within a new, expanded notion of what modernism might become. We perceive the lapse that has occurred in the past decades as the consequence of a lack of adequate paradigms by which to drive the project of modernism forward.

Just as the sciences have experienced a sea change due to models of complexity first developed in the mathematics of dynamical systems, we, too, benefit from their revolutionary employment in architecture. A parallel development already underway in the building industry would replace strict confines of construction within defined scales (interior, building, urban, regional) with a more lateral traverse across these scales. We understand the scalar and organizational hierarchies of architecture not as given and separate but rather as rigorously connected and codependent in complex and differentiated ways. This interconnectivity has far-reaching effects and is especially integral to an understanding of a new urbanism.

Architecture must reengage the urban scale of the city, not simply to repeat existing patterns but as a comprehensive project to envision coherent public space. Our aspiration is to work with the city to develop and implement building proposals of real and lasting value. We feel that strong and clear design can and should mobilize the necessary planning bodies to construct new urban space

Historically, the greatest examples of urbanism at this scale have prioritized design. All too often, design has followed on plans generated by committees, with the unfortunate consequence of the result being piecemeal, nonintegrated, and therefore less effective. Design, however, is not an isolated discipline. While we as designers operate primarily in the realm of the qualitative, we rely heavily upon quantitative input supplied by established planning bodies to assure our work's viability in the complex milieu of public space.

Since the nineteenth century, infrastructure has been overtly used as a model resulting in the amplification of systems of movement, distribution, and control. While the proliferation of these systems has necessarily been attendant to modernization, they are rarely questioned or seen as anything other than discrete components of a hierarchy no greater than its parts. Reflexively, the aftereffect of such thinking has been the intensely stratified conception of the city and how its systems relate to one another. While the city has always been an engine for the flow of capital, this is not its only reason for being. There are very real benefits to loosening this stratification, which is ultimately as social and political as it is functional. It is at this level then, that of the urban substrate, that we operate to produce change in the form of the city.

It is critical that public work exist in the first place as cohesive, coherent, and forward-looking—affirming not only strength of design but also integrity as a product of the thoughtfully assembled and very specific desires of communities. Our work addresses the imperative for integration in a fundamentally different way. It is our contention that planning that is based around generic and preestablished programs vitiates the very reason for such programs' implementation in the first place, for rather than responding to that which distinguishes one area from the next, this mode of operation erases difference altogether. For us, all space is singular and unique and must resist homogenizing influences from the reductive mechanisms of simple, unquestioned standardization. This is not a rejection of standardization altogether but rather a call for its modulation within a larger continuum.

EAST RIVER CORRIDOR
1998

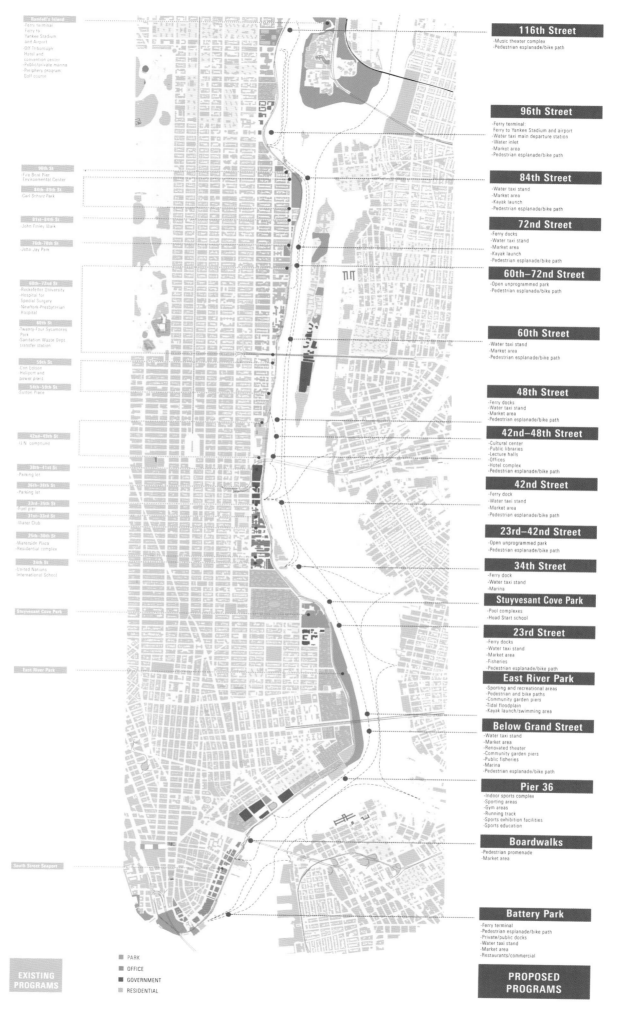

Randell's Island
-Ferry terminal
-Ferry to
Yankee Stadium
and Airport
-Off Triborough:
Hotel and
convention center
-Public/private marina
-Periphery program
Golf course

90th St
-Fire Boat Pier
Environmental Center

84th–89th St
Carl Schurz Park

81st–84th St
John Finley Walk

76th–78th St
John Jay Park

69th–72nd St
-Rockefeller University
-Hospital for
Special Surgery
-NewYork-Presbyterian
Hospital

60th St
Twenty-Four Sycamores
Park
-Sanitation Waste Dept
transfer station

59th St
-Con Edison
Heliport and
power plant

54th–59th St
Sutton Place

42nd–49th St
U.N. compound

38th–41st St
-Parking lot

36th–38th St
-Parking lot

33rd–35th St
-Fuel pier

31st–33rd St
-Water Club

25th–30th St
-Waterside Plaza
-Residential complex

24th St
-United Nations
International School

Stuyvesant Cove Park

East River Park

South Street Seaport

■ PARK
■ OFFICE
■ GOVERNMENT
■ RESIDENTIAL

116th Street
-Music theater complex
-Pedestrian esplanade/bike path

96th Street
-Ferry terminal:
Ferry to Yankee Stadium and airport
-Water taxi main departure station
-Water inlet
-Market area
-Pedestrian esplanade/bike path

84th Street
-Water taxi stand
-Market area
-Kayak launch
-Pedestrian esplanade/bike path

72nd Street
-Ferry docks
-Water taxi stand
-Market area
-Kayak launch
-Pedestrian esplanade/bike path

60th–72nd Street
-Open unprogrammed park
-Pedestrian esplanade/bike path

60th Street
-Water taxi stand
-Market area
-Pedestrian esplanade/bike path

48th Street
-Ferry docks
-Water taxi stand
-Market area
-Pedestrian esplanade/bike path

42nd–48th Street
-Cultural center
-Public libraries
-Lecture halls
-Offices
-Hotel complex
-Pedestrian esplanade/bike path

42nd Street
-Ferry dock
-Water taxi stand
-Market area
-Pedestrian esplanade/bike path

23rd–42nd Street
-Open unprogrammed park
-Pedestrian esplanade/bike path

34th Street
-Ferry dock
-Water taxi stand
-Marina

Stuyvesant Cove Park
-Pool complexes
-Head Start school

23rd Street
-Ferry docks
-Water taxi stand
-Market area
-Fisheries
-Pedestrian esplanade/bike path

East River Park
-Sporting and recreational areas
-Pedestrian and bike paths
-Community garden piers
-Tidal floodplain
-Kayak launch/swimming area

Below Grand Street
-Water taxi stand
-Market area
-Renovated theater
-Community garden piers
-Public fisheries
-Marina
-Pedestrian esplanade/bike path

Pier 36
-Indoor sports complex
-Sporting areas
-Gym areas
-Running track
-Sports exhibition facilities
-Sports education

Boardwalks
-Pedestrian promenade
-Market area

Battery Park
-Ferry terminal
-Pedestrian esplanade/bike path
-Private/public docks
-Water taxi stand
-Market area
-Restaurants/commercial

**PROPOSED
PROGRAMS**

A FDR Drive/local road interchange

B Butterfly pier

C 72nd Street ferry dock
with commercial programming over

D 96th Street boat basin

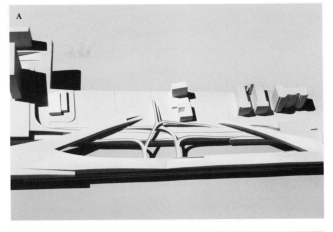

BATTERY PARK

SLOW-SPEED CAR/BIKE LOCAL
ROAD
Pushed to the edge of the city grid,
enabling connections to major
streets as well as the new
program

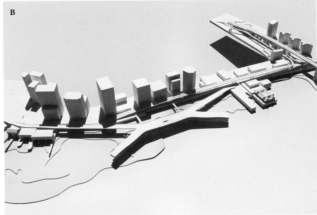

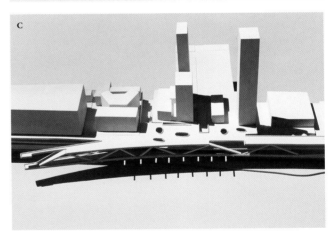

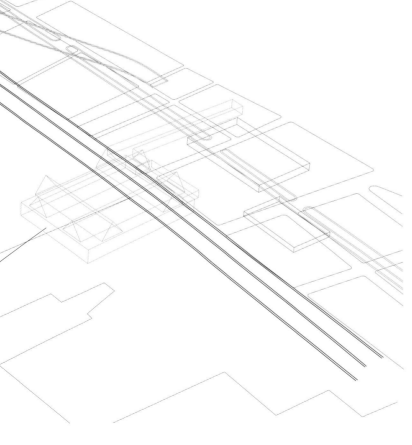

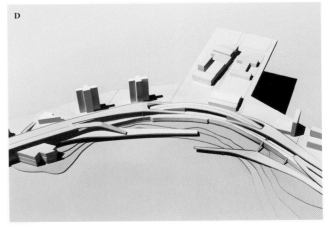

Southernmost segment of East River Corridor at the Battery with Butterfly Pier

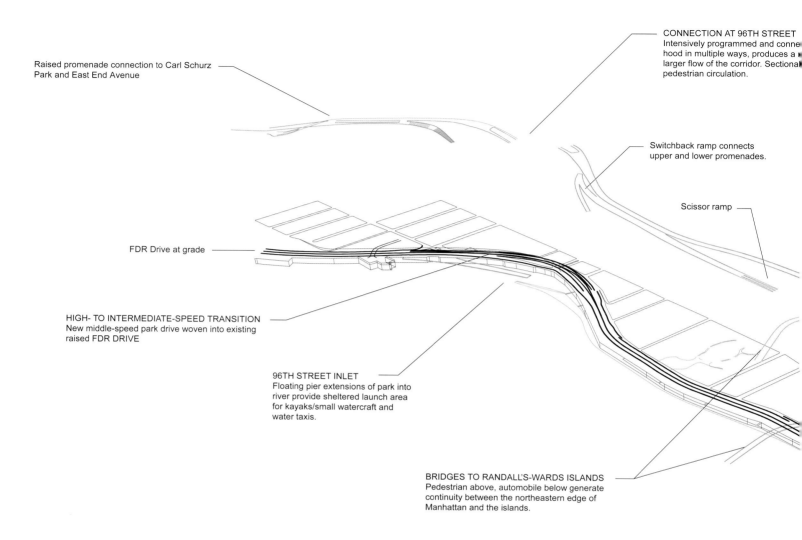

CONNECTION AT 96TH STREET
Intensively programmed and conne
hood in multiple ways, produces a ◖
larger flow of the corridor. Sectional
pedestrian circulation.

Raised promenade connection to Carl Schurz
Park and East End Avenue

Switchback ramp connects
upper and lower promenades.

Scissor ramp

FDR Drive at grade

HIGH- TO INTERMEDIATE-SPEED TRANSITION
New middle-speed park drive woven into existing
raised FDR DRIVE

96TH STREET INLET
Floating pier extensions of park into
river provide sheltered launch area
for kayaks/small watercraft and
water taxis.

BRIDGES TO RANDALL'S-WARDS ISLANDS
Pedestrian above, automobile below generate
continuity between the northeastern edge of
Manhattan and the islands.

Modulated landscap

weaving system that negotiates the topographical rise and fall and incorporates public programming for a textured integration of multiple systems.

While our proposal might seem to fix a certain form or strategy as a finished design, it was meant to be a possible development within a flexible system. The dilemma in a project of this magnitude is the necessity of developing the specifics of a proposal to a certain degree in order to understand the systems in operation and the feasibility of propositions. Our working hypothesis is that urban proposals of any significance—and certainly any attempt at doing something new—must emerge out of design and not from generalized planning schemes. This is fundamentally a design methodology that develops infrastructural logics

permitting a certain range of possible urban outcomes. As opposed to more traditional planning strategies, which provide only fixed templates for limited sets of desires, this model presents the capacity to handle change over time—a quality that is necessary for a vital and evolving urbanism.

Projects like the East River Corridor challenge developmental models born within the paradigm of master planning. Infrastructuralism suggests a staged series of projects already enmeshed within systems of distribution and growth. These projects operate at a range of scales, producing immediate urban effects that are localized yet already embody the logics of the fully extended project, thus functioning not as isolated objects but as moments structured within a continuum.

neighbor-
within the
mobile and

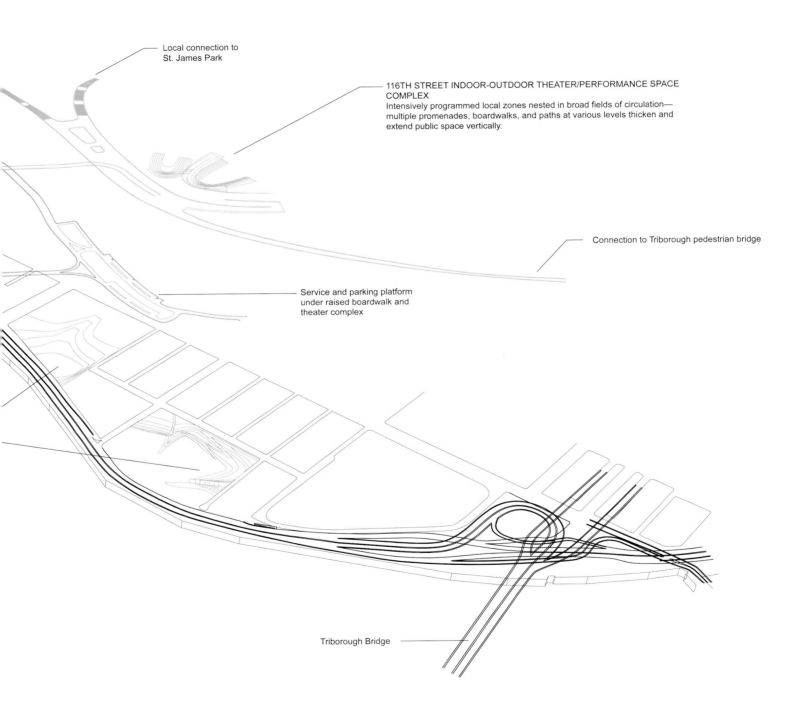

Local connection to
St. James Park

116TH STREET INDOOR-OUTDOOR THEATER/PERFORMANCE SPACE
COMPLEX
Intensively programmed local zones nested in broad fields of circulation—
multiple promenades, boardwalks, and paths at various levels thicken and
extend public space vertically.

Connection to Triborough pedestrian bridge

Service and parking platform
under raised boardwalk and
theater complex

Triborough Bridge

Northern segment of East River Corridor with connection to the Triborough Bridge

In Conversation with
Jesse Reiser & Nanako Umemoto

Andrew Benjamin

BENJAMIN: How do you understand the relationship between architecture and materials? If there are changes in the materials, how do you adapt the architecture to them? Or do you think that the architecture should determine the materials?

REISER: Well, it's an interesting question. The popular conception of the development of architecture relative to the development of technologies and the material developments that accompany them acts more or less as a baseline for any serious practice in architecture, which is to say that at least we have a modernist framework. There is a general acceptance of developments within material technologies, but typically those get incorporated into models of design that are already fairly known. In other words, many times you'll simply see the same modernist organizational principles acquiring a new material sheath.

BENJAMIN: And so those materials are not exploited for their potential. They are in some sense restricted by the same old envelope or deployed in the same old way.

REISER: Right. The material becomes more or less coded into the architecture, and the way it is deployed becomes symbolic. The internal developments of the material wouldn't necessarily be exploited. What I find more interesting than the material innovation per se is the way in which we as designers can begin to harness the abstract

potential of the material systems—meaning that it's not the use of a new material in a building that is of greatest interest to me, but rather that the matter itself, as a dynamic substance and principle, can actually inform how buildings can be organized. So it's not entirely about the literal use of the material, although at the end of the day that has to happen if you're talking about an actual building. It's more about how we understand the relationship of matter and force in a design process.

BENJAMIN: OK, let's take that point a step further. What is an abstract potential? I understand that it's a possibility that is there in the material, but I think this opens up questions that have to do with experimentation and research and architectural theory. So tell me a bit more about what an abstract potential would be.

REISER: In the design process, you have to find a kind of currency within architecture, some vehicle to express change in the development of a project. And that currency is generally manifest for us in the way that geometry and materials work with each other. So in contrast to a more classical way of thinking, in which a geometric diagram defines the lineaments of a building, here we are looking at the way in which matter and force can inform geometry and can actually begin to develop a notion of organization within space that's based on those issues.

BENJAMIN: Is this development and organization only possible if one uses computers and specific programs, such as animation or CAD software? How much of this has been realized only because it's possible with a computer?

REISER: Well, these kinds of issues have become thematic to a generation because of the advent of the software and the computer. But there is more to computing than the actual boxes sitting in our office. One of the things that we find very interesting in our practice is that we can make models that are actually physical analogues that compute themselves; the model is equally a kind of computer. That doesn't mean that we're rejecting the computer. Far from it; we use computers every day in our practice. But we find a very productive relationship between physical modeling and certain kinds of modeling that index forces in a literal way and how those inform our practice and the design we're making. What I mean by indexing is that we set up models that are sensitive to external forces, gravity among them. Using these models allows us, first of all, to understand the structural capacities of the design we are generating and, more importantly, to register a wide range of influences, both programmatic and organizational.

BENJAMIN: When I look at your models, I can see that they contain a potential for representation but they're not representations themselves. They are in some sense only potentiality. So should I look at these models diagrammatically rather than as small versions of what will come?

REISER: Well, I think they tread both sides of the issue, depending on your point of view. All objects have a representational quality if you choose to look at them that way. In practice, however, the only way these types of models become generative is if they are understood on a very particular scale and with a very particular direction. They are in some sense miniature versions of what will finally be generated, but these kinds of diagrammatic models are changeable: they're flexible, they can be edited. In other words, it would be a question not of taking one of those models wholesale into the project but rather of using the model in a generative sense, which means that its geometries can achieve a materiality in ways that the classical relationship between geometry and materials cannot. You get transitions that cannot be understood as moving from the ideal to the real. In an idealist architecture, such as Mies van der Rohe's, geometry seeks to transcend the accidents of matter. What we are doing is releasing potentials within matter understood as an abstract machine.

BENJAMIN: Your recent work has involved both large-scale buildings and urban projects and small-scale buildings and houses. How do you move between the two scales? How does your approach differ when it's a large urban project, as opposed to something small?

UMEMOTO: The bigger projects require a more direct relationship with moving components in the environment: cars, visitors, employees. It's similar with small projects and the movement systems within them. Smaller projects take more time to develop materially, since, typically, they require detailing in ways that large-scale projects do not.

REISER: We are dealing with the forces that shape a whole range of scales in any project. When you're working on a large-scale project, you have many more levels to deal with. But in a certain way, the organizational principles are very similar. If you line up a series of our projects, you'll find that while they might be radically different in terms of their scale—say, the difference between a very finely scaled development like the water garden we built for Jeffrey Kipnis in Ohio in 1997 and the project that we proposed in 1999 for the west side of Manhattan (in the IFCCA competition for the design of cities), which would take up forty city blocks—they employ common geometric and organizational principles.

BENJAMIN: How do you understand the generation of form? And how do you prepare for a project on the level of techniques and premises? The interesting question will be how you generate the form and how you understand whatever answer you give to that question. It's not as if you have the form and then you put the program in, as though the form were indifferent to the program. This relationship needs to be articulated in some way.

REISER: As we develop our projects, we look first toward typological models, not in any strict sense of a historical typology but more along the lines of what Rem Koolhaas would call a crude typology, and what others have called a formal typology: we take an initial look at the kind of project we would generate, then we begin to give, just roughly, a certain kind of grain to the project. For example, the East River Corridor Project in New York in 1998. It's twelve miles long, and it deals with multiple layers in the city; we knew from the outset that in some form or other we were going to be dealing with stratification, that it would be a densely layered project that would be predominantly horizontal. And so that gives us, from the outset, a sense of where we're going with it. It isn't as if we're pulling associations out of thin air.

UMEMOTO: The smaller projects demand a more direct use of materials but also a concern with the program. Within a certain limitation you have to push communication as well as the architecture, so that's more challenging. Whereas we didn't need to deal with smaller concerns with the East River Corridor Project; in a way, because it's so big, it becomes much more simple.

BENJAMIN: Can you clarify how you understand program?

REISER: There are different degrees of fitness of a program or an activity to an architecture. My sense is that program is something that's spelled out by people or institutions, and it's what they expect to happen in a space; the relationship of that to architecture has always been a very approximate one, to my mind. In a certain way, it's almost impossible to conceive of architecture as architecture via program. There is a desire for that to be the case, but I can't think of any great architecture that's essentially programmatic in origin.

BENJAMIN: My question is more polemical. It seems to me that something like Frank Gehry's Guggenheim Bilbao, while visually remarkable and while being an organism that has transformed Bilbao, is programmatically uninteresting in that it's two very large boxes clipped onto an extraordinary entryway. There's a failure to think through what the program would be. Now let's turn it around. Take Daniel Libeskind's Jewish Museum in Berlin. He had a very specific understanding of program, not simply of the museum's program but program having to do with representing absence.

REISER: Yes.

BENJAMIN: The architecture has a tight relationship to the program, not just program as function but the way program itself is understood, and I think that the building is exemplary for that reason.

REISER: I agree. When a program is understood as such or, in Libeskind's case, as iconography, it would be thematic, which has to do with deep content.

BENJAMIN: This is what I mean by program, a thought-through conception of what will be. I wonder how that has an impact on your understanding of form. Would you ever conceive of doing as much research on program as you would on form generation?

UMEMOTO: Normally there's a certain kind of space that we try to reprogram into material and structure. Sometimes we break the program down so that it's not necessarily just one program. Program is unthinkable without some intersection with matter. Matter is all we have to work with. Matter and program do not have a one-to-one relation. And that is the saving grace of architecture.

REISER: There's a close tracking of how the substance of the building would develop, but it's not completely based on the stated activities of the space. That wouldn't be a fully adequate way of generating what we're after. If there were an immediate relationship between matter and program, architecture would be so constraining that any trace of freedom would be eliminated.

BENJAMIN: I want to talk about how you understand research and experimentation in architecture. I'm

interested in experimentation in the sense of finding something out, of research. Both of you have at times taught; you're both teaching now, I think, at Princeton and Columbia. Are there ways in which you would link your research to teaching? How do you understand, in general terms, the relationship between research and experimentation in architecture?

UMEMOTO: When we ran our joint studio at Columbia, we knew what kind of path the students should take. So we directed them in that way.

BENJAMIN: But is it linked to what you as architects are trying to do? Do you use your teaching situations, your studios, almost like laboratories, like scientists would in order to discover something?

REISER: Absolutely. One really important thing has to do with the issue of invention. This follows the discussion on program and functionalism. I was very impressed with *Guns, Germs, and Steel*, by Jared Diamond. It's basically an anthropological book. There is a chapter called "Necessity's Mother," in which a litany of inventions are described in terms of their history. It turns out that most of these inventions weren't created with their final use in mind. The inventors of the phonograph went through a whole series of possible uses: recording the last wishes of a dying man, capturing animal sounds…Finally, after many, many tries, they realized it could be useful for recording music. But that came much later than the invention itself. That relates very much to the way we understand the studio that we teach and the work that we do in our own studio. Many things come up in a design, some of which we tuck away for later use, some of which we opportunistically incorporate into the work. There's simply a level of openness in the design process if you're attentive to it, which allows for a multiplicity of things to arise. I think that's part of what a new practice should be doing. It should have an awareness of the multiple possibilities.

UMEMOTO: We also have limitations. We figure there are only three ways a project can go, but when we bring it to students, one of them will have a completely different understanding of things, and the surprise is that they bring a different solution to the project, a new discovery that opens our eyes again. It's fun.

REISER: Absolutely. I mean, there were truly profound inventions that occurred in my last semester in a very modest class that was devoted more to the design of furniture than to architecture. One of the student's projects caused me to rethink the relationship of materials and geometry in design.

BENJAMIN: Both of you talk about the importance of materials and the way in which materials become both a source and a site of invention, of prompt thinking. Given that material is in some sense linked to engineering knowledge, I wonder how you see the relationship between architecture and engineering. One of the ways I've always understood it, from my own position of teaching, is that a student should know when to ask an engineer to come in rather than feel that he or she can do it alone. How do you understand the relationship, formally and practically, between architecture and engineering?

REISER: Engineers can come into an existing project either as analysts or as physicians. The most exciting prospect is that they can enter into a project from the outset. We're finding that it's actually much more productive to work on architectural projects with engineers from the beginning, very particular engineers who aren't simply problem solvers, who are not caught up in what I see as a modernist aspiration to design under the constraints of maximum efficiency and minimal materials. There are innovative and experimental engineers like the people from the British firm Arup—Cecil Balmond, Charles Walker—who really are using the rigors of engineering in idiosyncratic ways in relation to architecture. It isn't simply problem solving or a technical discipline. Engineers today have an expanded notion of the relationship among matter, forces, and space. Although of course they still have to solve the problems, and they are extremely good technicians.

BENJAMIN: What you're talking about could almost be described as another way of understanding practice.

REISER: Yes.

BENJAMIN: You're saying that the truth of architecture is that it's collaborative, and that relationships with engineers or environmentalists or even philosophers would be productive in thinking about contemporary practice.

REISER: That's absolutely true. I would say that architecture is interdisciplinary but in a very particular way. I think the most successful projects do arise out of the contributions of architects and philosophers, engineers, musicians, and social scientists. Each works strictly within his or her own field of expertise, contributing that expertise within the overall project. No one actually leaves his or her own discipline. I don't try to do amateur philosophy, nor do I expect a philosopher to do my job.

BENJAMIN: What that indicates is that the thing about interdisciplinarity was always nonsense. One works collaboratively by letting something arise out of the relationship rather than out of synthesizing so that everything becomes a bland mixture.

REISER: Yes, it's not about arriving at a consensus.

BENJAMIN: Right, quite the opposite. We no longer believe that architecture can change the world in any instrumental way, yet we also have to realize that only about 20 percent of buildings are done by architects. And so architecture, if it's going to flourish, has to define itself in relation to culture; it can't be a pure form. How do you understand the specificity of architecture? The question I'm asking is about the nature of architecture. How do each of you think about it, both as an activity and as a pedagogy? How do you understand what it is that you're doing, given that it's not building, even though it's kind of linked to creating buildings. Buildings can be created without architects—so what is architecture doing?

REISER: Architects, in both their building and nonbuilding work, are looking at problems that extend beyond problem solving or making society more functional, although that is part of our responsibility. This may sound very metaphysical, but I think there is simply a desire at some level to know what a new kind of space is. The universe is stranger than we can know, and one of the motivating desires in architecture is to somehow bring forth new realities in the most general sense.

UMEMOTO: It shouldn't be just repeating work the builder is doing; it should be more challenging. It should push things forward rather than always having to work within given limitations.

BENJAMIN: So, new architecture is bound up with something like innovation, and that's what distinguishes it from simple repair to the back of a building.

UMEMOTO: I don't know if it's innovation or not, but something that you push forward...

BENJAMIN: Discovery.

UMEMOTO: It could be that we're discovering something that's old.

Published in *BOMB*, no. 84 (Summer 2003): 64–69.

TYPOLOGIES OF SINGULARITIES

The phenomenon of the singularity, as compared to a merely additive architecture, assumes that local difference emerges out of changes to regions of a continuous field of similar elements. As such it is an excellent model for dealing with repetitive systems like spaceframes. An associated model is the inclusion/singularity. Here a foreign organization is "included" in the field, but in contrast to a mere juxtaposition, its presence, like a stone in a flow of water, creates a local disturbance pattern. This boundary organization at once mimics the organization and incorporates it into the field, such that even if the foreign element were removed, its effects, both locally as a mould and as reverberations across larger regions, would remain.

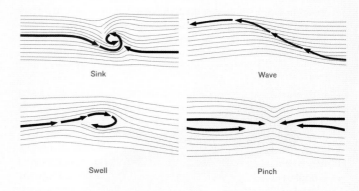

Sink   Wave

Swell   Pinch

UNILATERAL   AUTOINCLUSIONS
Disturbance Zones   Differentiation Achieved
around a Foreign Object   through Intensive Transformation
                                        of a System at a Local Level

REGULARITY · SPACEFRAME

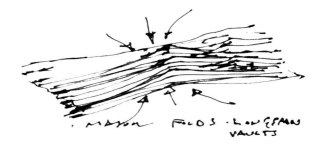

· MASON FOLDS · LONGSPAN VAULTS

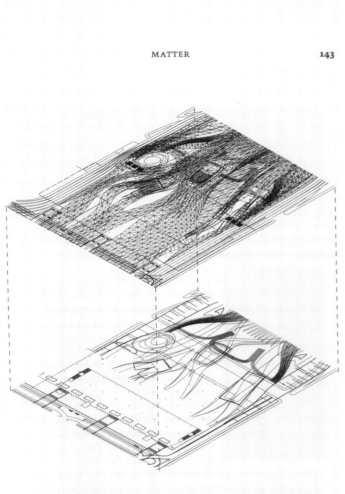

The regular field of structural elements established in a long-span space frame is interrupted by the inclusion of programs (theaters, museums) below. The resulting boundary organizations in the flow of the structures comprise the lobby and public spaces.

REGULAR FIELD W/INCLUSIONS

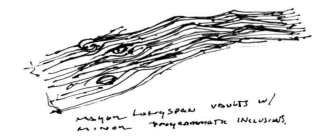

MAJOR LONGSPAN VAULTS W/ MINOR PROGRAMMATIC INCLUSIONS.

MANHATTAN
MEMORIOUS

[VOICEOVER] "I don't remember very much about New York before the project.

Was it really the relentless passage of years? The unending cycle of work? The tragedies and triumphs, large and small, that made a city forget?

"Our distinguished guest for this evening is Mr. Robert Moses, the nation's foremost city planner. Mr. Moses, of course you've had many years of experience in New York, both the city and state, as a planner of parkways and housing. I'm sure that our viewers tonight would like to hear you talk about some of the public planning problems."

Or could there have been other more persistent factors at work... quieter, subtler...hovering just behind the walls of the streets...eroding time and events, not violently, not so anyone would notice, but ever so quietly...like the careful closing of a thousand doors.

Moses: "We're way behind. We've been falling steadily behind for years, and now the...situation is more or less desperate."

"Is some of that due to the Second War, sir?"

And yet there are signs, portents among the derelict leavings...a clear message in amongst a rot of trash and advertising, or elsewhere in a violent scribbled message cut short on the placid asphalt.

Moses: "No, I would not include South America in this particular...uh, discussion. The fact is that unless we begin to, uh...unless we launch a new program, a much larger program, we're going to face a situation where we can't accommodate older people."

Yes, the signs are there... if you know what to look for.

What was Fitzgerald saying about the Valley of Ashes before he was silenced? And what would rise from the cinder fields? Would the trial on in Paris be really monuments after all?

[MUSIC] *I can't forget the night I met you.
That's all I'm dreaming of
And now you call it madness,
But I call it love...*

What went wrong there, on an oppressively hot evening in August, 1939? Was there another body subtly at work beyond the League of Nations? And isn't it strange that worldwide economic chaos inevitably precedes world war? What were we being prepared for now? These and so many other questions hang over the enterprise...

an enterprise so vast and so encompassing...

that it's hard to imagine now...

how the smallest gesture and nod...

set it all in motion.

You may be amused at yesterday's wonders, worlds of tomorrow have been delivered... have become our everyday.

There was another meeting that evening that did not make the headlines.

As far as the minutes show, the only things discussed were the place cards for the skyscraper banquet, and the initiation fees for new members.

Of course, there were leaks.

And yet, might they be the hardware?

The gross, physical machines...moving what could be moved?

Building what could be built?

Men, women, programs, and policies...

are inevitably doomed to failure.

But mute material is entirely reliable.

Most of the projects were an open secret. After all, how could you hide constructions that big?

Laying the groundwork for—

But what the public didn't know were the end uses...

that is, in the future, when all the parts were in place.
So many unexplained events.
So many unexplainable disappearances.
Coincidence?

Much that is on record is open to doubt.
Yet there were a few who tried.
Fabrication, even if it's not true, has its own history.
The only truth is the means.

As to the ends...

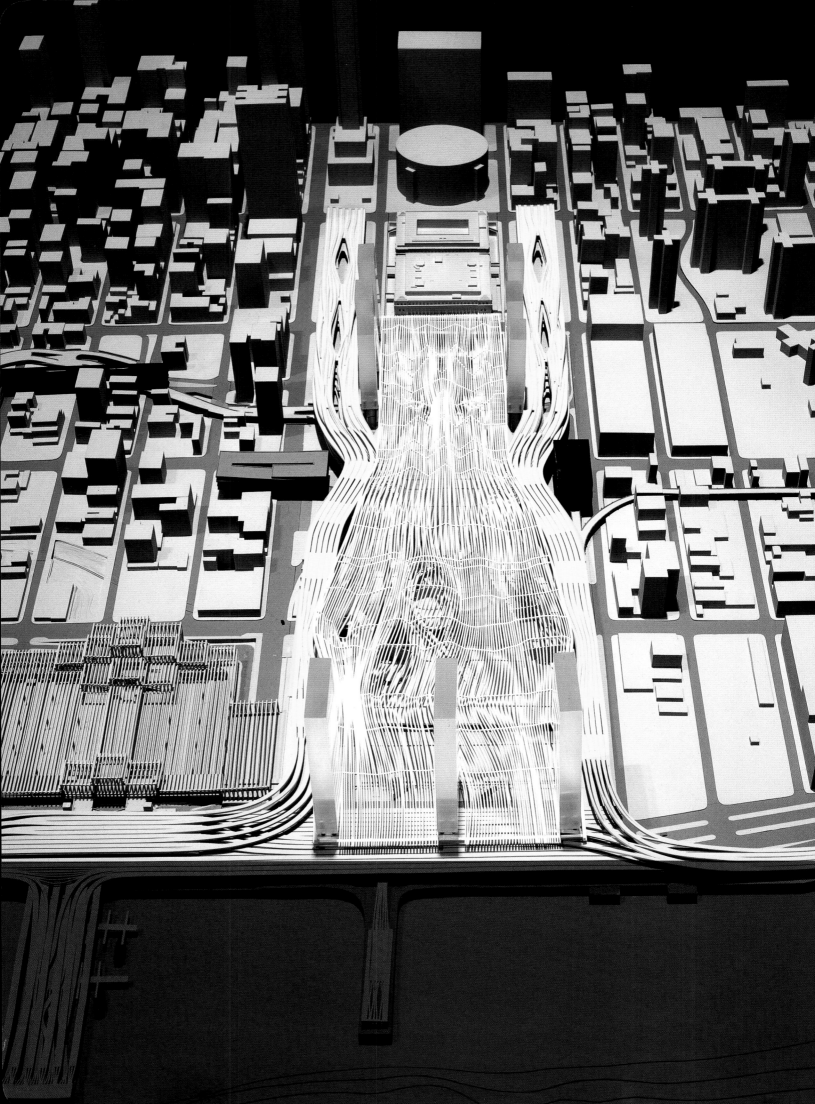

WEST SIDE
CONVERGENCE
1999

Wax study model of West Side Convergence

West Side Convergence

This competition was a preamble to the excitement around this neighborhood in western Midtown Manhattan—an attempt by Phyllis Lambert and the Canadian Centre for Architecture to rethink an urban area through architecture rather than through developers' plans.

The International Foundation for the Canadian Centre for Architecture (IFCCA) Competition for the Design of Cities presented the opportunity to reinvent this site by transcending the separation and monofunctionality of many of its large infrastructural elements through a mode of operation we term "infrastructuralism." Even developers shy away from the area surrounding the Javits Center, seeing its radical segmentation (in both time and space) as an insurmountable obstacle to the kind of urban activity that would ensure a return on their investment. While the city has always been an engine for the flow of capital, this is not its only reason for being. There are very real benefits—social and political as well as functional and economic—to the loosening of infrastructural stratification and the integration of activity in the area. It is thus at the level of the urban substrate that we operate to produce change in the form of the city.

The Javits Center (like convention centers in general) has been criticized for its lack of connection to the rest of the city and for the underutilized no-man's-land surrounding it. Immersed in an amalgam of park space, our proposal blends a group of programs that would traditionally remain distinct and isolated. Periods and patterns of use unique to each space overlap to produce a zone of continual activity.

Coplanar with the existing main exhibition floor of the Javits Center, our proposal would double its current area and its capacity for exhibitions and events. Our proposed mezzanine overlooks a recently completed Javits Center extension (the exhibition floor) on the west side and the event space on the east. This extension is subsumed within a region of our proposal that is heavily programmed with civic, cultural, and leisure uses: an "endless" (spiral) museum, a full-size concert hall, a flexible, multifunctional performance hall, and an IMAX theater. A cinemaplex stands nearby on the corner of Tenth Avenue and West Thirtieth Street. Within the immediate vicinity of this civic complex, three hotel towers overlook the project on the east and the Hudson River on the west and are intended to serve conventioneers and visitors to the city. The bases of the hotel towers and the ends of the mall arms share this common surface. The proximity of these structures produces intense potential combinations of use, while the density of programs incentivizes people to visit from distant parts of Manhattan and the greater metropolitan area.

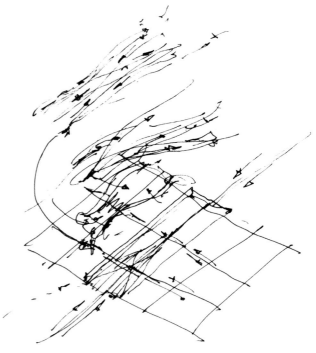

Concept sketch of West Side Convergence, knitting together a site comprising multiple grounds

The Hudson Rail Yards are part of the proposed site for the West Side Convergence project. Our West Side Convergence proposal links the Hudson Rail Yards to the Javits Center, creating a multiple-use space that integrates transportation, shopping, athletics, and cultural programming.

Park/Event Space

A number of park and landscape settings woven throughout the project provide recreation and leisure opportunities. Most generally, the park space runs along the Hudson riverfront from West Twenty-Eighth Street to West Thirty-Ninth Street at two levels. At grade are amenities for water-based recreation, and elevated above is green space. Both levels act as a continuation of the proposed Hudson River Park, which will ultimately extend the entire length of the island. The upper level turns into the city grid, still elevated, at West Thirtieth Street and at West Thirty-Fourth Street, bounding the entire proposal to the site limit at Eighth Avenue. The drawing in of Hudson River Park effectively pulls the island's edge into the site, generating continuity with the western shore of Manhattan.

The park surface serves a number of purposes. It is always in close proximity to more structured programs, including retail, commercial, and civic/cultural spaces, as well as the Javits Center. This encourages greater complexity among these otherwise isolated programs, generating mixtures and hybrids of program and organization. Surrounding the proposal on the west, north, and south sides, the park produces the zone of the project, which (at its upper levels) is not defined by the scale or order of the surrounding city blocks. A larger, cohesive identity emerges that, while fitting within and responsive to the surrounding neighborhood, transcends local limitations to become an attractor for all of Manhattan. The urban and regional scales of the surrounding uses, flows, and infrastructures provide a unique opportunity in their ability to support such a proposal.

The event space is a vast, open, yet articulated surface for recreational, sport, and leisure activities with varying degrees of structure. The event space lies at the heart of the proposal, bounded on the west by the civic programmatic complex and the Javits Center extension, on the east by the James A. Farley Post Office and Pennsylvania Station on Eighth Avenue, and on the north and south by the wide arms of the park, retail, and commercial structures. Underneath the event space's artificial surface lie the tracks of the rail yard. The continuous yet highly differentiated

blanket of a space frame spans the structure overhead and is partially glazed, partially clad in steel. The event space thus seems both inside and outside and operates as such. Sports requiring open fields, such as softball or soccer, can be played as in an outdoor park, whereas large, stadium-type concerts requiring protection from the elements in winter are also possible. Modulations in the surface create articulated areas more conducive to smaller-scale activities. We envision the use of the event space to resemble that of the meadows in Central Park, but amplified due to the proximity and variety of other programs in the surrounding structures.

Ludwig Mies van der Rohe's 1954 collage for his Convention Hall project in Chicago

OPPOSITE: Collage rendering; beneath the space frame roof are a vast enclosed all-weather park and event space, an expanded Javits Center with three hotels, leasable office space, five cultural institutions, and shopping mall links to the new Pennsylvania Station.

ABOVE: Collage rendering of the event space (with a capacity of 90,000 people) and space frame during a public concert

Commuters

Our approach to Penn Station, a major rail transportation hub in the New York metropolitan area, is an effort to blur the boundaries between the hard corridors of pedestrian traffic moving to and from platforms by locating retail programming along these currents of movement. A development tactic already successfully implemented in similar locations such as Grand Central Station, placing shops along commuter flows tends to draw people out of straight lines and vary their speeds, provoking more complex use of infrastructural public spaces such as circulation corridors. We propose an intensification of this effect through a fully developed mall that flanks the site on both the north and the south sides, leading from the platforms below grade up over the event surface and into the mezzanine area of the civic complex.

Each new program we propose requires a certain number of parking spaces, the majority of which are in elevated lots. It is possible that this increased amount of parking could be used to accommodate automobile commuters during hours in which various spaces are in low use (the concert hall and theaters during the weekdays, for instance).

Ferries from New Jersey as well as from northern and southern points in Manhattan would stop at Pier 79. From here, commuters would walk through the parks and gardens to either Penn Station or the surrounding streets, or alternately could pass through the common mezzanine area around the civic programs and then through the mall to the platforms. Paths above and within the space frame covering the event surface and rail yards also lead from the park on the Hudson, over the project, and down into the station.

At the scale we propose, the mall would compete with other full-scale malls in the metropolitan area as a shopping destination. This is especially important in maintaining density of use on weekends, during which the site is currently underused. The mall would also act as an attractor for conventioneers, who are increasingly drawn to multiuse convention sites such as those in Atlantic City and Las Vegas.

The emerging trend of extended retailing combines product-related activities (or themes, in some cases) with retail outlets. Mountaineering stores with climbing walls or ski stores with artificial slopes are being developed by the most ambitious retailers. Our mall's adjacent event surface—a large, open, green area intended primarily for sports and leisure activities—provides the type and amount of space necessary to house the equipment for this form of retail programming. We imagine that these specialized and highly visible retail installations will produce spectacles or structured, focused events within the larger, less structured space surrounding them, breaking down the conventional boundary between private retail and public corridor. Storefronts become inconsequential.

Collage rendering: a vast, flexible, enclosed public space under a space frame

Role in Midtown

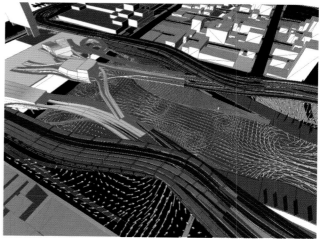
Flow diagram through the West Side Convergence development

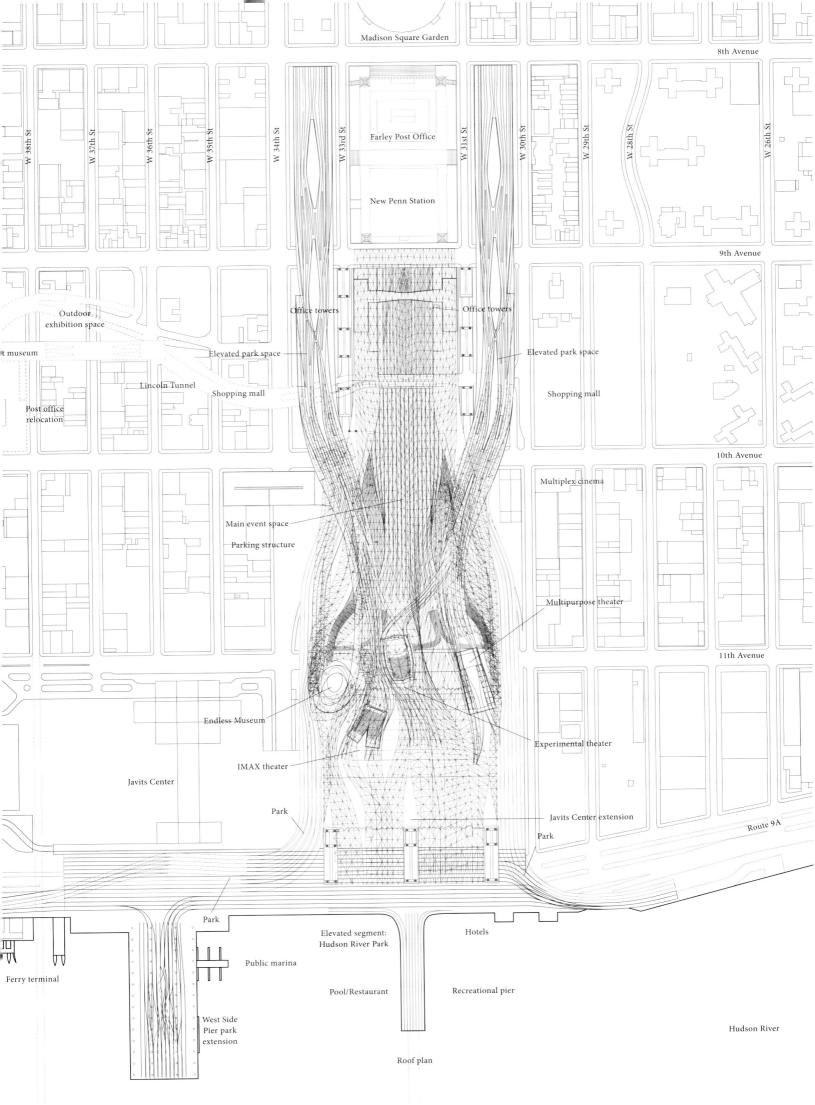

Madison Square Garden

8th Avenue

W 38th St
W 37th St
W 36th St
W 35th St
W 34th St
W 33rd St
W 31st St
W 30th St
W 29th St
W 28th St
W 26th St

Farley Post Office

New Penn Station

9th Avenue

Outdoor
exhibition space

t museum

Office towers

Office towers

Elevated park space

Elevated park space

Lincoln Tunnel

Post office
relocation

Shopping mall

Shopping mall

10th Avenue

Multiplex cinema

Main event space

Parking structure

Multipurpose theater

Endless Museum

Experimental theater

IMAX theater

Javits Center

11th Avenue

Park

Javits Center extension

Route 9A

Park

Park

Elevated segment:
Hudson River Park

Hotels

Public marina

Ferry terminal

Pool/Restaurant

Recreational pier

West Side
Pier park
extension

Hudson River

Roof plan

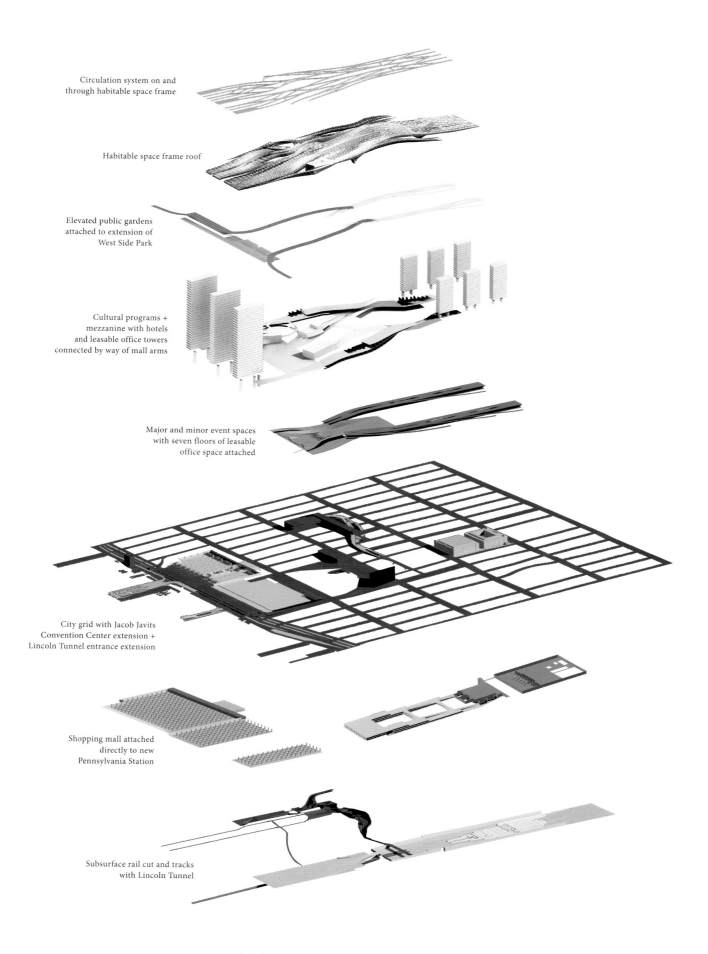

Circulation system on and
through habitable space frame

Habitable space frame roof

Elevated public gardens
attached to extension of
West Side Park

Cultural programs +
mezzanine with hotels
and leasable office towers
connected by way of mall arms

Major and minor event spaces
with seven floors of leasable
office space attached

City grid with Jacob Javits
Convention Center extension +
Lincoln Tunnel entrance extension

Shopping mall attached
directly to new
Pennsylvania Station

Subsurface rail cut and tracks
with Lincoln Tunnel

Exploded isometric view of the development

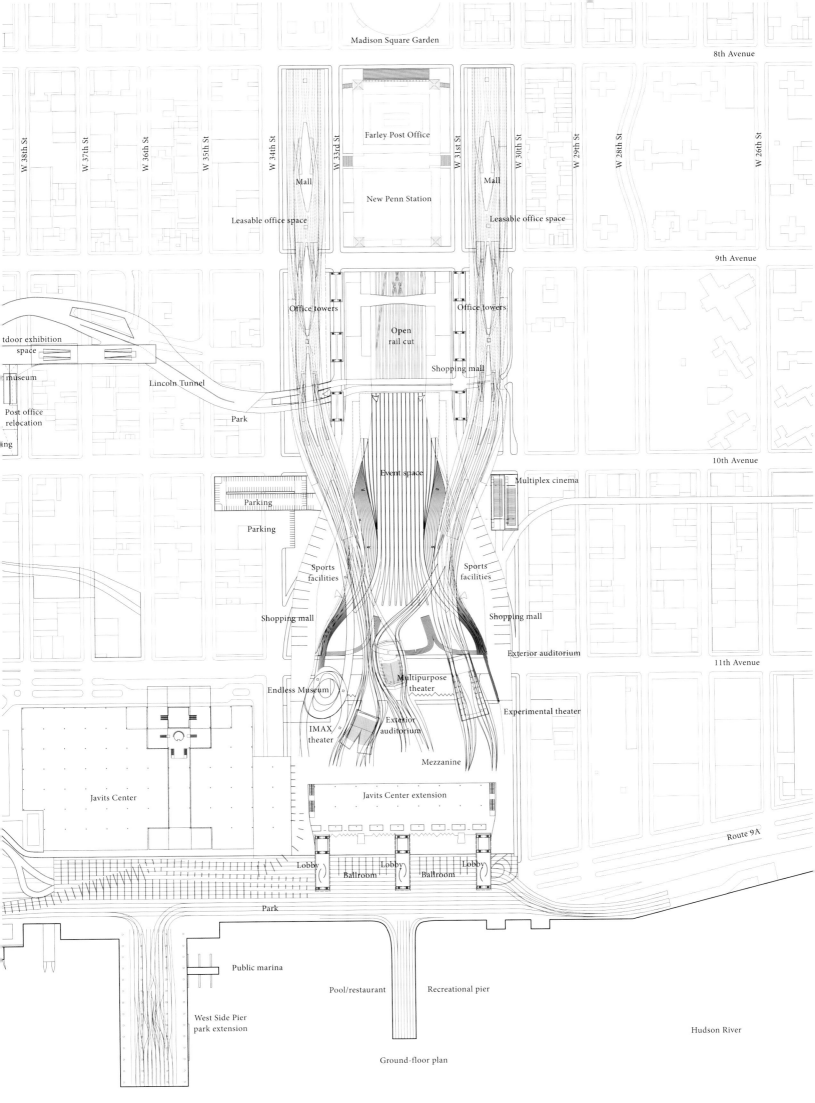

Madison Square Garden

8th Avenue

W 38th St
W 37th St
W 36th St
W 35th St
W 34th St
W 33rd St

Farley Post Office

W 31st St
W 30th St
W 29th St
W 28th St

W 26th St

Mall

New Penn Station

Mall

Leasable office space

Leasable office space

9th Avenue

Office towers

Office towers

Open
rail cut

tdoor exhibition
space

museum

Lincoln Tunnel

Shopping mall

Post office
relocation

ing

Park

Event space

10th Avenue

Multiplex cinema

Parking

Parking

Sports
facilities

Sports
facilities

Shopping mall

Shopping mall

Shopping mall

11th Avenue

Exterior auditorium

Multipurpose
theater

Endless Museum

Experimental theater

IMAX
theater

Exterior
auditorium

Mezzanine

Javits Center

Javits Center extension

Route 9A

Lobby

Lobby

Lobby

Ballroom

Ballroom

Park

Public marina

Pool/restaurant

Recreational pier

West Side Pier
park extension

Hudson River

Ground-floor plan

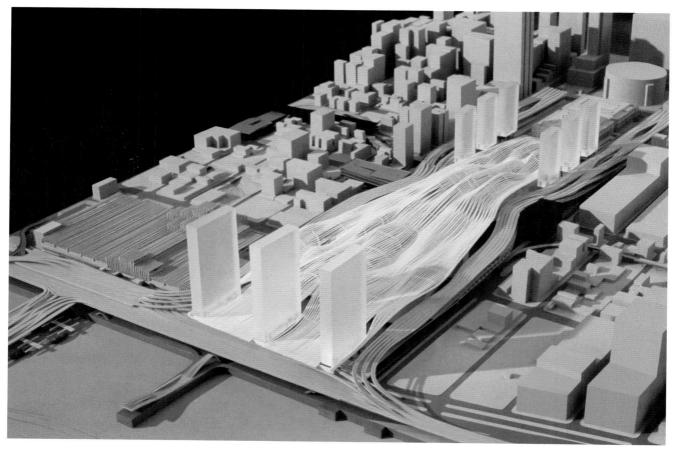

Site model of the West Side Convergence development

Neighborhood Residents

The neighborhood in the immediate area of the site has more residents than one might think, given the distinctly nonresidential scale and programs in this area. Rather than propose new housing (we propose none) in an attempt to ameliorate the scale and create an "urban fabric" suggestive of conventional images of neighborhood, we instead choose to build within the artificial geography of the site, with programs and scales tuned to the surrounding infrastructural elements. The rail yard, Penn Station, the Lincoln Tunnel, the West Side Highway, and the Hudson River all operate at scales, intensities, and speeds not commonly associated with residential use. Yet it is these specific conditions that set this neighborhood and its residents apart from every other in Manhattan. Our proposal takes advantage of these various features, augmenting them in ways that will produce more inhabitable and desirable neighborhood occupation than was possible with the existing vast, monofunctional structures.

As Central Park has shown, green space that is continuous with a large portion of the city—and which penetrates neighborhoods—fosters further growth. Combing the Hudson River Park deep within the site and differentiating it from the rest of the continuous waterfront, the proposal integrates green space with this neighborhood. While its users will come from all points on the island and beyond, its insertion into the grid provides a local focus around which the neighborhood will develop.

More important still, the residents of a city such as New York traverse many neighborhoods, as each one is to a greater or lesser degree an extension of their own. Very few neighborhoods in the city are self-sufficient, and those containing unique amenities become increasingly important. Park space in New York is the rarest of commodities; it is especially important for the city's children. Our project's vast all-weather landscape will establish this neighborhood's urban identity in terms of use for all New York residents, both local and remote.

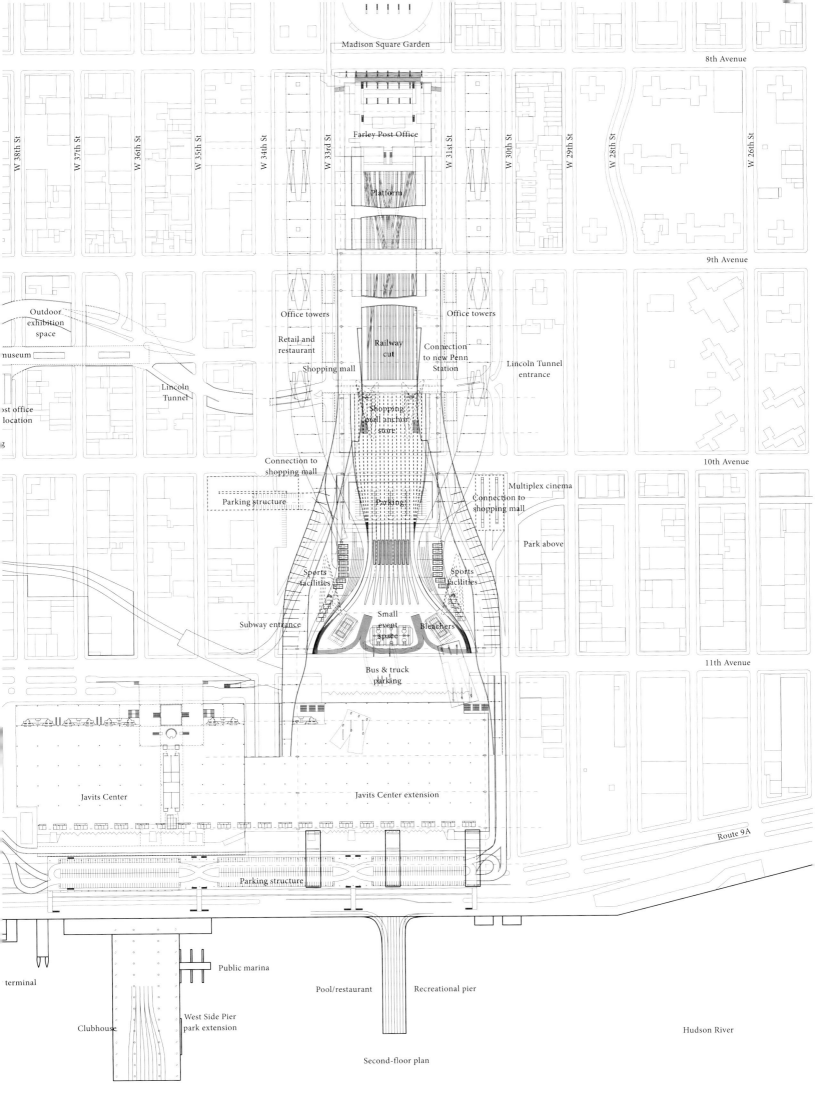

Madison Square Garden

Farley Post Office

Platform

Office towers   Office towers

Railway cut

Retail and restaurant

Connection to new Penn Station

Shopping mall

Outdoor exhibition space

museum

Lincoln Tunnel entrance

Lincoln Tunnel

Shopping mall anchor store

ost office location

Connection to shopping mall

Multiplex cinema

Parking structure   Parking   Connection to shopping mall

Park above

Sports facilities   Sports facilities

Subway entrance

Small event space   Bleachers

Bus & truck parking

Javits Center

Javits Center extension

Route 9A

Parking structure

Public marina

Pool/restaurant   Recreational pier

terminal

Clubhouse   West Side Pier park extension

Hudson River

Second-floor plan

8th Avenue

9th Avenue

10th Avenue

11th Avenue

W 38th St

W 37th St

W 36th St

W 35th St

W 34th St

W 33rd St

W 31st St

W 30th St

W 29th St

W 28th St

W 26th St

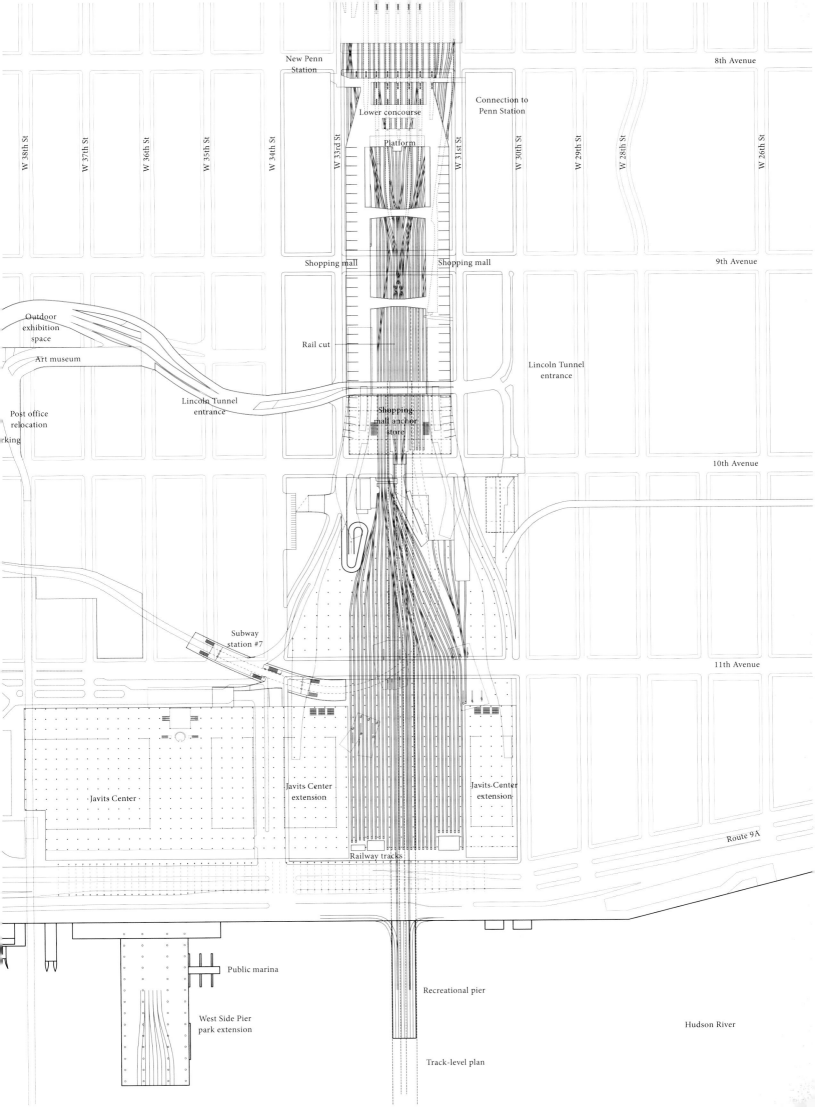

W 38th St
W 37th St
W 36th St
W 35th St
W 34th St
W 33rd St
W 31st St
W 30th St
W 29th St
W 28th St
W 26th St

8th Avenue

New Penn
Station

Connection to
Penn Station

Lower concourse

Platform

Shopping mall

Shopping mall

9th Avenue

Outdoor
exhibition
space

Art museum

Rail cut

Lincoln Tunnel
entrance

Post office
relocation

rking

Lincoln Tunnel
entrance

Shopping
mall anchor
store

10th Avenue

Subway
station #7

11th Avenue

Javits Center

Javits Center
extension

Javits Center
extension

Railway tracks

Route 9A

Public marina

Recreational pier

West Side Pier
park extension

Hudson River

Track-level plan

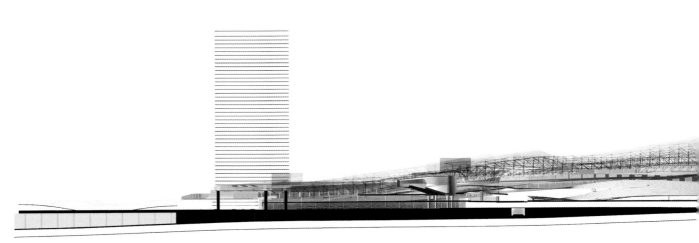

EAST-WEST SECTION

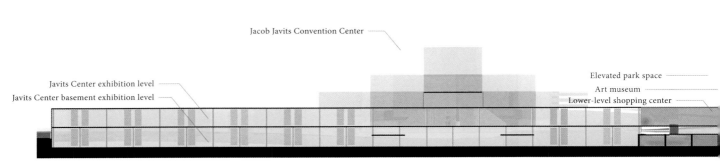

Jacob Javits Convention Center

Javits Center exhibition level

Javits Center basement exhibition level

Elevated park space

Art museum

Lower-level shopping center

NORTH-SOUTH SECTION

Javits Center exhibition hall extension

Basement exhibition extension

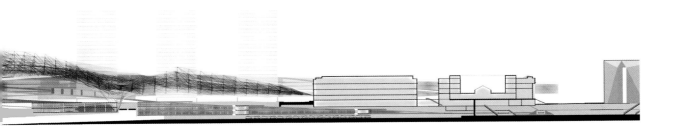

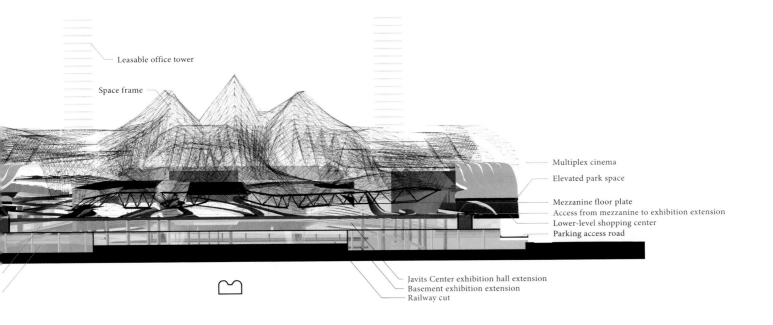

Leasable office tower

Space frame

Multiplex cinema

Elevated park space

Mezzanine floor plate

Access from mezzanine to exhibition extension

Lower-level shopping center

Parking access road

Javits Center exhibition hall extension

Basement exhibition extension

Railway cut

SAGAPONACK HOUSE
2002

Sagaponack House

Located on a two-acre wooded site within a subdivision, the Sagaponack House addresses the synthesis of two potentially antagonistic conditions: the modernistic model of the house as a discrete pavilion, and a formal and organizational strategy that promotes no clear boundary between interior and exterior, building and landscape.

We employed topological models that operate at two scales in the project. A volumetric organization allows continuity between landscape and building, while a fine-scale surface striation integrates and articulates geometry and materials as they shift from the intensive space of the interior to the extensive space of the exterior.

The concept for the house derives from our interest in Mies van der Rohe's American houses—specifically the typology of the freestanding pavilion—stemming from a long-standing admiration for Mies's work and the recognition that within the classical idealist canon, it has achieved a level of perfection (despite our intuitive resistance to this idea). But if the type has already been perfected, where is the possibility for innovation? As Jeffrey Kipnis has pointed out, an analogous situation occurs in music, and particularly in the waltz form, which arguably reached its final definition as a type three hundred years ago. Current innovations therefore are directed not at reinventing the waltz but at elaborating its form. Mies's classical conception of universal space, where the lived world is but an approximation of a higher idea, may be reformulated by shifting the conception of universality away from idealism and toward materialism. Thus, universal space becomes, for us, the space of ubiquitous difference. The architecture of such spaces relies on diagrams derived from material systems whose repetition establishes a field of similarity that has the capacity to develop internal difference.

The design of the Sagaponack House has continuously evolved since its initial inception. Our earliest studies attempted to establish connections between the ground surface and a freestanding pavilion through a series of earth ramps that connected the pavilion's lower and upper floors without violating the perimeter of its volume. Dimensional constraints in both plan and section forced us to abandon this approach. The project moved away from a discrete volume made of surface connections toward a scheme that extends surface-oriented programs associated with landscape into the volume's short end. Notionally, a series of strips extending from the cantilevering volume of the living/dining room become the ceiling and floors of the bedroom volumes, the main entrance stair, the grass ramp to the roof, and the pool volume (which is a continuation

of the internal staircase). These surfaces thus define the principal volumes of the house, which communicate spatially around the nexus of the stair through a literal weaving.

While continuity at the volumetric level is achieved by weaving, continuity among interior and exterior surfaces is achieved through introducing a striated geometry into the surface models. Striation provides a system of repetition that is continuous yet can acquire different materiality depending on location—from roof cladding on one extreme to turf on the other. Striation allows smooth transitions from one material to another through meshing.

The Sagaponack House is thus an extended elaboration of the way in which relations between interior and exterior can be actualized through the action of new architectural paradigms on a modernist type.

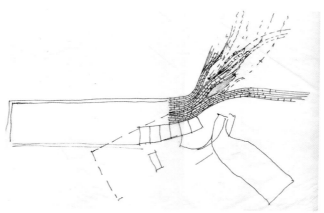

Preliminary sketch of the Sagaponack House's paving scheme

Preliminary sketch of the swimming pool with bathers

OPPOSITE: Preliminary study model

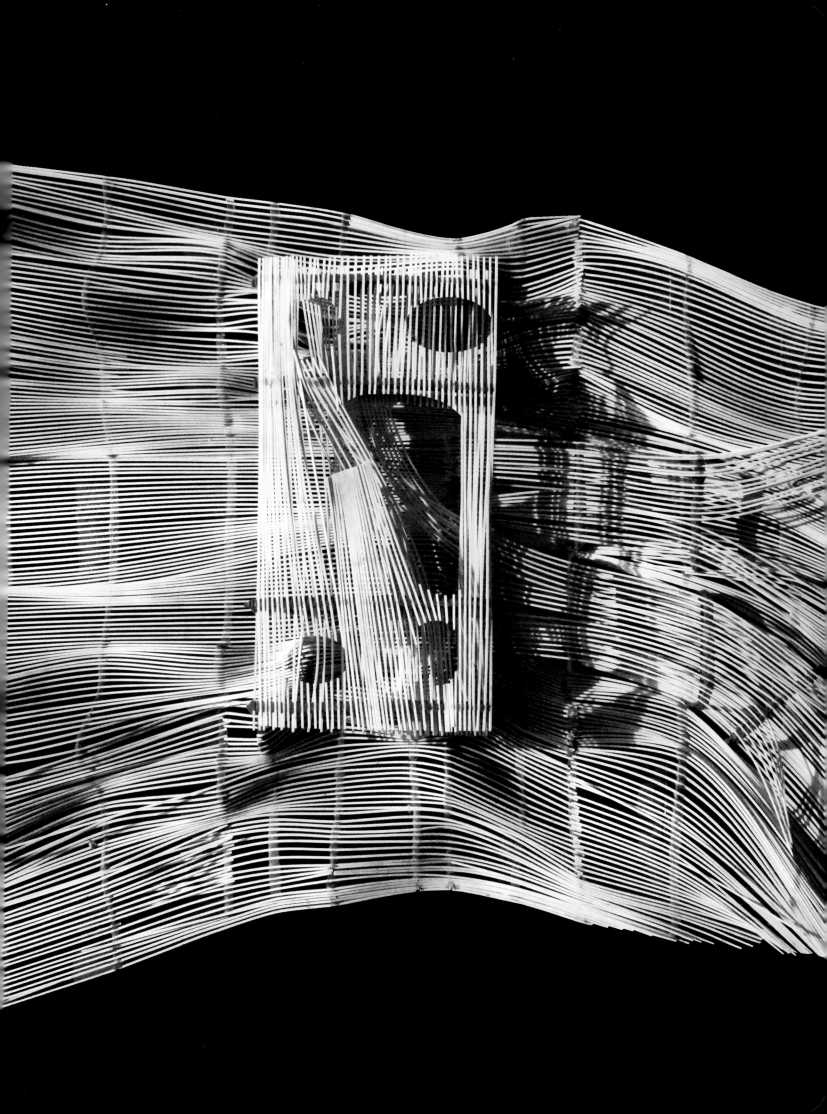

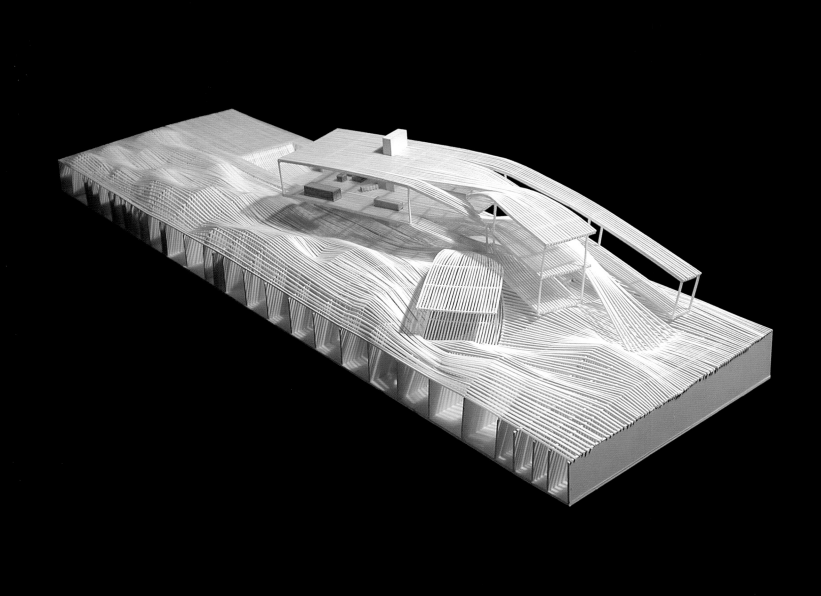

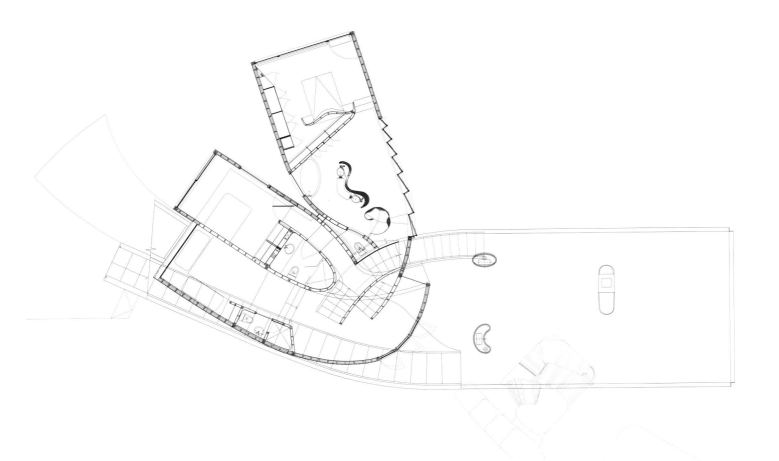

Top-floor plan

OPPOSITE: Lathing model of Sagaponack House

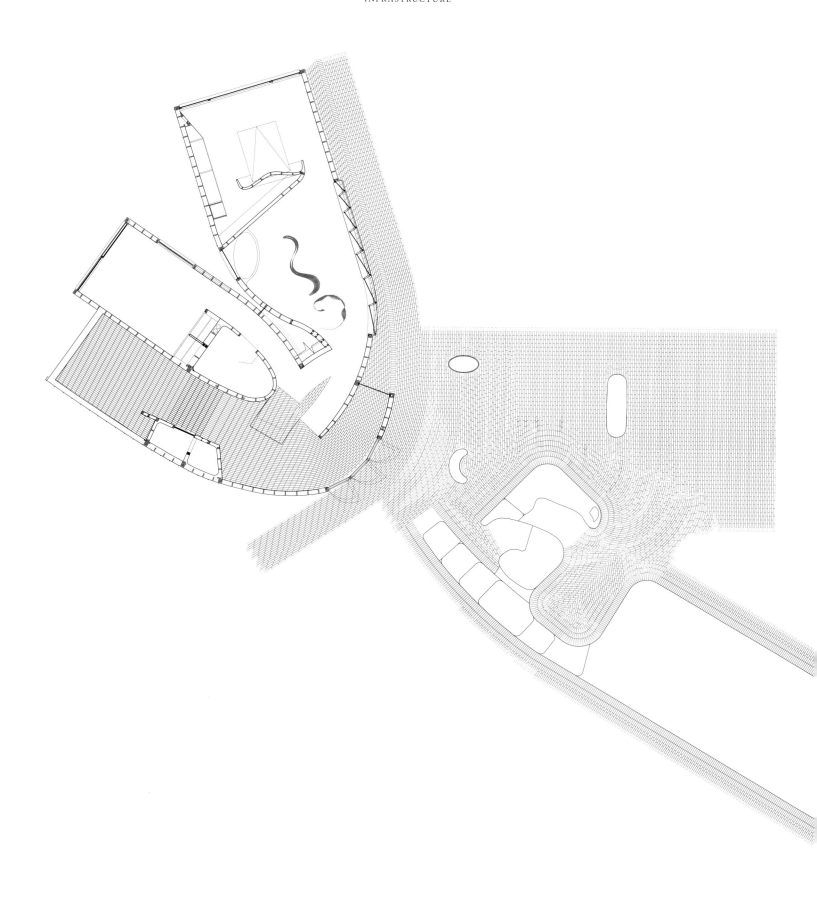

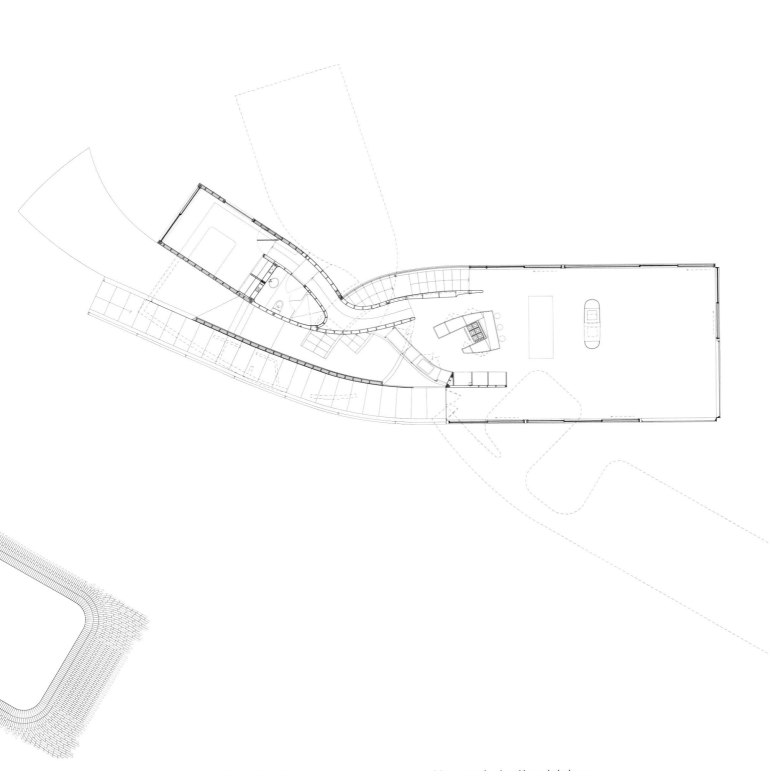

OPPOSITE: Ground-level plan showing the paving pattern of the courtyard and pool beneath the house

ABOVE: Second-floor plan showing living/dining room and bedroom

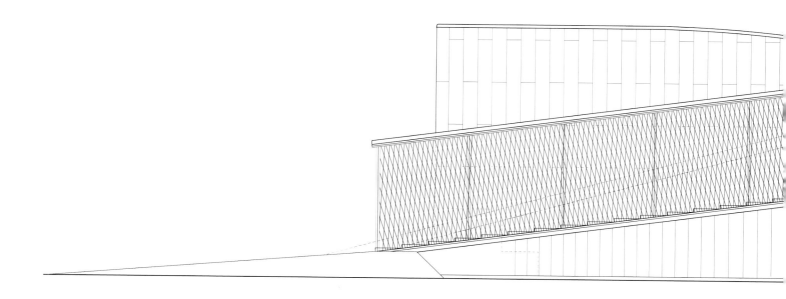

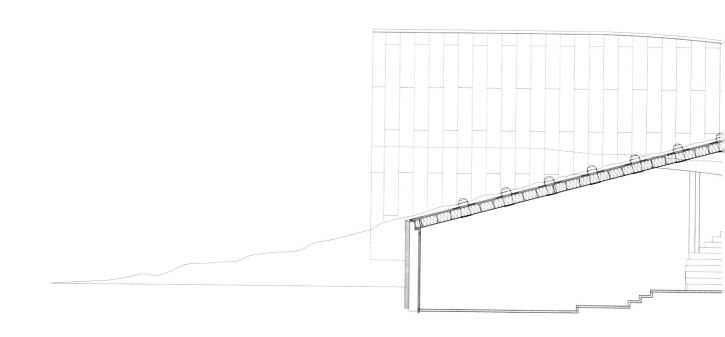

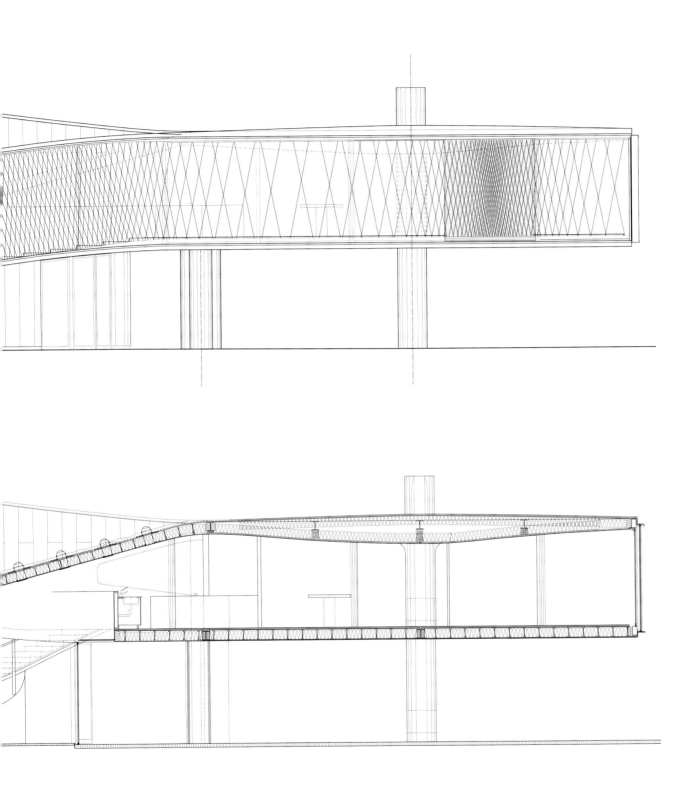

TOP: West elevation

BOTTOM: North–south section

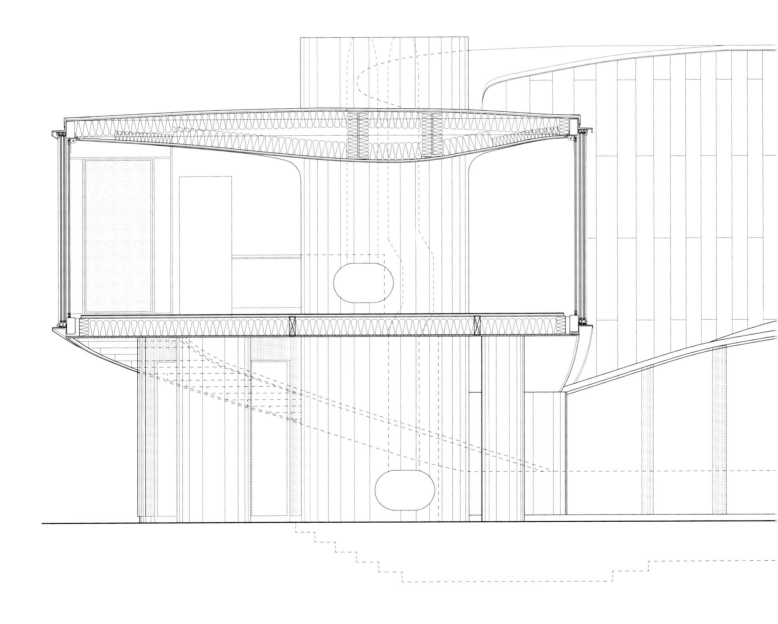

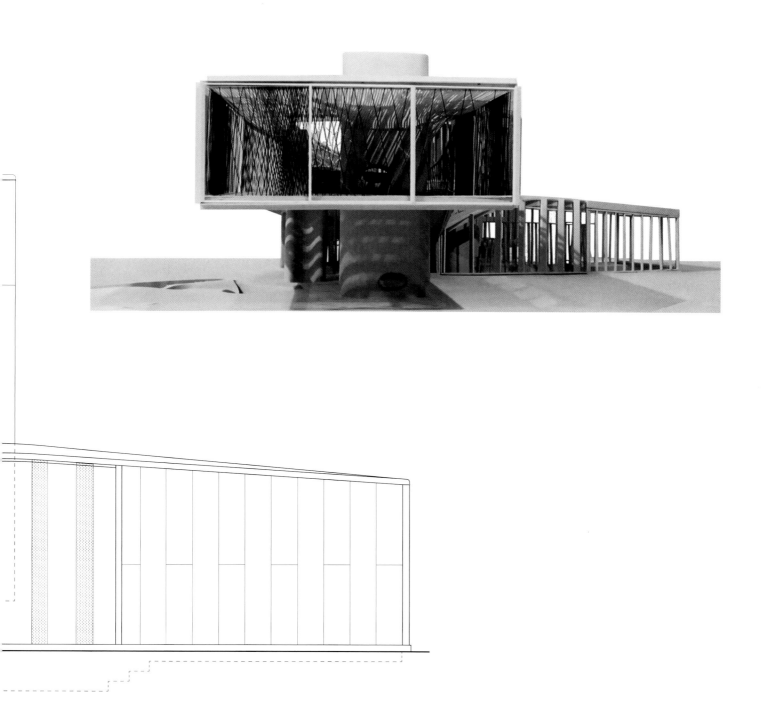

OPPOSITE: East–west section

ABOVE: South elevation

ALISHAN
TOURIST ROUTES
2004

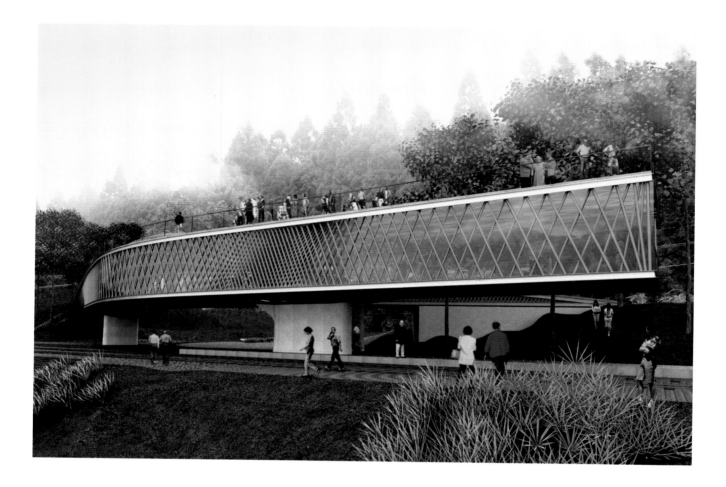

Alishan Tourist Routes

Taiwan is at a cultural and architectural crossroads. As the nation's economy emerges from a legacy of industrialization dependent on low-cost construction and transforms into a service economy based on modern, world-class institutions, cities such as Taipei have experienced accelerated growth and exist in marked contrast to the abundant natural beauty and rich cultures of the rest of the island.

As Taiwan's first wave of industrialization is now complete, we found it crucial to move building culture into a flexible new ecological modality. Our proposal for the development of new tourist infrastructure at Alishan, along an existing railway, acknowledges the site's unique situation. The rail line ascends more than two thousand meters, passing through a global climatic spectrum. Alishan's varied environment has the potential to support an integrated economic model that synthesizes tourism with a textured local ecology.

Originally constructed for the logging industry, the Alishan railroad persists as a corridor through the landscape, passing through four distinct ecosystems as it climbs the

mountain. Our proposal approaches the train line not as a window to its past as a corridor of industry, nor its surroundings as a discrete and untouched landscape. Instead, our plan treats the right-of-way as an opportunity to mediate the space of the cut. A re-creation of a nostalgic architecture and landscape is neither possible nor desirable, as the projection of a strict binary between the natural world and the built environment—between nature and culture—no longer holds. It is thus necessary to fundamentally rethink how technical systems work with and through nature and how nature operates as a technical system.

The beauty of the Alishan landscape is the result of complex systems of relative permanence and impermanence. Its logic of fluctuations and successions is echoed along the thin line of the rail right-of-way. The railroad exists in constant dialogue with contexts both internal and external. Much of the territory through which it passes is agricultural, blurring distinctions between the natural world and the built environment; what might be perceived as natural is bound to production and industry. Instead

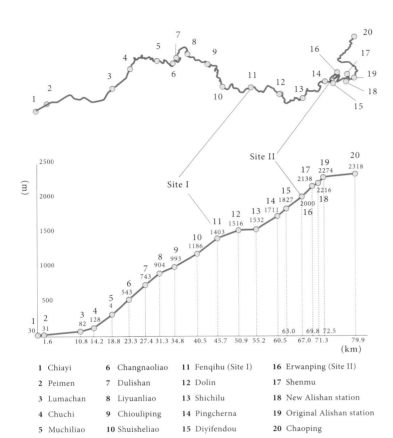

1 Chiayi
2 Peimen
3 Lumachan
4 Chuchi
5 Muchiliao

6 Changnaoliao
7 Dulishan
8 Liyuanliao
9 Chiouliping
10 Shuisheliao

11 Fenqihu (Site I)
12 Dolin
13 Shichilu
14 Pingcherna
15 Diyifendou

16 Erwanping (Site II)
17 Shenmu
18 New Alishan station
19 Original Alishan station
20 Chaoping

of viewing the railway as an autonomous object, we see it as a rich continuum, coexistent with nature and other infrastructures in space and time. Our design smoothly integrates the ecological and technological along a spectrum, ranging from the relative permanence of the corridor itself to the relative impermanence of its flora. As it is impossible to return to an absolute concept of the natural, our project seeks to engender a unique identity for the line that integrates its natural qualities with a novel type of ecological architecture.

The production of various crops from around the globe suited to each climatic shift as the railway increases in elevation enables the Alishan rail line to serve as an infrastructure for the development of locally grown international restaurants and a vibrant ecotourism economy along the line.

OPPOSITE: Rendering of Erwanping Station

ABOVE: Alishan Mountain Railroad, distance and altitude

RIGHT: Climatic zones of the railroad, from tropical (bottom) to temperate (top)

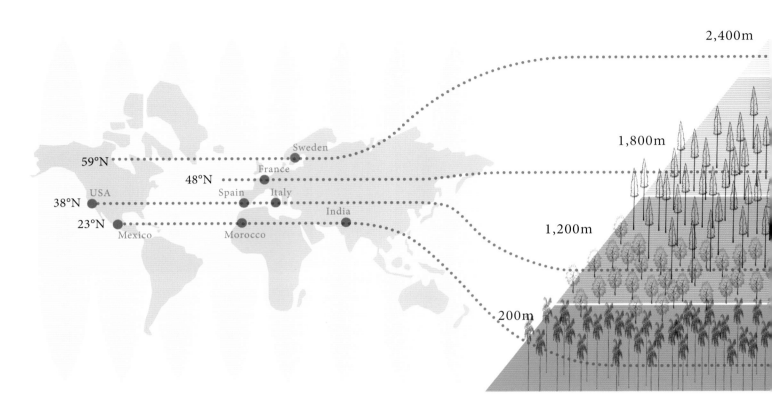

One Degree of Latitude = One Kilometer of Altitude

This equation is crucial to understanding the potential of Alishan Mountain as a tourist site. The ratio allows for ecological, cultural, and material exchange among Taiwan and a family of nations; we maintain that new regionalisms can be constructed at all levels of material practice.

We feel that in order for Alishan to compete as a major tourist destination, the connection between the train line and its ecosystems must be foregrounded in a comprehensive tour experience. It is as important to bring new ecologies to the site as it is to celebrate the existing ones—not through a superficial or invasive overlay of uses but through a projection of new and exciting possibilities that emerge from a coherent engagement with the inherent ecological structure. Our proposal is for an agricultural strip that integrates local food production with farm-to-table international restaurants as a microeconomy of taste tourism. Farming and consumption thus are condensed in an economically productive corridor (rather than creating sprawl) that reconfigures the relationship between sites of food production and consumption into a more integrated system specific to the site.

Agricultural production and distribution no longer follow the antiquated model in which produce grown in the "periphery" (rural space between urban hubs) is shipped to cities for consumption. Today, food production claims about half of the world's landmass and is a complex global system. The development of farming technologies has enabled mass agricultural production at a previously unimaginable scale, yet these modes of production and distribution have had grave environmental and political consequences. With the current world population at 7.2 billion and projected to reach 9.6 billion by 2050, one of the major challenges facing us will be the sustainable production and distribution of food. In our current climate, however, food scarcity is artificial, as farming technologies enable production to the point of excess. Nearly half of all food produced worldwide is wasted each year, while 795 million people (roughly one-ninth of the world's population) are malnourished.

We believe our proposal for Alishan could serve as one of many possible models for rethinking agricultural production, distribution, and consumption. Whereas farming—and specifically monoculture—tends to homogenize the landscape, we propose to accentuate the ecological variety of the four distinct ecosystems through which the Alishan Railway passes, so that each change in climate is marked by a shift in agricultural production. A journey up the Alishan Mountain thus directly reflects the

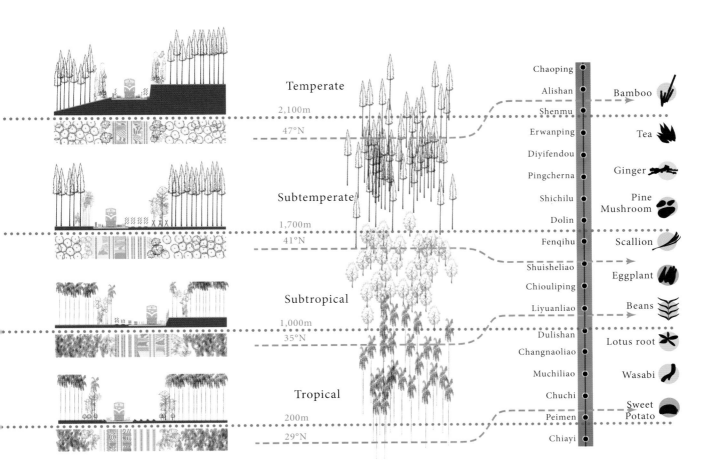

Temperate

2,100m
47°N

Subtemperate

1,700m
41°N

Subtropical

1,000m
35°N

Tropical

200m
29°N

Chaoping
Alishan
Shenmu
Erwanping
Diyifendou
Pingcherna
Shichilu
Dolin
Fenqihu
Shuisheliao
Chiouliping
Liyuanliao
Dulishan
Changnaoliao
Muchiliao
Chuchi
Peimen
Chiayi

Bamboo
Tea
Ginger
Pine Mushroom
Scallion
Eggplant
Beans
Lotus root
Wasabi
Sweet Potato

journey through the mountain's four distinct ecosystems in a gradient of culture, cuisine, and landscape.

Site I, Fenqihu Station, at 1,403 meters (4,603 feet) above sea level, falls within a subtemperate forest climate similar to certain areas of Italy and France. It is therefore possible to grow produce similar to that found in French and Italian cuisine, opening up possibilities for the development of a fusion restaurant featuring locally farmed ingredients. Site II, Erwanping Station, rests at 1,827 meters (5,994 feet) above sea level, falling within a subtemperate/temperate forest climate, similar to areas of France and Sweden. The land surrounding Erwanping Station is ideal for tea cultivation.

As the tourism industry develops along the Alishan Railroad, a new cultural fusion will take hold across a spectrum of practices, including eating, entertainment, and relaxation. A program of cultural fusion entails not simply the transplanting of culture from other countries to Alishan but the production of a wholly new culture. Creative experimentation with cuisine, accented by locally grown ingredients at different levels of the climatic gradient and influenced by cultures from around the globe, will render this site an international destination.

TOP: This climatic section illustrates Hopkins's Bioclimatic Law relating altitude and latitude.

BOTTOM: A proposed restaurant at the Fenqihu Station serves dishes made from ingredients locally grown along the train line.

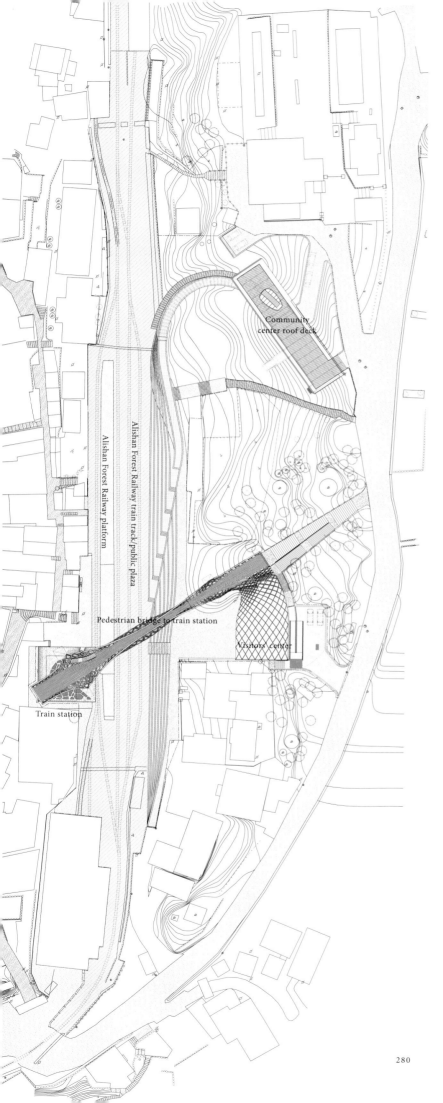

Community center roof deck

Alishan Forest Railway platform

Alishan Forest Railway train track/public plaza

Pedestrian bridge to train station

Visitors center

Train station

Fenqihu Station: Routes through the Site

Historical inertia has kept this vast public space a train yard, but our proposal reimagines it as a piazza. Given that only two trains a day pass through the site, there is an incredible opportunity to transform the space into a resource for tourists, residents, and travelers. In our proposal, paving the right-of-way at Fenqihu with Grasscrete and suppressing the tracks creates a continuous flow of green from the parking areas, a bamboo forest, and a community center to the station and the town. Bleachers line the edge of the piazza along the natural slope of the topography, creating an amphitheater for performances and events. The arching footbridge forms both an enclosure and a gateway.

The high route through the site leads from automobile and tour bus parking down through the new panoramic restaurant and community center building. Across the bridge is a spectacular lookout over the Dustpan Valley. Stairs from the bridge lead down to the station. People arriving by train ascend stone stairs past a bamboo forest to the restaurant, or down into a shopping arcade leading through town. During festivals spectators fill the terraced edges of the piazza and circulate freely. The site can host at least three scales of events on the piazza, the restaurant, and the route through town.

Aerial view of Fenqihu Station site

LEFT: Site plan of Fenqihu Station, the eleventh stop along the train line

OPPOSITE: One-half full-scale model of Fenqihu Bridge, shown at the 2000 Venice Biennale

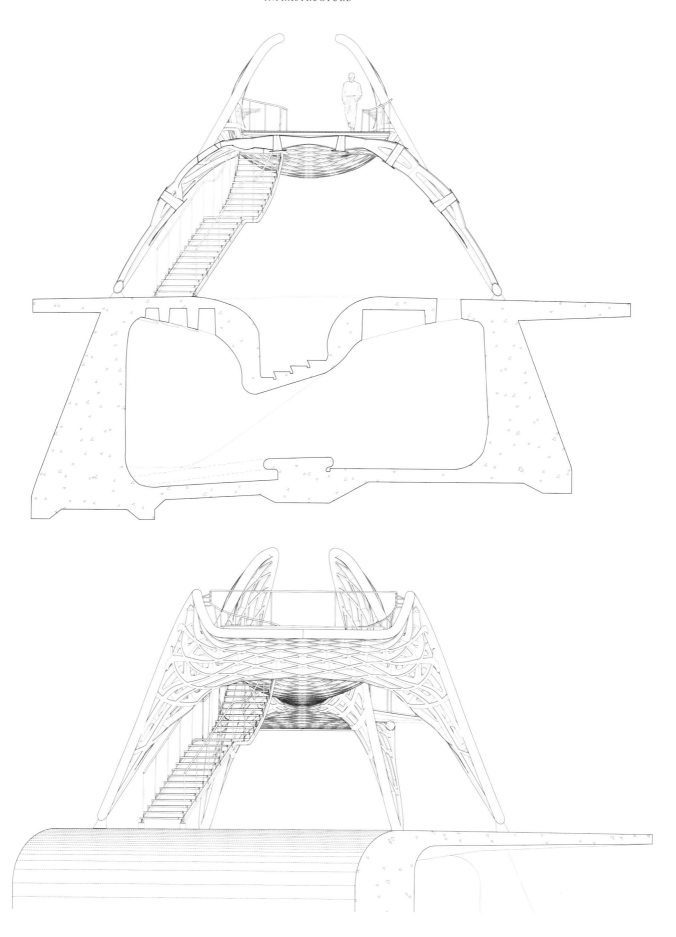

TOP: Cross section through bridge at Fenqihu

BOTTOM: End elevation

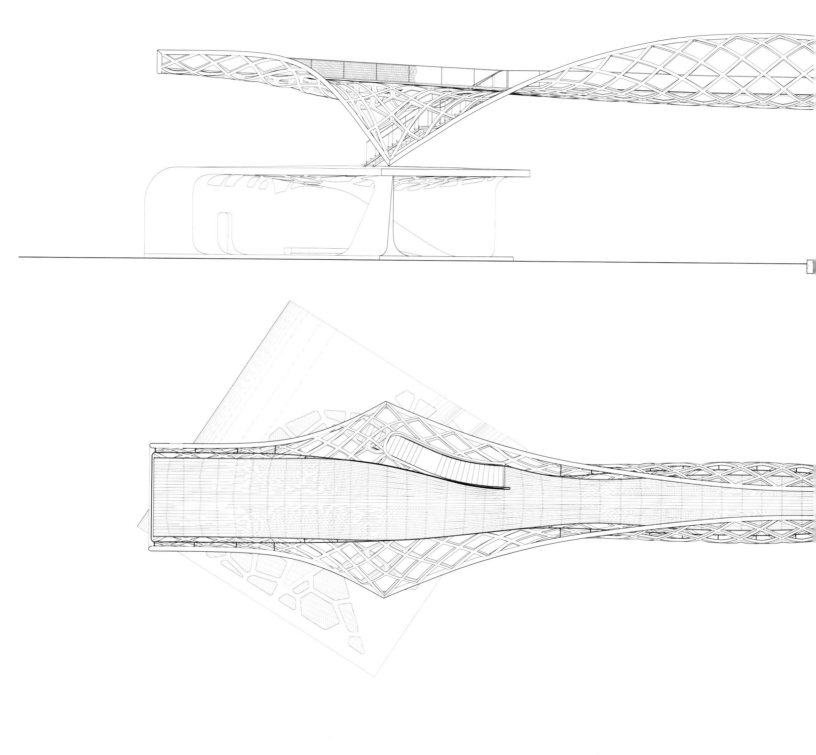

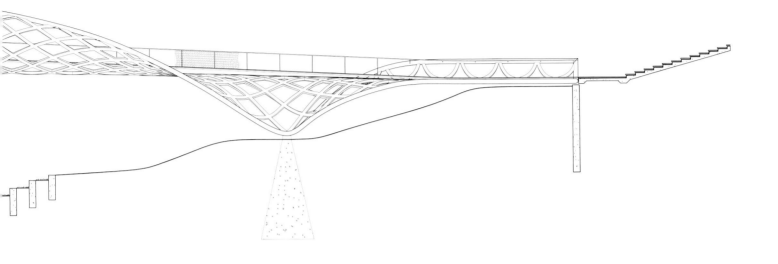

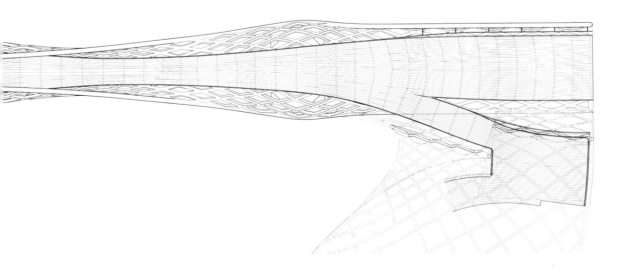

TOP: Elevation of bridge at Fenqihu showing station and scenic lookout

BOTTOM: Plan of bridge showing connections to station and restaurant

Legend

	Existing tree
	New tree
	Existing building
	Grass
	Asphalt paving
	Bluestone paving
	Wood deck

0 m   10 m   20 m   30 m   40 m   50 m

Erwanping Station

Rather than assembling functions in a collection of separate buildings, we propose an economical glue-laminated (glulam) decking system to integrate buildings smoothly with each other and into the landscape. Zones for centralized functions and for rest, including the station, greenhouses, and a hostel, branch off of a central spine. An elevated boardwalk forms a platform that allows for spectacular panoramic views of the sunrise. The boardwalk, in turn, leads down into recreational spaces, including gardens, a circuit of paths through the landscape, and a swimming pool. The building itself is openwork, with low appreciable building mass and minimal foundation impact.

ABOVE: Site plan of Erwanping Station complex

OPPOSITE TOP: Preliminary study model of the station and observation decks

OPPOSITE BOTTOM: Laminated object models of Fenqihu Station

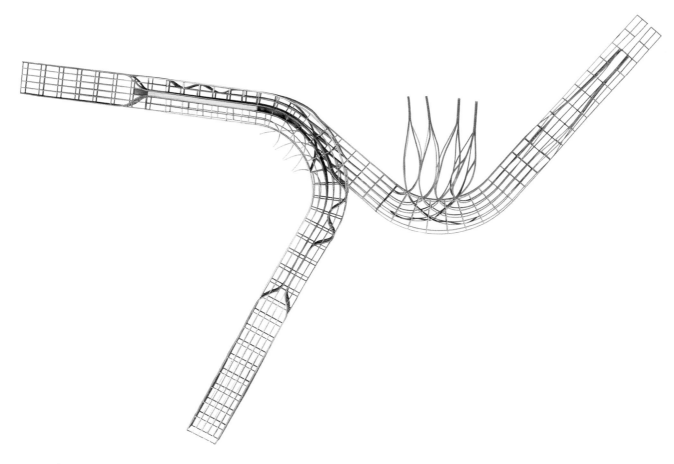

Materials

Wood is the primary construction material for the buildings and infrastructure in both sites. Rather than employing it in a traditional manner, our design treats wood as a flexible organic element in a spectrum of constructional systems: geodetics, glulam, and ruled surfaces.

The existing gravel rail bed is resurfaced with a Grasscrete system of planting and masonry blocks modulated to create varying densities of green and paved surface; denser areas of paving become principal axes of movement across the site. The existing rail tracks are depressed into the Grasscrete system, allowing pedestrians to move across the track areas without disturbing the operation of trains and opening up the formerly monofunctional space to major public uses. The train line, regarded as a barrier since its inception, now becomes a space for celebration and connection.

Each geometry locks into a certain material system: spacing, periodical fluctuation, course, and the forms over which the train line travels. Elements of graphic integration include structural spacing and planted rows. Their complex overlap creates new patterns, which are no longer reducible to their constituent parts.

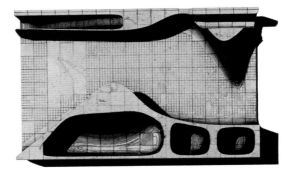

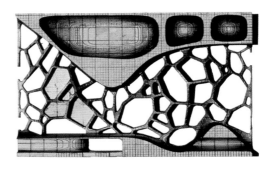

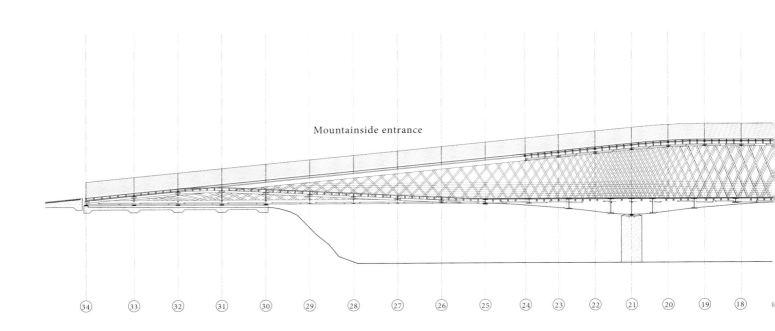

Mountainside entrance

| 34 | 33 | 32 | 31 | 30 | 29 | 28 | 27 | 26 | 25 | 24 | 23 | 22 | 21 | 20 | 19 | 18 |

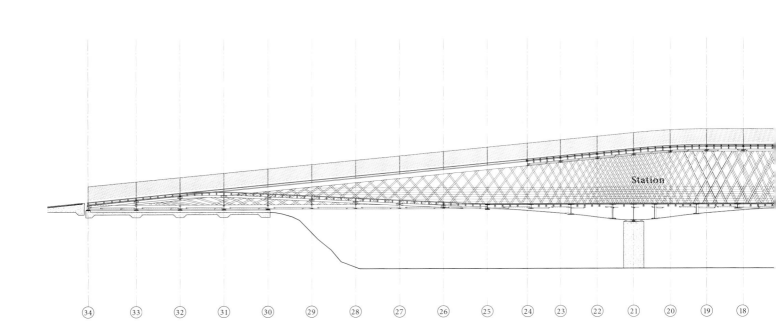

Station

| 34 | 33 | 32 | 31 | 30 | 29 | 28 | 27 | 26 | 25 | 24 | 23 | 22 | 21 | 20 | 19 | 18 |

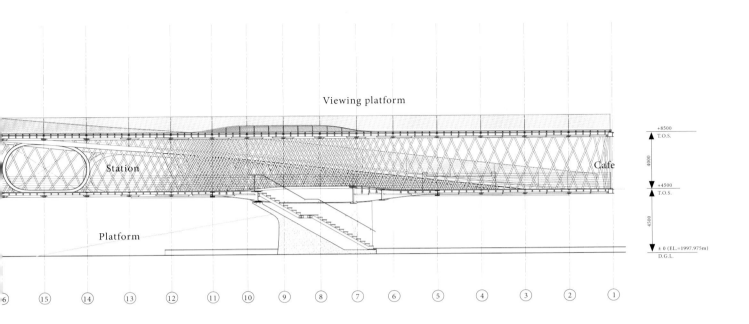

Viewing platform

Station

Platform

Cafe

+8500
T.O.S.

4000

+4500
T.O.S.

4500

± 0 (EL.=1997.975m)
D.G.L.

(16) (15) (14) (13) (12) (11) (10) (9) (8) (7) (6) (5) (4) (3) (2) (1)

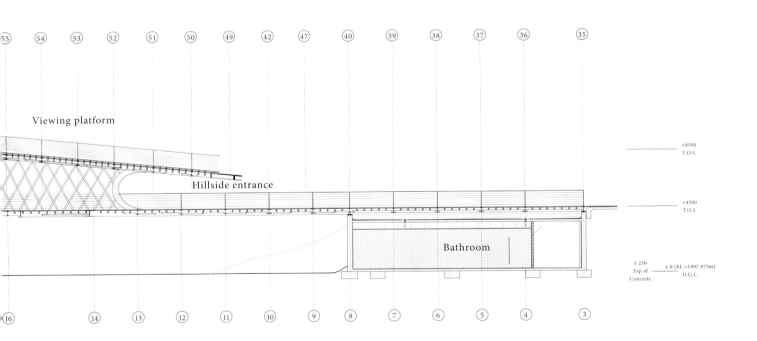

(55) (54) (53) (52) (51) (50) (49) (42) (47) (40) (39) (38) (37) (36) (35)

Viewing platform

Hillside entrance

Bathroom

+8500
T.O.S.

+4500
T.O.S.

± 230
Top of
Concrete

± 0 (EL.=1997.975m)
D.G.L.

(16) (14) (13) (12) (11) (10) (9) (8) (7) (6) (5) (4) (3)

TOP: Longitudinal section through West Fork, containing Station

BOTTOM: Longitudinal section through East Fork

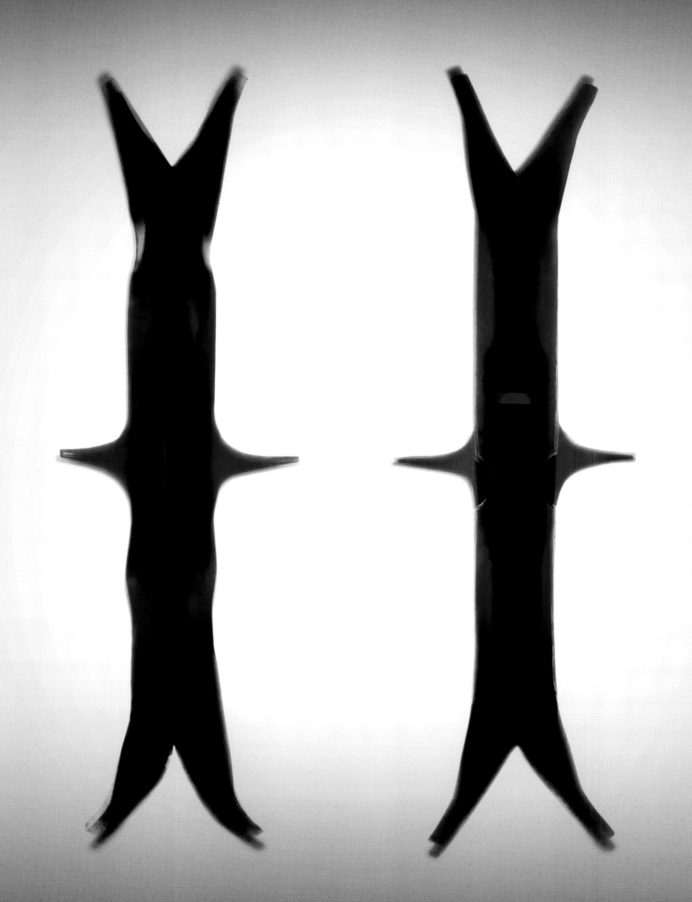

IIT STUDENT CENTER
1998

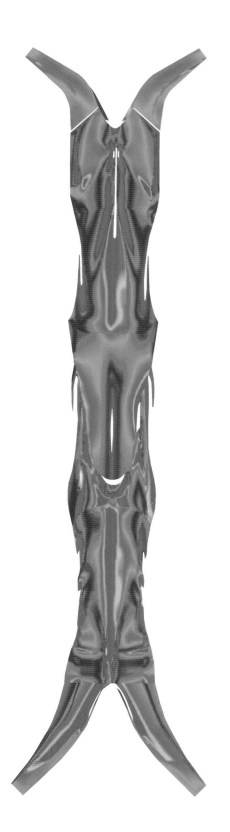

Top surface draws interior activity to roof garden.

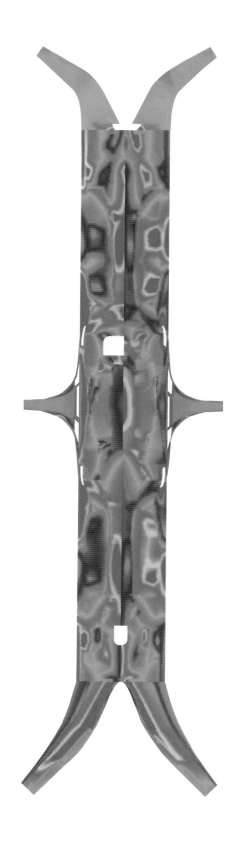

Waveform generates structural and programmatic
continuity across all floors.

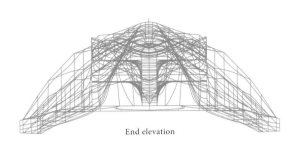

End elevation

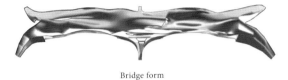

Bridge form

Bridge densities

Located at the geometric center of the IIT campus, this highly trafficked bridge will serve as a concourse and the hub of student activity, providing central access to all parts of the campus.

The new Student Center for IIT will be a programmed bridge over State Street—a human infrastructure enlisting service, circulation, and landscape to connect the two sides of the Miesian campus. This new construction connects into the streets, feeding the existing pattern of discrete buildings on the ground created by Mies, yet remains stylistically distinct from the architecture of the campus.

The highly programmed bridge over State Street deploys permeable edges to manage flows of activity, redressing the split (created by the El train and cold weather) between the east and west areas of IIT. Flow-based organization, interlacing "fingers" of space, and new terrains inside and out provide multiplied opportunities for users and adjacencies.

It was essential for us to develop an approach by exploring specific operations on the proposed site, rather than setting up abstract procedures to be played out later. Given the importance and particularity of the program and context, we have presented our design research at length.

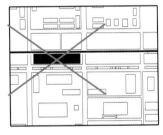

NOT OBJECT...

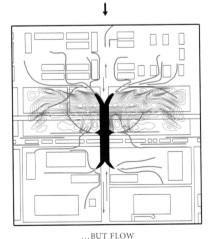

...BUT FLOW

Student center straddles central axis of campus, managing major circulation routes.

CULTURAL INSTITUTIONS

———

ENVIRONMENTS

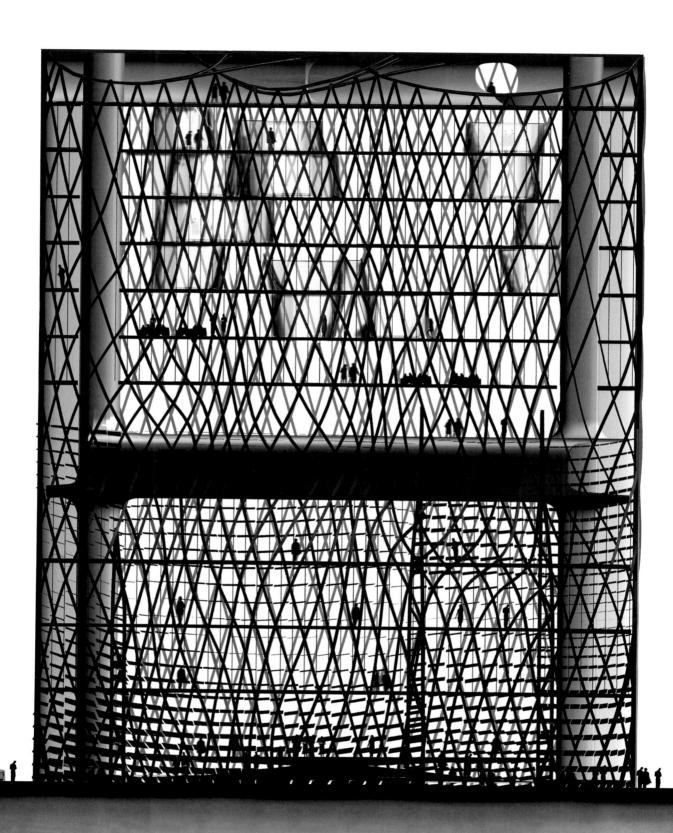

EYEBEAM MUSEUM
2001

Eyebeam Museum

The crucial question facing the design of a museum of art and technology paradoxically does not center on technology per se but foregrounds the physicality of space itself. As technology constantly remakes itself on both material and immaterial levels, it is pointless to fix the configuration of a building based on technologies that are fugitive in their effects and whose software and hardware undergo continuous replacement. The spaces of this new type of museum must balance flexibility of use with environments that are highly specific in terms of mood and character. Such a balance between the generic and the inflected has only recently become possible. The model of flexibility propagated by neo-modernists involves a neutral and inert scaffolding, which by attempting to be good for everything is in the end good for nothing. Avoiding this impoverished model, we propose instead a series of flexible yet qualitatively vibrant environments for exhibition. Neutral exhibition spaces thus can exist in this museum without determining overall architectural effects.

Our proposal for the Eyebeam Museum embodies a comprehensive conception of media. Beyond the relatively familiar associations of media with electronic technologies and dematerialization, there is a more inclusive model founded on the logics of material computation (of which electronic media is a subset). Architecture as building is coextensive with this model and was our motivating concept. Above all, the building is based on flows: of people, energy, matter, technology. Its envelope and major public spaces synthesize the apparent opposition between the impermanence of electronic media on the one hand and the material presence of a museum building on the other.

Architecture has traditionally been conceived of as a material practice, and our work incorporates dynamics as a material bloom enlisting structure, organization, and space. One outcome of this is that here, our ethic is not to overdetermine space as a rigid container for new media or as an attempt to *be* new media. Rather, we recognize the importance of the architecture for a museum of art and technology as a properly physical venue for engaging new media in embodied social space. We are living in a time of profound change brought on by advances in technology and the resulting social and cultural changes. A museum of art and technology requires at the very least a critical reassessment of the relationship between technology and architecture. We felt that following safe formulas would not only fail organizationally and economically but would (perhaps more importantly) be a lost historical and cultural opportunity. The architecture for a museum of art and technology must be quantitatively specific yet qualitatively

ineffable, producing the conditions and ambiance essential to the reception of the new, yet open enough to accommodate whatever it might become.

The ground floor is the nexus of all activities. The major functions—exhibition, education, and public uses— are both visible and directly engageable from the street. Spatially, the lobby extends horizontally and vertically, incorporating three connected yet distinct scapes. Horizontally, the groundscape—a vast, open space gently rising toward the rear of the building—incorporates a large, flexible area for exhibitions and events, the cafe, and the store. Vertically, the north- and south-facing facades are mediascapes developed along similar formal and organizational principles, yet animated by disparate systems of flow. Both are modulated screens designed to respond to and regulate minute fluctuations of information. The south-facing facade regulates environmental fluctuations of solar and wind energy, serving as a vast heat pump for the building's interior. Conversely, the north-facing facade—extending six stories behind the street entrance—develops a vast surface that carries a fully automated and interactive digital exhibition system: the mediascape. These scapes and the volume that they describe are not disconnected elements but a coherent series of public environments. Indeed, an exchange across systems—from digital technologies to environmental effects—reaches beyond the visible into the realm of the physical. For instance, heat that bleeds off the north-facing media wall heats the building in winter and cools it in summer.

The lobby provides direct access to exhibition spaces above and below through two elevators located on the east and west sides. An escalator bank on the far western edge of the lobby provides access to and egress from a black box theater, which is located below grade. A dedicated lobby is on an intermediate level between the ground floor and the theater level. The theater is versatile: it can be rearranged to accommodate any type of content and uses the latest technology in display systems, including digital film and HDTV projection, as well as the latest acoustic sound systems. A sector of the ground floor on the far eastern edge of the building serves as a tenant lobby, for which there is a dedicated entrance and elevator (these zones will convert to museum use after fifteen years).

Our concept for changing uses over time emphasizes simplicity and adaptability. The building's floor plates above grade are separated into two semiautonomous volumes. The volumes, comprising five and seven stories respectively,

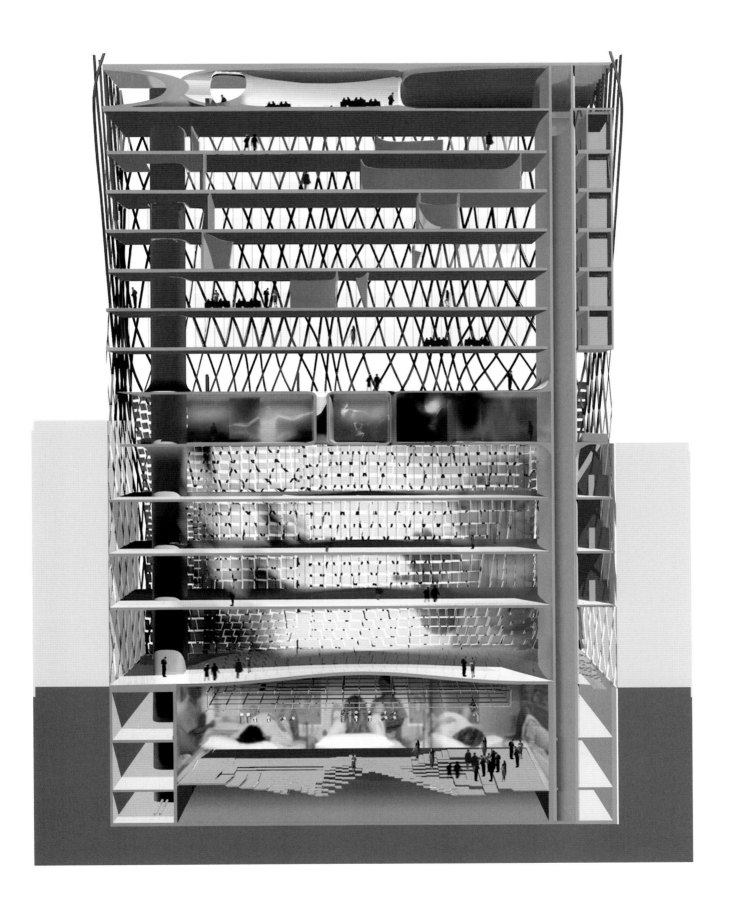

Section of the Eyebeam Museum reveals the various specialized gallery spaces, auditorium, and virtual reality and multimedia rooms.

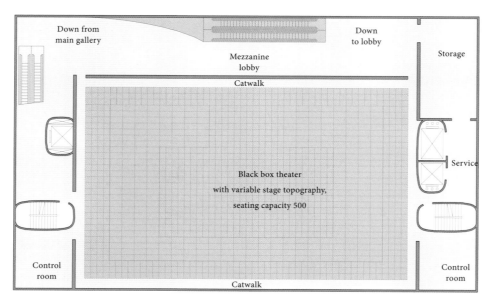

Black box theater plan

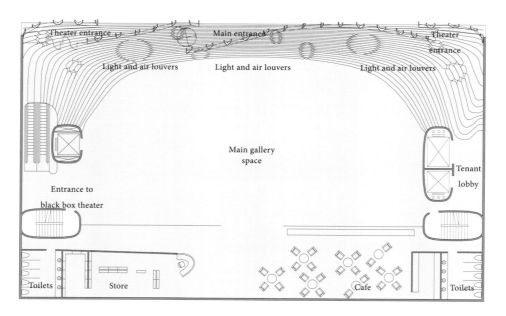

Main gallery plan

Mixed Media and Digitized Matters: Eyebeam Museum

Ila Berman

In their Eyebeam Museum competition proposal, Reiser + Umemoto question the presumption that the relationship between art and technology should be limited to digital and electronic media and instead attempt to locate these within a larger definition of the technological on the one hand and a broader context of media on the other. Their strategy compresses the attenuated spectrum that links the nonphysical dimension of digital and electronic media to its physical material correlates, using architecture as the instrument to then conflate the manifold effects of the digital with other structural, technological, and environmental matters. In this context, electronic and digital media are not limited to being referents of architecture, nor to being diagrammatic, generative, and representational tools in design. Rather, these media are reconceived as synthetic building materials with intrinsic formal properties and functional capacities, returned to matter to conjoin the informing potential of the diagram and the physical medium to be manipulated. It is here that notions of media (as a form of information) and medium (as both a mode of material expression and a matter to be expressed) are conflated.

The idea that the digital and electronic might be integrated with the architectural as a material medium rather than a conceptual or formal tool is certainly not a novel concept. It is a tactic that has been employed by many architectural practices, including those of Rem Koolhaas and Herzog & de Meuron, most often as a method to dematerialize (as well as rematerialize) the surfaces of architecture. The building structure is reduced to a cinematic prop for an immaterial skin—a canvas or "white wall of signification"—that collects graphic and semiotic information simultaneously in order to materialize a surface of perceptual affects. If, in the era of the mediated billboard architecture of Venturi, Rauch and Scott Brown, the proposition was to reduce the materiality of architecture to the thinness, and potential clarity, of the semiotic, in its current reformulations (despite the propensity of the digital toward the immaterial), information has been recast in perceptual and material terms. Thus, the criticality of this strategy revolves around the inversion of traditional architectural hierarchies, that is, the displacement of frame with surface and structure with skin, while continuities between previously delineated oppositions are simultaneously engendered, as the sign is immersed in matter and the optical embedded in tactility.

Rendering of the virtual mediascape (left), lower galleries (right), and lobby below

Although these conditions are strategic effects of Reiser + Umemoto's Eyebeam proposal, what is perhaps more significant is the notion that the rethinking of the digital in both logistical and material terms (in opposition to the inverse proposition that considers its significance in its capacity to dematerialize architecture) might enable its synergistic communion with other composites of matter, both architectural and nonarchitectural, artificial and natural. In this context, the building becomes both the technological instrument and the synthetic medium of exchange. In order to do so, the catalogue of architectural materials must be opened to incorporate the limits of an ever-widening spectrum that seemingly separates the most artificial and immaterial technologies of our "infozoic era" from the most primitive and primordial of natural matters, both of which, for different reasons, have traditionally remained in the realm of the nonarchitectural.

Rendering of the Eyebeam Museum from across the West Side Highway

That we equate the electronic and the digital with the immaterial and the impermanent renders the intangible and transient nature of their technologies inherently antiarchitectural. Architecture has traditionally been aligned with the tectonic, the material, and the permanent as opposed to the informational, the insubstantial, and the fleeting. Although the digital, in particular, has the capacity to inform space, to computationally generate and diagram its formal parameters and to represent these within a virtual world (which includes the realm of holographic projection and all forms of extended virtuality), in the physical world, the digital remains mute—a mode of mathematical, semiotic, and graphic consistency without embodiment. It is perceived as a form of expression that lacks substance and thus is dependent on the corporeality of the surface of its projection or transmission. Nature, on the other hand, constituted by a protean and polymorphous manifold of matter, has, despite its intrinsic and complex structural logics, been traditionally defined, within the realm of architecture, in terms of "molecular" material composites that precede "molar" organization. Apparently lacking the other side of architectural embodiment, they require the delimiting capacity of form and the geometric stability of structure in order to fix their mutability and produce the possibility of inhabitable space. Nature is perceived as the variable flux of matter—potential fluid substance without form or meaning, lacking a stable form of expression. Or so it would seem. Perhaps these definitions persist only from the perspective (the frame and vantage point) of architecture, since it is the "architectural"

itself that divides up the world into oppositional propositions and that limits our understanding of both the artificial matters of the digital and the natural forms of expression of the environment. We must understand, however, that each of these simultaneously contain variable modes of both expression and content, form and substance, and that when both are conjugated with those of the architectural, they produce multiple forms of media mixed with the digitized flows of matter.

In the Eyebeam proposal, the emphasis shifts from the horizontality of the earlier occupiable landscapes (Yokohama Port Terminal, West Side Convergence, and the Water Garden) to the verticality of the optical skin. The notion of visibility, especially insofar as it crystallizes the programmatic focus of the art museum, was critical to the thinking of the project. Architecture not only became a prop for the visible but also the filter through which visibility was actualized. Just as Reiser + Umemoto's Flux room makes visible an ever-changing magnetic field activated by its occupants, the interactive media wall on the north and thermodynamic sun shades on the south of the Eyebeam project materialize and make palpable the continuous rhythmic modulations and interactions of the flows of human occupation and atmospheric flux. Taking its formal clues and geometric form of expression from the insistent pixelization of the digital (which translates material intensities into mathematically distinct gradients), the architecture of the thermodynamic sun shades produces a diagrammatic digital field that translates the fluidity of atmospheric flows into quantifiable attributes and optically perceptible movements. Atmospheric traits of expression such as environmental fluctuations of solar and wind energy are thereby regulated and materialized by systems and technologies that are simultaneously architectural and digital. Air flow, triggered by temperature differentials and their resulting gradients, is spatially and optically registered by this architectural matrix of lightweight elements that rarefies ambient matters (through the geometry of the diagram) at the same time that it materializes the invisibility of its flows. The index produced is a digital analogue of the flow of environmental matters, embodied through the tectonic geometry of an architectural mode of expression.

This environmental screen is proposed as an alternate interactive media wall. It is linked to the digital, not only by its pixelated form and the discrete individuation and limited set of potential positions of its constituent elemental units but also by the initial homogeneous consistency of the projective field that indexes these flows of matter and energy. This homogeneity is critical to the way in which the digital rarefies and diagrams matter by translating qualitative material differences (immanent differences in kind) into an abstract statistical field of smooth and rhythmic variation (abstract differences in degree). The repetition of the same is thus transformed into rhythmic difference, an itinerant geometry that divides material continuity into discrete bits of information, where movement is revealed through statistical microgradients (of position, spacing, and direction) that are incrementally yet continuously related across the field. Just as the superficial, repetitive, or rhythmic lines on the curved surface plot of the Water Garden describe the surface of its form by imbuing it with a structure and engendering its perceptibility, in the environmental screen, the forms of expression of fluid atmospheric events are made visible through the differential frequencies, rhythms, and directionality of this digital field of locally interacting architectonic elements. This might be understood as an alternative and inverted form of datascape. Rather than transposing information into form and then infusing it with material substance, this form of datascape provides a logical format, a digital field and architectural geometry for the distribution of fluctuating material information: from datascape to digitized matter. The environmental screen thus becomes an interactive media wall, an architectonic scanner that operates in real space and real time. Architecture emulates the technological form of expression of the digital and engages the material form of expression of the atmospheric.

In the Eyebeam project, the diagram is both geometric and material, in the sense that it doesn't simply index the geometry of a given or proposed matter-event to be substantiated by the permanence of built form (as is the case of the variegated trusses of Yokohama or the modulated space frame of the West Side project). Rather, it is truly a material diagram—not simply a diagram of matter that effectuates flows of matter-energy but a modulated geometry that lives, is actualized, and is immanently intertwined with the matter-event itself. Perhaps what is most critical is that this diagram not only imparts visibility to the imperceptible flows and exchanges of material and information, but that it also facilitates their circulation. The inverse effect of the architectonic digitization of this fluctuating ambient energy on the south wall is the simultaneous immersion of the material effects of the real interactive media wall within the environmental field. Despite the presumed immateriality of artificial electronic and digital media, they are real composites of fluid matter-energy (expressions of matter) that emit light and heat, which Reiser + Umemoto draw upon to literally heat and cool the building. Artificially produced matter-energy is thus circulated with natural atmospheric flows, which are then regulated, transmitted, and instantaneously cast in the digital and technological systems of an architectural machinic assemblage, where the extremes of the artificial and the natural, digital and environmental, immaterial and material, mechanistic and vital, are synthesized in a complex web of circulating exchanges of matter, form, and information.

The implicit negation of environmental and gravitational manifestations of matter in modern idealizations of space is both exposed and inverted in Reiser + Umemoto's proposal for the museum. The notion of environmental control is replaced by modulated environmental exchange and the stratification of systems (of circulation, structure, occupation) is replaced by their complex synthesis. As circulation systems and inhabited spaces are transformed into structural elements, the presumed weightlessness of the modern curtain wall, historically subordinate to the dimensionality of the Cartesian frame, is animated with space, impregnated with material, and imbued with weight. It is literally transformed into a hanging curtain, a fluid tectonic mesh impinged upon by the forces of gravity. Just as the inhabitable spaces of the museum achieve flexibility by being pulled away from the edges of the building's frame to be locally distributed in space, the framing system of the curtain wall on the exterior is intentionally pulled away from the orthogonally stratified plates that systematize the space of the museum, to locally express its own deformative animation. The smooth, floating fields of interior elements thus find their counterpoint in the smooth continuity and amorphous form of the layers of external cladding, both of which occupy rather than frame space. Similar to the thermodynamic screen, this cladding is another machinic assemblage that is simultaneously a real diagram of matter. The literal fluidity of the cable-net system locally responds to and expresses real deformations. It is conflated with an oblique geometry that facilitates lateral movements along and through the abstract mobility of the diagonal (such that the oblique generates curvilinear inflections) and also geometricizes them. That is, the system's immanent forces are organized and diagrammed in order to be drawn into the realm of the perceptible. This mutable, breathing skin, which oscillates between the mechanistic and the vital, transforms the face (facade) of architecture into an animate body that fluctuates between the presumed visibility of the digital and true hapticity of its matters.

Section of main level with black box theater below, showing variable performance terrain

CHILDREN'S MUSEUM
OF PITTSBURGH
2001

Site plan

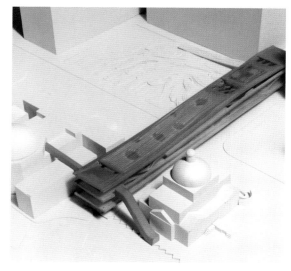

Overhead view of physical model

Pittsburgh is a city of bridges, both physical and spiritual. This characteristic is at once a historical feature and a potential model for future building. The present isolation of the new Children's Museum site calls for the implementation of a general conception of bridging at many scales and toward many ends. Architecture will be enlisted to join diverse communities, neighborhoods, and people of all ages.

Traditional museum design has generally fostered closed and static architecture—monuments separated from the public and the life of the city. Instead, our proposal involves an innovative building that is light and inviting, a place of activity and flow that stimulates new forms of perception in children and encourages activities in a real-world setting. Hovering over the site, the new museum establishes the Allegheny Center neighborhood as a focal point for the joy of childhood, rejuvenating the surrounding neighborhoods and serving as a critical link to the stadiums and developments along the river's edge.

The new museum bridge spans the western edge of historic Allegheny Center, effectively linking the existing children's museum, the Buhl Planetarium, and a newly conceived parkscape, and replacing a defunct fountain at the southernmost end of the site. The distinguished classical character of the existing Children's Museum building makes it an ideal ceremonial space and principal entry into the new architectural domain. Visitors entering at ground level through its domed central space pass through a glazed link, then ascend to the new structure above.

While the rectilinearity of the bridge answers the need for a discreet yet elevated volume between two historically significant buildings, the new museum's internal organization speaks to an entirely different set of conditions. Instead of filling the building volume with conventionally stratified floor plates, a rhythm of

interwoven slabs and structure offer an architecture of visual and physical connectivity. The architecture for this building is not simply another neutral scaffolding. At once bounded and safe, it provides an active, flexible environment able to contain many varied activities and programs within a simple enclosure. The museum's internal organization is thus a hybrid between the logics of landscape design and normative building. The result yields fluid, ambient spaces, not institutional in character but productive of varied environments of light, tactility, color, and terrain—essential components of a child's world.

Central to the philosophy and performance of the new museum, "real stuff" programming has been designed so as to directly communicate with all museum functions, including galleries, classrooms, studios, party rooms, and a public cafe. These nodal points in the building not only allow direct physical communication among programs but also engender a palpable thematic link to permanent and changing exhibitions in the gallery spaces. This crucial proximity produces an entirely new kind of museum experience, where "real stuff" is taught to the child in a tangible way, practiced by the child in "real stuff spaces," and potentially demonstrated by the child in the open galleries.

For example, floor surfaces in a gallery might hold earth for planting; the architectural materiality thus supports "real stuff" programs carried out amid blooming flowers. Color, texture, and materiality all contribute to a child's heightened awareness of ambient space. The grand can be combined with the intimate, the hard with the soft, the light with the dark, the smooth with the striated. Light, sound, and touch are not considered extraneous to architectural concerns; instead, these qualities can be made to correlate with issues of sustainability. The articulated roof louvers we designed maximize solar gain during the

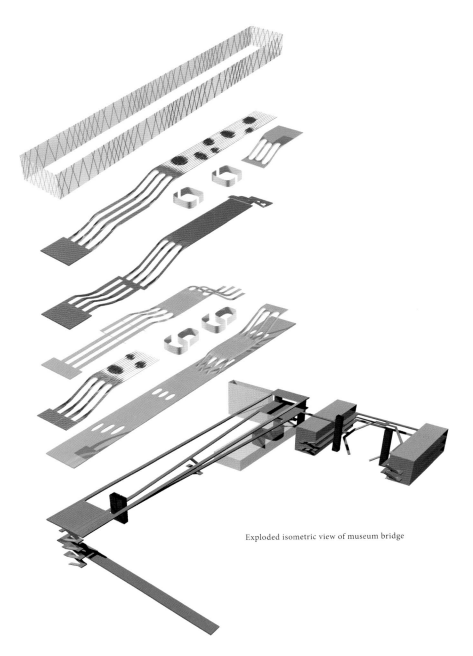

Exploded isometric view of museum bridge

day. Positioning the louvers to open to the east heats up the building in the morning during winter and protects the building from afternoon heat in summer. Far from being neutral to the program, this element demonstrates sustainability as a pedagogical concept exceeding the role it plays in architecture.

Significant buildings throughout Pittsburgh testify to the legacy of steel and glass in the city's economic history. Our choice to use these materials for the structure and envelope of the museum is particularly poignant in this context. The latest advances in these technologies have given new human qualities of texture, form, lightness, and color to what have been formerly considered cold, hard, and unemotional substances. This alchemy, when properly expressed in building, imbues spaces with excitement, warmth, and intimacy.

Children are our most precious resource and our hope for the future. In a world increasingly saturated with chimeras of the disembodied, the immaterial, and the virtual, it is important to assert the primacy of embodied activities in space. Contrary to popular opinion, the most innovative architectural projects in recent years focus on dynamic models of matter—or "stuff"—in order to develop new forms of space and experience. As the epitome of such a project, a children's museum illustrates our responsibility to foster future creativity by building spaces that nurture children's imaginations and allow them to realize their greatest potentials.

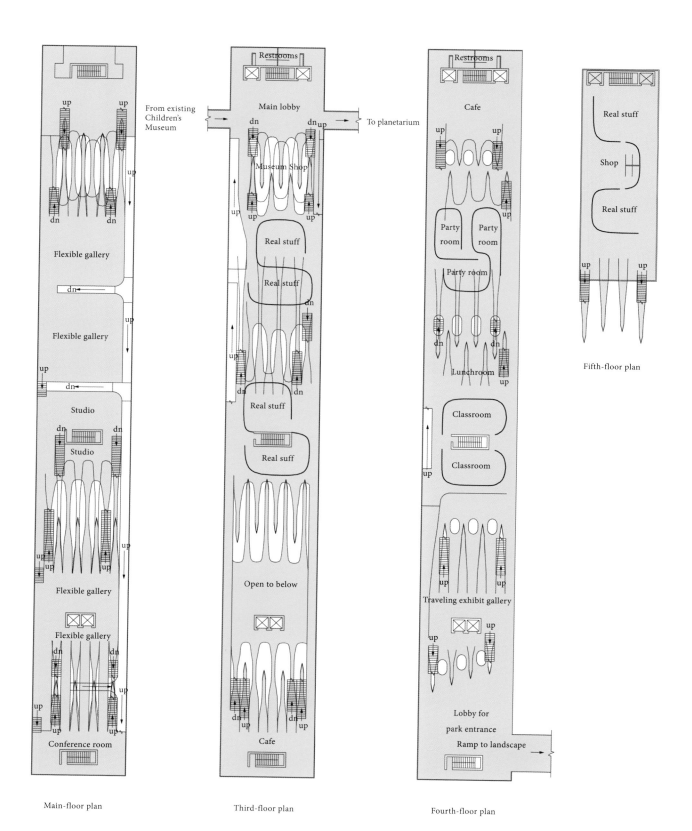

Main-floor plan

Third-floor plan

Fourth-floor plan

Fifth-floor plan

TOP: Rendering of top-floor children's play area

BOTTOM: Rendering of flower garden in "real stuff" space

THE NEW MUSEUM
2003

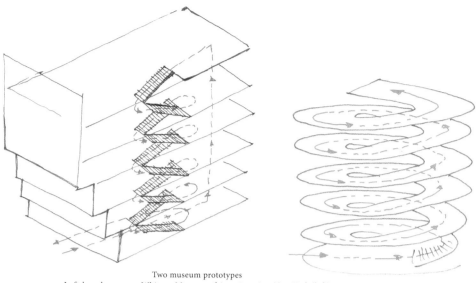

Two museum prototypes
Loft-based museum: Whitney Museum of American Art, New York (left)
Museum of movement: Solomon R. Guggenheim Museum, New York (right)

Facade as Public Space: the New Museum

We propose a new museum type for the New Museum: a dynamic hybrid between a museum of fixed movement process and one of neutral flexibility. These historic typologies, incommensurable and mutually exclusive, required an architecture that fixed the organizational structures, curatorial possibilities, and spatial character of the institution. Exemplified by the Guggenheim and the (Breuer) Whitney models, respectively, the museums of fixed movement process and neutral flexibility are no longer viable. Our proposal for the New Museum allows the institution itself to change and fluctuate in accordance with the character of its exhibitions. This concept taps into a new paradigm of modularity, one that with equal ease generates spaces for existing exhibition typologies and provides for the deployment of the unforeseen.

The New Museum has the opportunity to configure itself within one typology as a whole or to display a continuous variety reflective of exhibition cycles and artistic and technological innovation. This flexible concept of display can accommodate not only traditional forms of art but also experimentation by both curators and artists.

The museum will occupy a signal position in the cultural revitalization of the Bowery in lower Manhattan. Located at the termination of Prince Street, its public facade announces its position as a vanguard institution and the focal point of the commercial and cultural axis extending from SoHo into the East Village. The facade is conceived as both a spectacular announcement of the New Museum's presence relative to the neighborhood and a filter to its activities. More than a sign or a window, it is a dynamic programmed zone that displays the movements and activities of people within. Viewed from the interior, it is an integral part of the architectural promenade, a space where the museum connects to the life of the city.

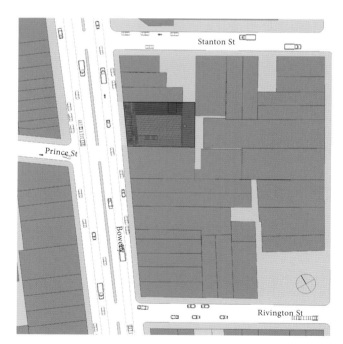

The New Museum building is located on the Bowery at Prince Street.

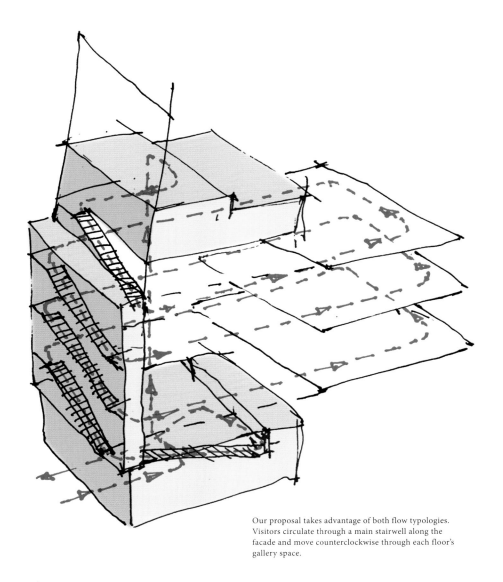

Our proposal takes advantage of both flow typologies. Visitors circulate through a main stairwell along the facade and move counterclockwise through each floor's gallery space.

Sequence

Museum visitors enter the lobby, passing under a media lounge to ticketing and coat check before descending stairs to a black box theater or entering the primary circulation elevator.

The gallery sequence is top-down. Visitors take the elevator to the sixth-floor special projects gallery, then begin to descend across the facade. A single, gentle run of stairs crosses the entire facade, ensuring that visitors must traverse each exhibition space before descending to the floor below. Thus, a spiral of descent not along but through the museum is established. Visitors emerge at the southwest corner of each story; moving counterclockwise, they circle the perimeter of the building to its northwest corner to descend again. Upon reaching the second floor, the spiral of descent shifts to the rear of the building, drawing visitors past a public program sequence starting at the mezzanine level that includes a media lounge, restaurant, and cafe. The rear stairs, passing between the media lounge and the restaurant, arrive at ground level overlooking a skylighted gallery; visitors pass the museum store before exiting to the street.

Lobby and streets are coextensive, with bookstore below, media gallery above.

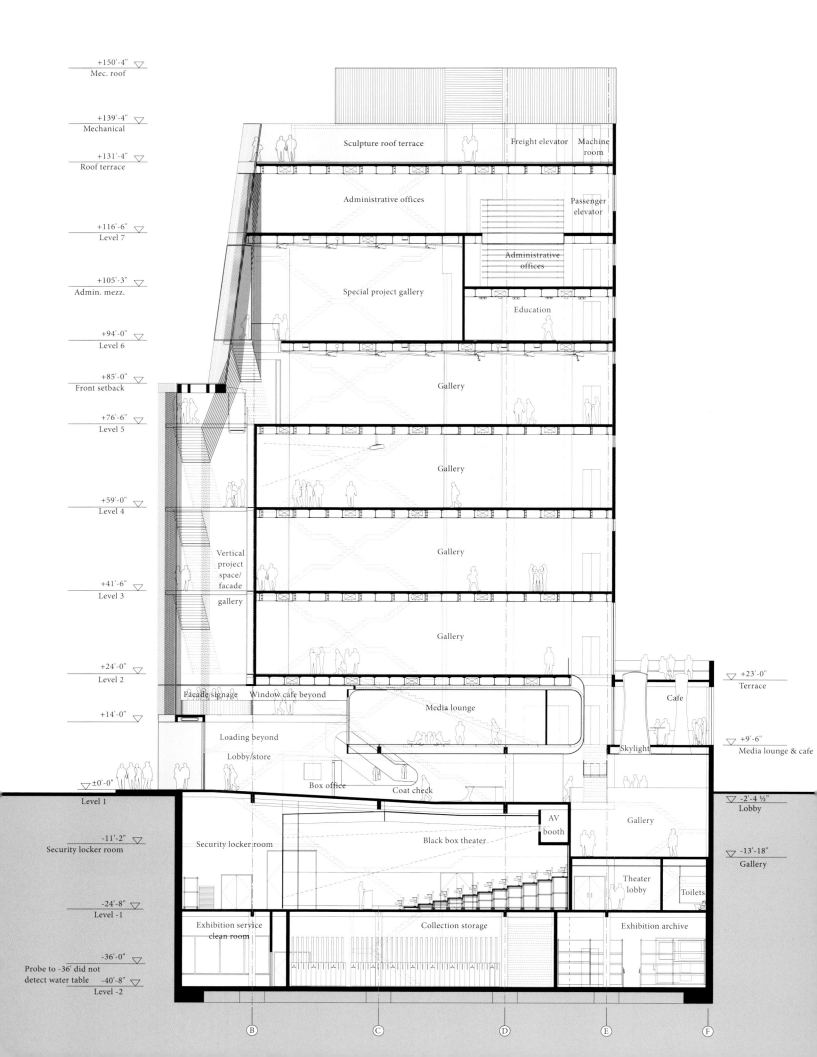

+150'-4" ▽
Mec. roof

+139'-4" ▽
Mechanical

+131'-4" ▽
Roof terrace

Sculpture roof terrace   Freight elevator   Machine room

Administrative offices   Passenger elevator

+116'-6" ▽
Level 7

Special project gallery   Administrative offices

+105'-3" ▽
Admin. mezz.

Education

+94'-0" ▽
Level 6

+85'-0" ▽
Front setback   Gallery

+76'-6" ▽
Level 5

Gallery

+59'-0" ▽
Level 4

Gallery

Vertical project space/ facade gallery   Gallery

+41'-6" ▽
Level 3

Gallery

+24'-0" ▽
Level 2

▽ +23'-0"
Terrace

Facade signage   Window cafe beyond   Media lounge   Cafe

+14'-0" ▽

▽ +9'-6"
Skylight   Media lounge & cafe

Loading beyond

Lobby/store

Box office   Coat check

±0'-0" ▽
Level 1

AV booth
Black box theater   Gallery   ▽ -2'-4 ½"
Lobby

-11'-2" ▽
Security locker room   Security locker room

▽ -13'-18"
Gallery

Theater lobby   Toilets

-24'-8" ▽
Level -1

Exhibition service clean room   Collection storage   Exhibition archive

-36'-0" ▽

Probe to -36' did not detect water table -40'-8" ▽
Level -2

Ⓑ   Ⓒ   Ⓓ   Ⓔ   Ⓕ

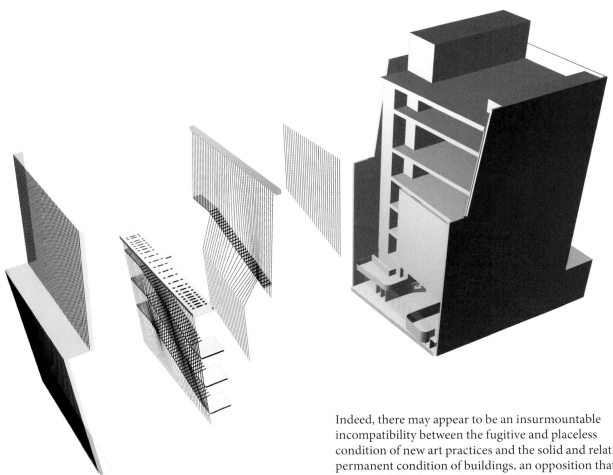

Recent high-profile museum projects in cities around the world have suggested no clear guidelines for the design of an institution as dedicated to the unprecedented as the New Museum. Indeed, the proliferation of new art practices has confounded both architects and curators alike. The simple fact that much new art is ostensibly portable has led many to erroneously conclude that a building is not only unnecessary but an impediment to its production and proliferation. This has produced a panoply of projects for the museum as object—an attempt through architecture to make the museum one more artwork among many. But we believe that architecture, far from being irrelevant, has a necessary role to play in integrating art and culture. This role requires that the museum building be more than just an object, but rather an active and novel component of the museum as an institution.

ABOVE: Axonometric diagram of the exploded facade. The moiré effect is created through the layering of rod-net screens, which are simultaneously structural and produce an atmospheric effect.

OPPOSITE: North section

Indeed, there may appear to be an insurmountable incompatibility between the fugitive and placeless condition of new art practices and the solid and relatively permanent condition of buildings, an opposition that has been upheld by both architects and avant-garde pundits. A reactionary model attempts to relocate architecture within the realm of new technologies, arguing for a "virtual architecture" that denies the power of spatiality altogether. It would be a mistake to extrapolate a fixed architecture from current trends in technological production; the very nature of innovation betrays the folly of such a strategy. Nor would it be productive to produce yet another neutral, flexible scaffolding that by attempting to be good for everything is good for nothing. Rather our project seeks new ways in which the spatial organization of the museum in its full context will allow for maximum integration of activities at all scales.

The design of the New Museum represents a unique opportunity to implement a fundamentally new museum typology, enhancing the relationship of the museum to the city and dynamically reimagining the institutional experience. New exhibitions must not only encompass a wide range of types and requirements but also do so in a context that will attract an increasingly diverse visitorship, whose expectations will become radically enlarged in terms of scope and interest.

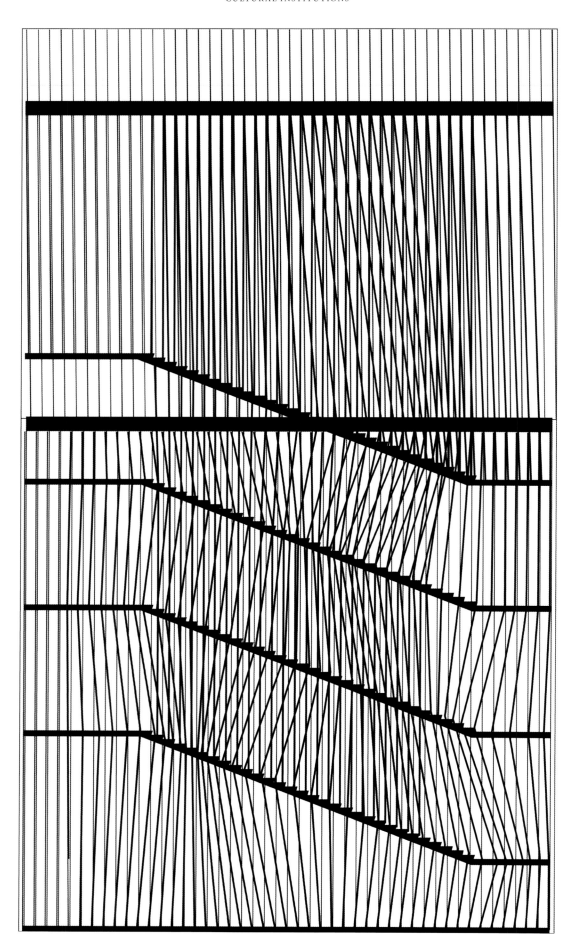

Facade moiré is created by optical interference between structural hangers and hullion system.

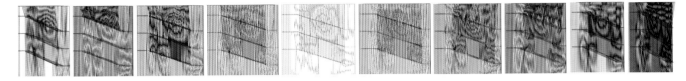

Views of the facade at various degrees. As one passes by the museum either on foot or by car, the layered rod-net produces a shifting moiré effect, such that the building expresses a continuously changing facade.

Gallery Design

Our overall spatial diagram for the New Museum is a C-shaped sectional volume of public spaces and circulation. The volume extends across the ground floor lobby and up the facade, then turns horizontally at the sixth floor into the double-height space of the special projects gallery. Within this C-shaped volume are clasped the principal gallery floors.

The neutral, white, boundless space of the principal galleries foregrounds the artwork and curatorial intent. Radiused baseboards and ceiling coves create seamless junctions between exterior walls and floors, ceilings, and interior walls. All air supply and return grilles are concealed, as well as switches, thermostats, and alarms. The large main gallery spaces are column-free, with proportions that maximize the potential for flexible partitioning. Galleries on floors 2 through 5 measure 15.5 by 23 meters (51 by 72 feet), with 4.5-meter (15-foot) ceiling heights. Special galleries at a more intimate scale are arrayed near public program zones, both in the interior and exterior spaces of the museum.

A Museum under Glass

We propose the moiré as a dynamic symbol of the New Museum's status as a mediator between the social and the cultural, the material and the immaterial. The facade moiré is created by the superimposition of the structural bars that carry the main stairs, the principal vertical circulation route through the building. These stairs, designed with a gentle slope typically used in landscapes, have generous tread depths that allow and encourage people to move slowly and pause midflight without the need for landings.

As they continually revisit the facade after passing through the sequence of galleries on each floor, it provides a reference and visual connection to the outside world, thrusting visitors into continual, variable reevaluation of the place of art within the city. A virtualized hybrid of city and institution, the facade comprises two exhibition spaces and a circulation system.

Night rendering of the museum showing facade gallery

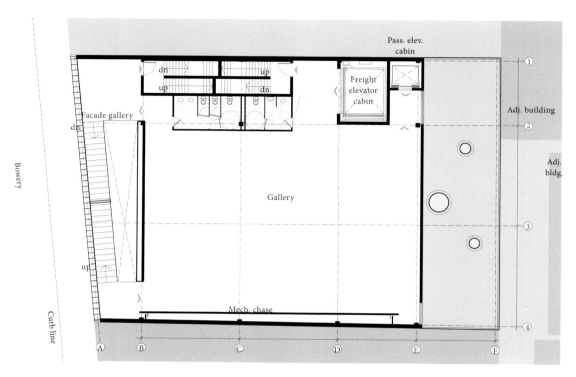

Fourth-floor plan: gallery

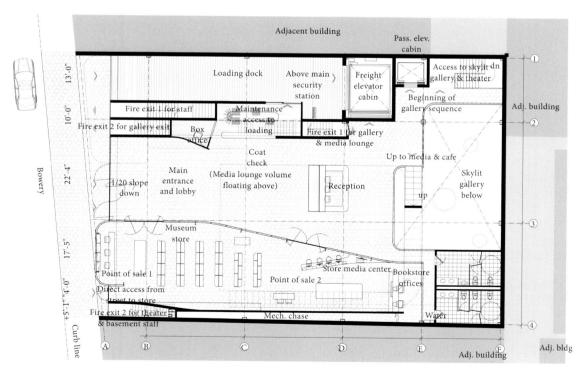

First-floor plan: lobby and store

UNIVERSITY OF
APPLIED ARTS VIENNA
2012

The Angewandte: University of Applied Arts Vienna

The University of Applied Arts Vienna (Universität für angewandte Kunst Wien, or UAAV) has undergone fundamental change from its beginnings as the Vienna School of Arts and Crafts to its present status as an internationally recognized art and design institution. Founded in 1867, the school was closely associated with the Imperial Royal Austrian Museum of Art and Industry, which was established in 1863 and eventually evolved into the MAK (Museum für angewandte Kunst). Since its founding, the UAAV has been at the forefront of Austrian art and design, serving in fin de siècle Vienna as one of the central institutions associated with Jugendstil and the Vienna Secession and evolving into a highly regarded international university. It has been the home of many highly influential artists and designers, among them Gustav Klimt, Josef Hoffmann, Otto Wagner, Oskar Kokoschka, and, more recently, Wolf Prix, Jil Sander, Greg Lynn, and Zaha Hadid. A competition for an extension to the UAAV presented an opportunity to develop a new architecture commensurate with the burgeoning international status of the school and its teachers.

Our proposal calls for a dynamic arrangement of a cantilevered bar branching out of an existing building designed in 1965 by Karl Schwanzer. It houses a library, an auditorium, and a two-level courtyard. The addition forms a new ground that links the school with its surroundings, confronting the vital challenge of incorporating new and old architectures and also developing new spatial opportunities to express three essential elements that define the culture of the institution: discourse, production, and display. These are not abstract concepts but palpable organizational principles that guided our design, from an overall urban concept to the tectonics of the building itself.

The three major buildings that occupy the UAAV campus are the MAK, the Ferstel (the historic origin of the school, built in 1867), and the Schwanzer (a utilitarian modernist loft building). Although the neoclassical facades of the Ferstel and the MAK and the grid of the Schwanzer building all are rigidly regular, the buildings are starkly dissimilar, thus calling for an extension that unites them and integrates them into the surrounding neighborhood.

The interior courtyard among the three buildings remained relatively under-engaged, functioning as an open space to be traversed rather than as a communal place for exchange and assembly. Our design for the addition to the Schwanzer building activates the interior courtyard as an intimate and textured environment that enables novel forms of engagement and discourse for students and teachers.

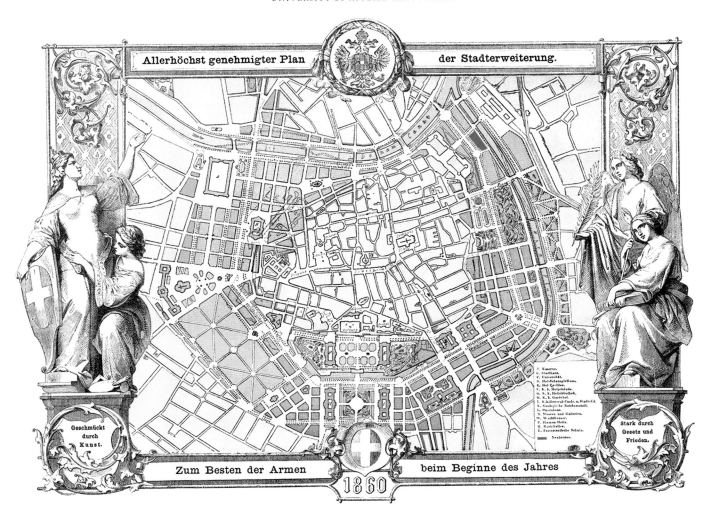

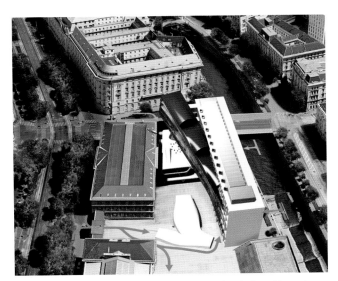

OPPOSITE: Rendering of street view of the University of Applied Arts Vienna from the corner of Oskar-Kokoschka-Platz and Stubenring

TOP: 1860 map of Vienna with the location of the UAAV indicated in red

BOTTOM: Flow diagram through the interior courtyard of the Angewandte

Situated on the Stubenring segment of the Ringstraße, the campus and its surroundings occupy a dynamic position in the city. The Ringstraße—Vienna's ring road, built in 1857 under Emperor Franz Joseph I to replace the medieval walls encircling the city—bounds the western end of the campus. Although the primary entrance to the campus is located along the Ringstraße, between the MAK and the Ferstel building, with a secondary entrance on the eastern end, which opens up to the Wien River, the school remains closed off on its southern and northern ends. Rather than limiting the school's connection with the city by funneling pedestrians through its main gate, we conceived of an active urban nexus that addresses the diverse demands of both the university and the general public. To this effect, we propose three different entrances into the complex. This larger urbanistic logic opens the institution to its surrounding public thoroughfares, from the original gate on the Ringstraße through to the Fritz-Wotruba-Promenade on the Wien River. A third entrance at Oskar-Kokoschka-Platz, framed by a floating library—an embodiment of the discursive side of education—will serve as a new monumental gateway into the courtyard for students and faculty members.

View from the lower courtyard. Across from the shell of the auditorium (bottom) is the cafeteria,
which looks out at the workshop spaces.

Prescribed Visibility of Public and Private Space

This proposed architecture considers the complex public role the Angewandte plays relative to the interactions among students, faculty, museumgoers, visiting intellectuals, and the general public, each of whom engages with the university in significantly different ways. We drew inspiration from depictions of postwar Vienna in Carol Reed and Graham Greene's 1949 film *The Third Man*. Mapping the hidden psychology (or, perhaps more aptly, psychosis) of the subject onto the city, the film's portrayal of the Viennese urban landscape illustrates a break from the apparently rigid and logical (Apollonian) planning scheme of its Ringstraße and regular neoclassical facades, revealing in its place a warped (Dionysian) psychology of Vienna's courtyards, alleyways, interiors, and tunnels.

Our scheme for the Angewandte calls for adding a point of entry along Oskar-Kokoschka-Platz, while maintaining a separation between public exhibition space and the places of learning and experimentation. Our proposal attempts to balance the public and private aspects of the institution, preserving the privacy of the students while simultaneously prescribing transparency through opening up additional exhibition space on the ground floor of the Schwanzer building. With this in mind, we designed the new courtyard to comprise two different levels. The upper, public level, which surrounds and overlooks the activities of an excavated student courtyard, celebrates the spectacle of production and student life at the Angewandte. The lower, "monastic" courtyard, which serves the students and brings light into the surrounding cafeteria and workshops, is given over to the life of the school. This lower space is not accessible to the public, giving students an opportunity to meet and produce their works in view of but separate from passersby who are on their way to lecture halls and exhibition spaces.

The main auditorium is the most prominent feature of the sunken courtyard and is accessible from both the lower student level and a continuous upper public ground. This new, connected public interface forms the heart of the urban strategy of the project, extending from the Wien River on one side through the galleries and into the main auditorium, then continuing out to the MAK and the arcade on the Ringstraße.

Stills from Carol Reed and Graham Greene's 1949 film *The Third Man*, showing a nocturnal Vienna framed by "Dutch angles"

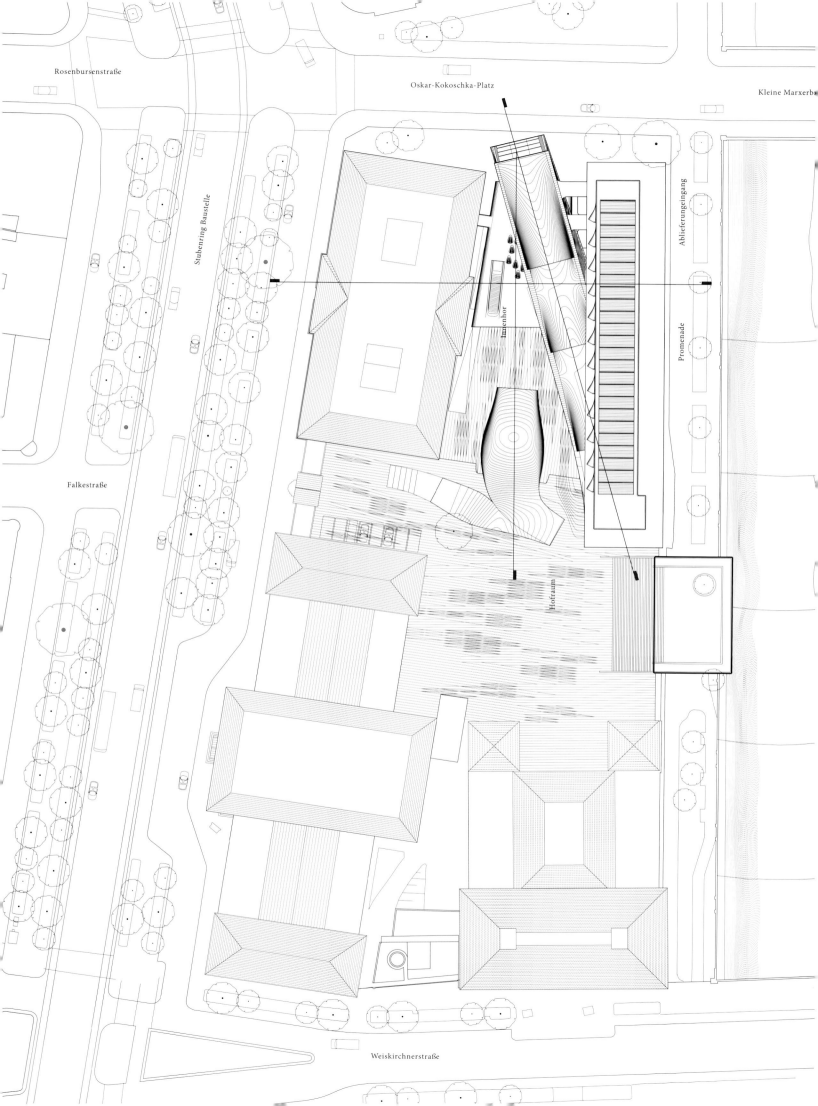

Rosenbursenstraße

Oskar-Kokoschka-Platz

Kleine Marxerb

Stubenring Baustelle

Ablieferungeingang

Innenhor

Falkestraße

Promenade

Hofraum

Weiskirchnerstraße

Gravity structural system

Floor slabs are supported by beams spanning the short direction.

Primary floor beams are supported by hangers connected to the chords of the primary X elements.

The primary X elements are supported by a combination of new columns (blue) and reinforced existing columns (green).

Gravity loads from discontinuous existing columns to be supported by new trusses at attic level and new transfer beams at Level 3

The Structure

Grafted onto the rigid uniformity of the Schwanzer building, the proposed extension is a dynamic foil to its modernist regularity and produces an integrated space in the courtyard between the two existing buildings. An addition should not merely be new but should fundamentally reread its context. This bar is at once continuous with the Schwanzer building and discrete— a catalyst that activates the existing buildings. A rod-net truss on the facade of the extension integrates the two distinct architectural styles of the Schwanzer and the Ferstel, producing a coherence through recasting the residual space between the buildings as the central focus of the institution's activities and ambitions. As the building extends above the courtyard, it forges new connections, not only between buildings but also to the city, opening views out, above, and below. Its pedagogical intent is to disrupt the routine experience of the city and the homogeneous modernism of the Schwanzer.

The structure that supports the existing bar extends through the floor plates, crossing in the middle to free the envelope from opaque bulk. Each level of the Schwanzer is uniquely affected by the presence of this skeleton, a new structural typology: a cruciform Vierendeel that, while spatially coextensive with the Schwanzer, is structurally autonomous, imparting no gravity or lateral loads on the existing building. On the outside, a variegated rod-net modulates light and provides structural support to the slab edges. Inside, the bar is populated with studio spaces.

The diagonal envelope of the bar opens the ends of each floor to views of both sky and ground. On the upper level of the bar, vaulted hoods bring light into the studios. The bar connects to the Schwanzer building with discrete bridges— a significant contrast with its fused origins. In a move appropriate to its modernist origins, we render the base of the Schwanzer building visually transparent and replace its existing program with exhibition spaces and galleries.

Below the outer extent of the bar, a library connects the second levels of the Schwanzer and Ferstel buildings, replacing an existing wall-like link that previously blocked the courtyard. Within the Schwanzer and flowing out from the library, the second level is a dedicated space for discourse, filled with study spaces and lecture rooms.

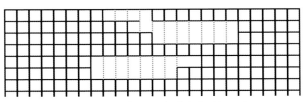

Discontinuous column elevation: the dashed red line indicates existing columns in the Schwanzer building to be demolished.

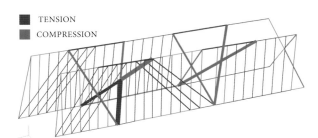

TENSION
COMPRESSION

Axial sorce: a series of vertical hangers and diagonal ties transfer the gravity load to the chords of the X elements, which in turn are supported by a combination of new columns and reinforced existing columns.

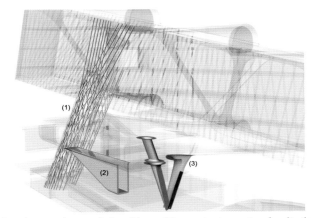

Lateral structural system: the lateral forces of the new structure are transferred to the foundation by three structural components: (1) sloped diagrid, (2) braced frame at the library stair, (3) braces below library.

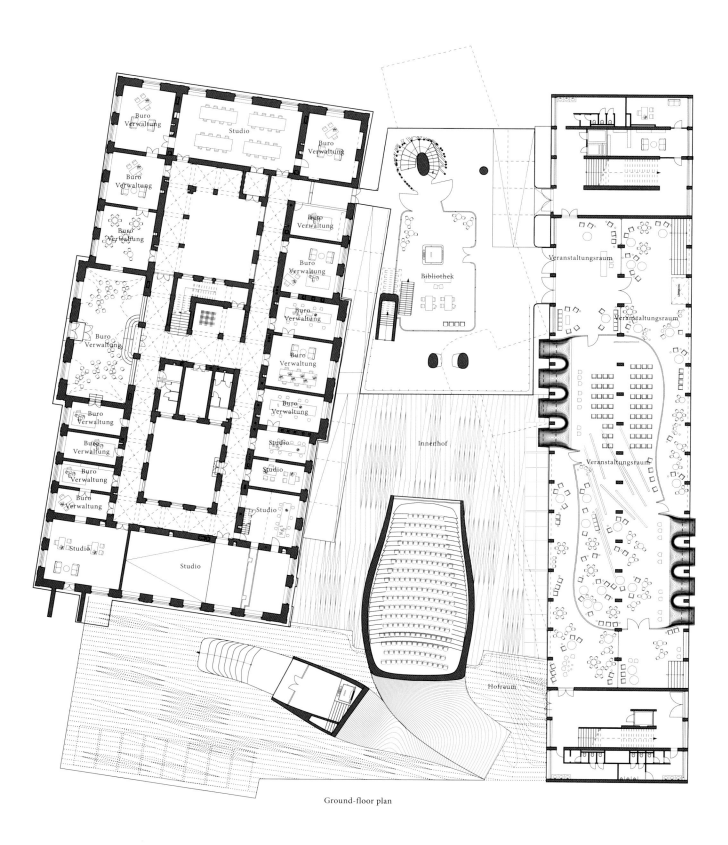

Ground-floor plan

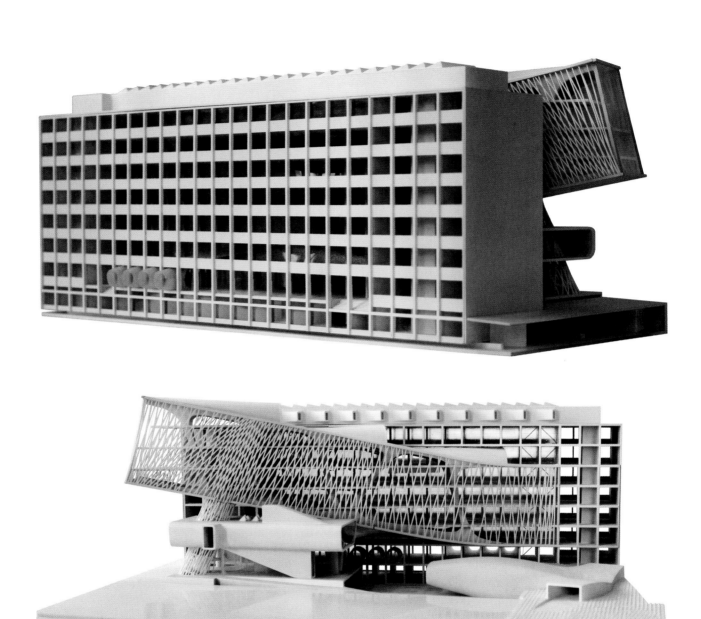

Physical model: canal facade (above) and courtyard facade (below)

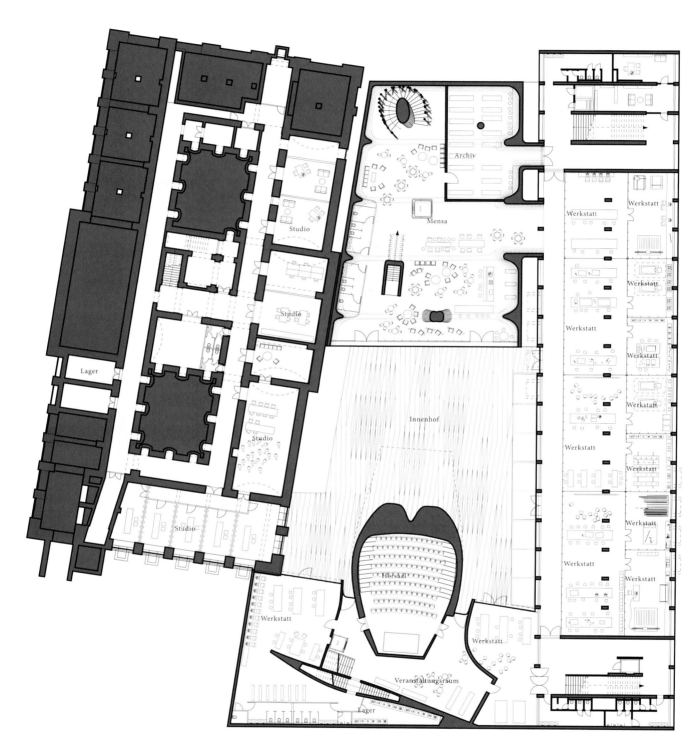

Basement plan

Student and faculty entry from Oskar-Kokoschka-Platz.
The elevated library serves as a gateway.

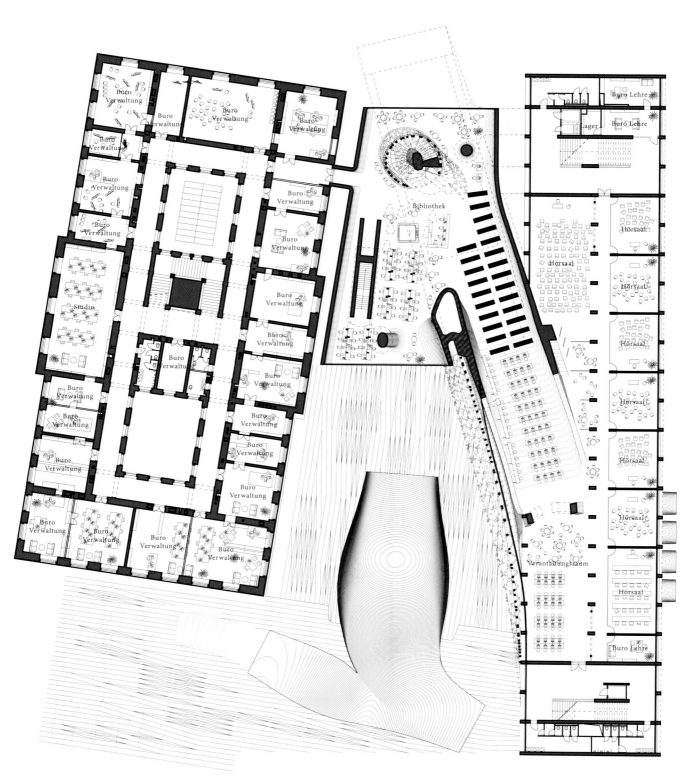

Second-floor plan

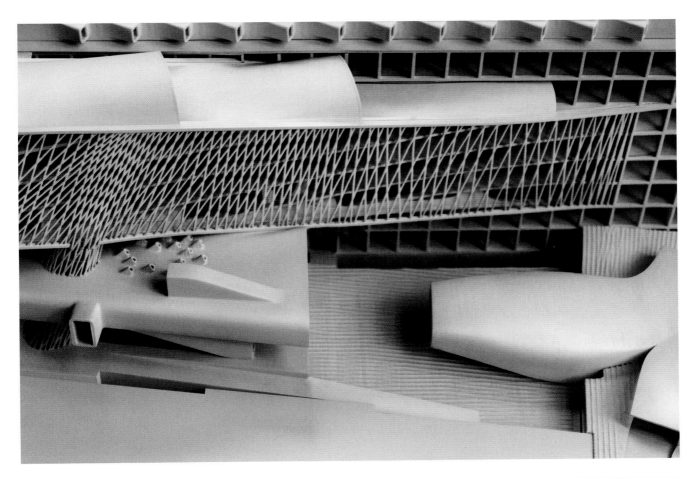

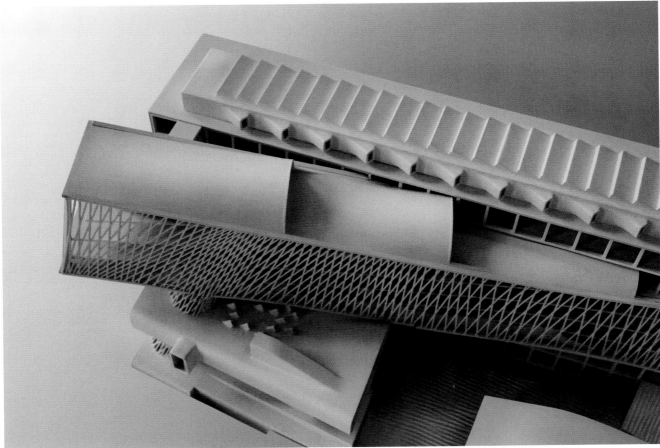

Overhead views of the courtyard (top) and of the angled bar and library (bottom)

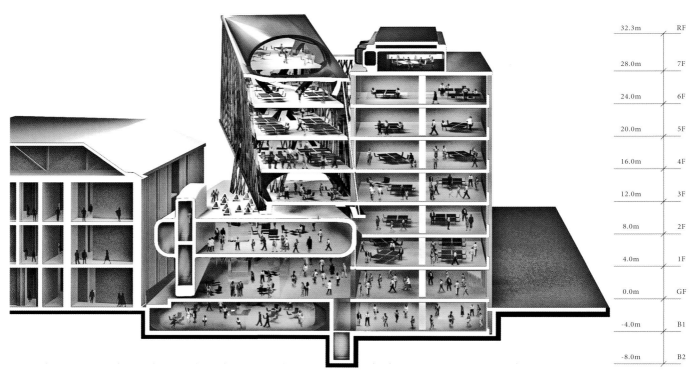

32.3m	RF
28.0m	7F
24.0m	6F
20.0m	5F
16.0m	4F
12.0m	3F
8.0m	2F
4.0m	1F
0.0m	GF
-4.0m	B1
-8.0m	B2

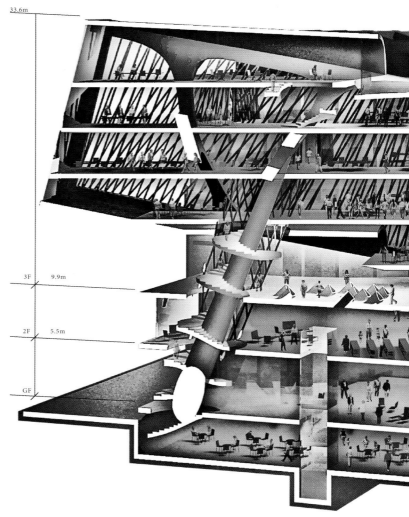

33.6m	
3F	9.9m
2F	5.5m
GF	

TOP: Transverse section

BOTTOM: Longitudinal section

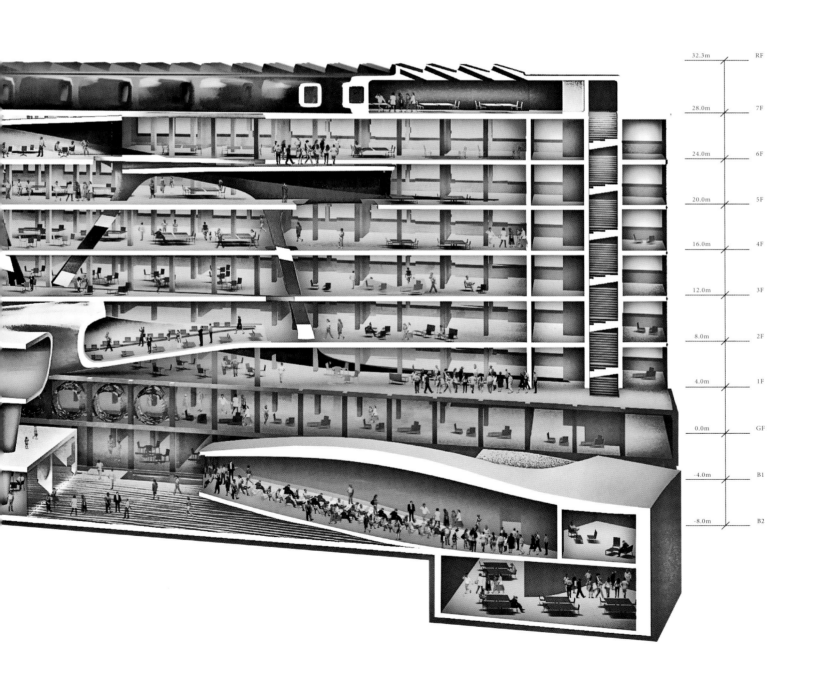

32.3m	RF
28.0m	7F
24.0m	6F
20.0m	5F
16.0m	4F
12.0m	3F
8.0m	2F
4.0m	1F
0.0m	GF
-4.0m	B1
-8.0m	B2

Project Credits

258 SAGAPONACK HOUSE
Sagaponack, New York, USA, 2002
Principals:
  Jesse Reiser + Nanako Umemoto
Design team:
  Matthias Blass, Eva Perez de Vega Steele
Interns and assistants:
  Ade Herkarisma, Saran Oki, Akira Nakamura,
  Hidekazu Ota, Yuzuru Kobayashi,
  Kenji Nonobe, Mikiko Kajikawa, Yuya Suzuki
Structural engineer:
  Robert Silman Associates, P.C., Nat
  Oppenheimer, Pat Arnett, Tim Shenk
Mechanical consultant:
  Mahadev Raman, Arup & Partners, New York
Plumbing consultant:
  Igor Kitagorsky, Arup & Partners, New York
Structure Model/Assistants:
  Rhett Russo, Jason Scroggin

274 ALISHAN TOURIST ROUTES
Alishan Mountain, Taiwan, 2004
Principals:
  Jesse Reiser + Nanako Umemoto
Design team:
  Eva Perez de Vega Steele, Jason Scroggin,
  Jonathan D. Solomon
Interns and assistants:
  Joe Kobayashi, Yuya Suzuki, Keisuke Kitagawa,
  Alver Mensana, Akari Takebayashi,
  Akira Nakamura, Aki Eto, Arthur Chu,
  David Nam, Ian Gordon
Structural engineer:
  Cecil Balmond, Charles Walker,
  Arup Ltd., London
Architectural consultant:
  Philip Fei, Fei and Cheng

292 IIT STUDENT CENTER
Chicago, Illinois, USA, 1997
Type: Offices
Length: 150 meters (492 feet)
Structure: Prestressed steel shell
Principals:
  Jesse Reiser + Nanako Umemoto
Design team:
  Jose Sanchez, David Ruy, Jason Payne
Structural engineer:
  Cecil Balmond, Arup Ltd., London

298 EYEBEAM MUSEUM
New York, New York, USA, 2001
Type: Museum
Size: 46,500 square meters (500,000 square feet)
Structure: Space frame, reinforced concrete
Principals:
  Jesse Reiser + Nanako Umemoto
Design team:
  Wolfgang Gollwitzer, Matthias Blass,
  Rhett Russo, Jason Johnson
Interns and assistants:
  Tomoro Aida, Hideto Aoki

310 CHILDREN'S MUSEUM OF PITTSBURGH
Pittsburgh, Pennsylvania, USA, 2001
Type: Offices
Scale: 5,575 square meters (60,000 square feet)
Structure: Concrete, glass
Principals:
  Jesse Reiser + Nanako Umemoto
Design team:
  Nona Yehia, Jefferson Ellinger
Interns and assistants:
  Akira Nakamura, Shizuko Takeyama,
  Khalid Waterson, Damon Van Horn,
  Gernot Riether

316 NEW MUSEUM
New York, New York, USA, 2003
Principals:
  Jesse Reiser + Nanako Umemoto
Design team:
  Rhett Russo, Eva Perez de Vega Steele, Jason
  Scroggin, Stephan Vary
Interns and assistants:
  Akira Nakamura, Kenji Nonobe, Aki Eto,
  Yuzuru Kobayashi, Dong Wook Yang,
  Josh Mckeown, Jonathan Solomon,
  Akari Takebayashi, Chris Sullivan
Structural engineer:
  Mahadev Raman, Markus Schulte,
  Arup & Partners, New York
Mechanical engineer:
  Mahadev Raman, Markus Schulte,
  Arup & Partners, New York
Associate architect: Peter Guggenheimer

330 UNIVERSITY OF APPLIED ARTS VIENNA
Vienna, Austria, 2012
Finalist, International Competition
Type: Extension of architecture school
Size: 8,323 square meters (90,000 square feet)
Structure: Multiple
Principals:
  Jesse Reiser + Nanako Umemoto
Design team:
  Michael Overby, Juan De Marco, Hillary Simon,
  Eleftheria Xanthouli, Joy Wang, Becky Quintal,
  Kris Hedges, Massimiliano Orzi
Interns and assistants:
  Ryosuke Imaeda, Shosuke Kawamura
Structural engineer: Arup & Partners, New York
Architectural consultant:
  Gollwitzer Architekten, Metzgergasse,
  Germany
Model fabricator:
  Re:art, Yasuhito Furuyama, Japan

Illustration Credits

CASA DA MÚSICA
Office of Metropolitan Architecture (OMA),
Heer Bokelweg 149, 3032 AD Rotterdam, The
Netherlands, www.oma.com

43 **SKETCH OF NANAKO AND JESSE**
TianYi Xie, 2017

76 **MARCEL DUCHAMP, *CIMETIÈRE DES
UNIFORMES ET LIVRÉES, NO. 2***
Yale University Art Gallery
Gift of Katherine S. Dreier to the Collection
Société Anonyme

JOHN HEJDUK, *VICTIMS* SKETCH
Canadian Center for Architecture

96 **WENCESLAUS HOLLAR, *LONG VIEW OF
LONDON FROM BANKSIDE***
https://allkindsofhistory.files.wordpress.com/
2011/11/bankside.jpg

114, 122–27 **HYPNEROTOMACHIA ERO/MACHIA/
HYPNIAHOUSE PROJECT**
© The Museum of Modern Art/Licensed by
SCALA/Art Resource, © Reiser + Umemoto, 1989

119 **SCHRAGE MUSIK CANNONS**
http://xplanes.free.fr/do335/do335-7.htm

DAME LAURA KNIGHT, *TAKE OFF*
© Imperial War Museums (Art.IWM ART LD
3834)

120 **STILLS FROM *THE WORLD AT WAR***
© FremantleMedia

121 **VIEW OF A SHORT STIRLING B.III**
William Green, *Famous Bombers of the
Second World War*, Vol. 2, (Garden City, NY:
Doubleday, 1960), 31

131, 247 **LUDWIG MIES VAN DER ROHE,
RESOR HOUSE PROJECT**
© The Museum of Modern Art/Licensed by
SCALA/Art Resource, 1949

135 **KURT SCHWITTERS, *THE CATHEDRAL
OF EROTIC MISERY***
© 2017 Artists Rights Society (ARS), New York/
VG Bild-Kunst, Bonn

HYPNEROTOMACHIA POLOPHILI
Yale University Art Gallery

136 **JOHN HEARTFIELD, *HURRAH, DIE
BUTTER IST ALLE!***
©2017 The Heartfield Community of Heirs/
Artists Rights Society (ABS), New York/ VG Bild-
Kunst, Bonn

139 ***SEMIOTEXT(E)/ARCHITECTURE***
Hraztan Zeitlian, editor/designer. Review of
experimental architecture. (New York: *Semiotext(e)*,
1992).

145 **AIRSHIP SHED WITH TRUSSES**
Architectural Association

AIRSHIP SHED UNDER CONSTRUCTION
Bauten Der Industrile, Verlag Georg
D. W. Callwey/Munich

GODDARD ROCKET INTERNALS
Man and Space, (New York: Time Incorporated,
1964), 72

184–85 **KANSAI LIBRARY SKETCH**
Canadian Center for Architecture,
© Reiser + Umemoto, 1996

200 **VILLA VPRO**
MVRDV, 1994

YOKOHAMA TERMINAL
Foreign Office Architects (FOA), 1995

201 **REDRAWN FROM ROBERT LE RICOLAIS**
Isoflex "cardboard model"

REDRAWN FROM KUNIO WATANABE
Folded Plate

REDRAWN FROM TOYO ITO
Grin Grin Park

REDRAWN FROM SANAA
Rolex Learning Center

REDRAWN FROM JUNYA ISHIGAMI
Kinmen Port Terminal

REDRAWN FROM SOU FUJIMOTO
House of Hungarian Music

REDRAWN FROM AKIHISA HIRATA
Foam Form

206 ***LA THÉORIE ET LA PRATIQUE DU JARDINAGE***
The Metropolitan Museum of Art. Presented in
memory of Daniel W. Langton, Landscape Architect,
by Mrs. Langton

216 **AERIAL VIEW OF NEW YORK CITY**
https://en.wikipedia.org/wiki/File:Manhattan_1931.jpg

244 **WEST SIDE CONVERGENCE MODEL**
© Georges Meguerditchian - Centre Pompidou,
MNAM-CCI /Dist. RMN-GP,
© Reiser + Umemoto, 1999

277 **ALISHAN MOUNTAIN**
Lienyuan Lee, 2015

335 **STILL FROM *THE THIRD MAN***
Studiocanal Films Limited.